Arnold

Arnold

Schwarzenegger and the Movies

Dave Saunders

I.B. TAURIS

LONDON · NEW YORK

Published in 2009 by I.B.Tauris & Co Ltd
6 Salem Road, London W2 4BU
175 Fifth Avenue, New York NY 10010
www.ibtauris.com

Distributed in the United States and Canada Exclusively by Palgrave Macmillan,
175 Fifth Avenue, New York NY 10010

ISBN 978 1 84511 948 5

A full CIP record for this book is available from the British Library
A full CIP record is available from the Library of Congress

Library of Congress Catalog Card Number: available

Typeset by JCS Publishing Services Ltd, www.jcs-publishing.co.uk
Printed and bound in Great Britain by CPI Antony Rowe, Chippenham

FSC
Mixed Sources
Product group from well-managed
forests and other controlled sources
Cert no. SGS-COC-2953
www.fsc.org
© 1996 Forest Stewardship Council

Contents

Illustrations

Acknowledgements

The many who have inspired and appraised this manuscript during its gestation must be commended *en masse* for their diligence and patience. For getting *Arnold* into the public domain, the always-supportive Philippa Brewster should be held accountable.

My family and friends naturally warrant praise for feeding, watering, talking to and indulging me during the period of cogitation that produced the ensuing book. Especial gratitude for supporting me in numerous, wholly appreciated ways goes to my late and much-missed mother Jill (a perceptive, witty and honest critic of both Arnold's films and an early draft of this book), my father David, my brother Tom, my sister Isobel, Les Whitham, Simon Messenger, Ben Cowdall, Tim and Kate Mason, Leon Daye, Hajnalka Elek, students and staff at the Department of Media Arts, Royal Holloway, University of London, Dave Green and Jim Hornsby of the University of Bedfordshire, and my brothers-in-law (past and present) Nick Joyce and Dave Wheeler. Lastly, Paco Nunez – with whom I had many productive discussions while a fellow postgraduate at Royal Holloway – in no small part stimulated this endeavour; I therefore dedicate this book to him.

Dave Saunders
2009

Introduction

There's Something About Arnold: Schwarzenegger's American Dreams

Every promise, every opportunity is still golden in this land. Our children can walk into tomorrow with the knowledge that no one can be denied the promise that is America.[1]

America was in my head always . . . I'd always had a claustrophobic feeling about Austria . . . It wouldn't allow me to expand . . . I knew I was a winner. I knew I was destined for great things . . . Never was there even the slightest doubt in my mind that I would make it.[2]

Humility does not become Arnold Schwarzenegger. No matter what nickname this awkwardly polysyllabic Teuton acquires – the 'Austrian Oak,' 'Shuwa-chan' (in Japan) and recently 'Governator' have all been in widespread usage – his presence, for better or worse, looms large in our culture, our material lives, and our collective unconscious: Arnold, as Michael Blitz and Louise Krasniewicz avow over the course of a lengthy disquisition, *matters*.[3] Schwarzenegger himself, of course, has seemingly always asserted this point with a perspicacity bordering on prognostic. Ever since his childhood veneration of Steve Reeves, so he says, he wanted to be a bodybuilding luminary and then a naturalised American film star; he always knew, purportedly, that he wanted to take a glamorous, equally resilient wife (preferably one of the Kennedys, the closest the United States has ever had to a royal family); and, from his twenties, he entertained a notion that he would eventually diversify into big-tent politics: he was, the logic follows, simply built to be a star.

How much the young Arnold could have been certain about his own future is open to conjecture, given the actor's tendency toward grandiloquent self-promotion and the resolute defence of all but his most embarrassing proclamations. Yet it is not without perceptible (if post hoc) justification that Schwarzenegger makes these claims. In the early twenty-first century – well past Arnold's box office zenith and theoretically peak years of film celebrity – commentators frequently observe that he occupies a stratum of renown quite above and beyond the normal echelons of Hollywood achievement based on conventional aptitude, artistic kudos and lowest-common-denominator sex appeal; 'Nothing and nobody,' concludes biographer Nigel Andrews, 'can iron the Arnold abnormalities into routine talent.'[4] Even discounting the resurgence of press attention that his gubernatorial tenure has inevitably brought, Arnold is, and in his own mind always was, an enchanting anomaly, a meta-star of hyperbolic proportions.[5] Amongst living actors, his regality is surpassed only by enduring male icons such as Sean Connery, Jack Nicholson and Clint Eastwood, all of whose prestige rests on similar ingredients, though all of whose attractiveness is nowhere near as mysterious, nor as transcendent of orthodox craftsmanship, as the boundlessly enthusiastic bodybuilder from the boondocks of Austria who came looking for providence across the Atlantic. If, as Raymond Durgnat asserts, '[t]he social history of a nation can be written in terms of its film stars,' then there is much to learn from an acute examination of the Schwarzenegger phenomenon.[6]

It is the purpose of this book to elucidate and explicate the primary vehicles of Arnold's allure: his films. Many extant and invaluable works – to which I am naturally indebted – deal with the bald facts of Arnold's life and times, and numerous academic papers have been published that explore, usually via necessarily cherry-picked analysis, the multifarious cultural implications of his deceptively protean roles.[7] But Arnold is, in the end, essentially always 'Arnold,' essentially always the democratically moulded Golem we most want him to be, no matter how his *métier* attempts to adjust to accommodate or pre-empt changes in intellectual discernment. This de facto immutability is, perhaps, why many spectators are charmed by his monadic, 'almost mystical charisma,'[8] and why his surname alone was, for a time, genuinely as potent a selling point as any in the annals of mass marketing. As Theodor Adorno and Max Horkheimer asserted, 'Anyone who doubts the power of monotony is a fool,' and it is a fool who dismisses out of hand Arnold's magnetism as either trivial or immaterial.[9] Notwithstanding a glut of scholarly application to the matter of stars and their 'direct or indirect reflection of the needs, drives and dreams of the American people,'[10] no single work has traced a comprehensive, exegetic delineation of Schwarzenegger's cinematic career arc. *Arnold: Schwarzenegger and the Movies* thus aims to consolidate and build upon what disparate critical studies exist, to form a cogent overview of Schwarzenegger's substantial filmic corpus; close textual readings of the films' content will be used to impart overarching political context.

By the late 1970s, I herein argue, the time was ripe for such a face ('the face of a medieval warrior – a face with great natural dignity')[11] to emerge and in due course dominate mainstream Hollywood action cinema. In the post-Marshall Plan climate of American pre-eminence, a number of imperative factors conspired in aiding Schwarzenegger's preternatural ascent: supply-side morality and the ongoing 'culture wars'; lingering ignominy thanks to the entwined legacies of Vietnam and Watergate; a revitalised but nonetheless newly absolutist popular conception of the American Dream (of which Arnold is the most famous living embodiment); Reagan's and Bush Senior's conservative economic and foreign agendas; widespread anti-liberal backlash after the Great Society's overselling of reform; and the death-throes of the Cold War. Yet how, exactly, did 1980s and 1990s America celebrate, co-opt and ultimately disavow the folkloric, imperial and literal power of the Teutons, in the shape of Arnold, for what I will assert are in essence hegemonic ends? The answer to this question lies not in sketching a Manichaean template of 'good' versus 'evil' in a battle of empires for the eyes and ears of a global audience, but in the ways that Arnold's film performances and the themes addressed by those films effect a bilateral synergy with the epoch in which they were made. Arnold became the definable, singular 'Arnie' for a reason: he was shaped, as he had sculpted his own enormous body, by forces emanating from the broader sphere of political and cinematic history; indeed, his often critically belittled films constitute politically legible works that reach out beyond the province of their contractual authors to embrace the shifting backdrop of the parent culture. As John Berger saliently points out, 'Hack work is not the result of either clumsiness or provincialism. It is the result of the market making more insistent demands than the art.'[12]

Arnold was, in congruence, embraced by the United States not solely because it needed him, but because he too needed *it*: Hollywood populism, he knew, was the way to the New World's heart, if not always its mind. Moreover, in a nation whose closest equivalent to Shakespeare is perhaps John Ford, a filmmaker predominantly of frontier Westerns, there is no finer way – if one has what it takes, and what it takes is the kind of immense determination only the visionary possess – to impress oneself upon the national character.[13] Arnold used the film industry as a means to inculcatory self-promotion, a conduit via which to implant his sizeable personality within the cult of celebrity that had so fascinated him as a boy; the Austrian Oak, a somatically archetypal yet psychologically subsumed vision of 'Aryan supremacy and Germanic strength of will,'[14] was happily lured to the shores of the USA by its syndicated promises of opportunities for the industrious. In a diverse but inequitable continent such as advanced-capitalist North America, where the determination of the well-motivated recent immigrant to exploit new vistas still potentiates its giant economies,[15] there might well be no more effective mode of displaying the benefits of a life lived in pursuit of freedom and happiness than having Arnold-as-movie-star, Styrian accent intact, broadcast an implicit, multipart libertarian Constitutional from the highest platform possible: that 'irrefutable prophet of the prevailing order,' the culture industry.[16]

More explicitly and in his private life, Arnold, notes Laurence Leamer, believed that 'American liberty was a fresh breeze in his face, not the air that he had always lived in . . . not a birthright he took for granted';[17] 'You have the best tax advantages here,' said Arnold to Studs Terkel in 1980, 'and the best prices here and the best products here . . . I am a strong believer in Western philosophy, the philosophy of success, of progress, of getting rich . . . It's a beautiful philosophy, and America should keep it up.'[18] 'He's chosen,' eulogised Arnold's friend and fellow muscle devotee Sven-Ole Thorsen. 'They don't come around too often.'[19] Heeding the 'call to adventure,' an epiphanic beckoning experienced by chronicled voyagers throughout history and apocrypha, Arnold intuited the auguries and set out to fulfil his American destiny. At no other place, and in no other time than the age of Reagan (fittingly an amiable former actor of limited range), could Schwarzenegger have bestridden the United States, and by extension the world, as he did.

Chapter I re-evaluates three of Arnold's earliest films, *Hercules in New York* (Arthur Allan Seidelman, 1970), *Stay Hungry* (Bob Rafelson, 1976) and *Pumping Iron* (George Butler and Robert Fiore, 1977), and assesses their import as foundational works. Establishing Schwarzenegger as a bona fide celluloid presence, these somewhat neglected offerings efficiently served to introduce the wider public to a burgeoning idol by variously positing him within the received discursive realms of competitive masculine physicality, individualist endeavour and quasi-classical myth. Chapter II covers the remarkable escalation of Arnold's film career and the apotheosis of his 'Arnoldian' incarnation, played out from *Conan the Barbarian* (John Milius, 1982), through *The Terminator* (James Cameron, 1984), to *Red Heat* (Walter Hill, 1988). Chapter III explores the variety of ways in which Arnold – or by this time frequently 'Arnie' – self-reflexively adapted to his iconic entrenchment and the concurrent semi-liberalisation of mandate and government, seeking out new ways to address problems of political identity, crises of masculinity and encroaching middle age whilst simultaneously retaining his proprietary 'Arnoldness'; films discussed herein include Ivan Reitman's *Twins* (1988), Paul Verhoeven's *Total Recall* (1990), *Kindergarten Cop* (Ivan Reitman, 1990), *Terminator 2* (James Cameron, 1991), John McTiernan's *Last Action Hero* (1993), and *True Lies* (James Cameron, 1994). The final chapter looks at Arnold's latter *oeuvre*, and evidence therein of shifts back towards earlier, tested tropes, as well-trodden but contested filmic territory is tentatively reclaimed amid a renewal of American calls to domestic, international and spiritual solidarity in the face of largely unfamiliar global dangers.

It is the directors, of course, who constitute at least the nominal authors of these films; yet their use of Schwarzenegger as vehicle and star can constructively be seen as paralleling Ford's and Howard Hawks's much-discussed use of John Wayne to retell the gamut of American history, or Sergio Leone's and Don Seigel's employment of Clint Eastwood in re-mythologising the gunslinger maverick within a variety of often ideologically nebulous yet nonetheless symptomatically replete works. '[A]ll the greatest American films,' observes critic Robin Wood, are 'fed by a complex generic tradition and, beyond that, by the fears and aspirations of a whole culture.'[20] Further, with pertinence to the kind of textual historicism in which this book engages, Steven Prince has produced the definite treatise; generally speaking, my approach and rationale echo those summarised in Prince's *Visions of Empire*:

> By recognising that contemporary narrative films, manufactured as entertainments with mass appeal, must necessarily draw upon and rework salient cultural values, the political implications of such films become clearer. 'Political' is understood here not just in terms of parties and electoral institutions, or the design of overt propaganda, but as the realm of collective values and fantasies that underlie and inform socioeconomic systems and behaviour in the real world.[21]

'[F]ilms,' concur Janice Hocker Rushing and Thomas S. Frentz, 'are to the cultural psyche what dreams are to the individual psyche.'[22] Arnold Schwarzenegger, however, in both his life *and* his congruent art, represents an embodied projection of such shared obsessions. He is contemporary cinema's foremost trans-narratory site of both conscious and unconscious cathexes: a self-made avatar brought forth from the post-war American id, devoted to a never-ceasing quest whose copious constituent stories may seem to digress, but whose Great American Grail – Freedom – stays the same. 'From the moment the [archetypal] hero learns of this prize,' observes Christopher Booker, 'the need to set out on the long hazardous journey to reach it becomes the most important thing to him in the world. Whatever perils and diversions lie in wait on the way, the story is shaped by that one overriding imperative.'[23]

Despite his many inimitable qualities, Arnold – *Der neue Mensch*, displaced and totemised – is no more or less than a contemporary protagonist in the eternal, cyclical narratives that spawned what Joseph Campbell called 'the hero with a thousand faces,' an 'echo of lost worlds, haunting an imagination invaded by excessive rationality and thus becoming the crystallisation point for thrusts of the archaic and of the irrational.'[24] Schwarzenegger's most enduring role is therefore vast and mythopoeic: he is an elemental hero archetype of *our* age, a serendipitously 'chosen' culture-borne recapitulation of legend. As Saul Friedlander writes:

[E]very approach to mythic narrative not tied to formal structure alone but leaning toward narrative content as the carrier of real significance – as in the work of Jung, Eliade, Barthes, Tournier – shows that through often insignificant, conjectural, or pedestrian narration, myth transmits (for the ideological purposes of asserting the power of the ruling class, Barthes would say; for the purpose of authentic disclosure, enhancing the primordial and sacred, as Jung, Eliade, and Tournier would say) a message that strives for universal significance.[25]

Since the birth of language, societies have told stories in order to promulgate systemic codes or to render axiomatic what is intrinsically relativistic; we thus create myths as tools of understanding, to locate us in a scheme and make moral sense out of chaos. When ancient fables have lost their potency, similar memes (expressed in the idioms of the current) must emerge to take their place. '[T]he logic, the heroes, and the deeds of myth survive into modern times,' avers Campbell; 'In the absence of an effective general [or *modern*] mythology, each of us has his private, unrecognised, rudimentary, yet secretly potent pantheon of dreams.'[26] However, we are cautioned by V.G. Kiernan in *America: The New Imperialism* (1978) that an 'economic system, like a nation or religion, lives not by bread alone, but by beliefs, visions, daydreams as well, and these may be no less vital to it for being erroneous.'[27] Now into its final phase, the political efficacy of the Schwarzenegger fantasy-quest is the basis of a story in itself.

The central treatise within this contextual work, then, is two-pronged: to delineate the process whereby a Rodinesque, stilted Austrian was taken – via the 'dream factory' of Hollywood – to the bosom of the world's most powerful nation, and to account for the nature and historical significance of his extraordinary appeal. There is, it must be said, something about Arnold, and that something, whether we are enamoured of him or not, lies as much in the oneiric, contradictory hearts of the American people as in the strong arms of Schwarzenegger.

Machina ex Deus
Rise of the *Übermensch*

I have not in my life set eyes upon a man with more might in his frame than this helmed lord. He's no hall-fellow dressed in fine armour, or his face belies him; he has the head of a hero.[1]

Pumping Iron was an exercise in brainwashing and we've never recovered from it.[2]

G rowing up in bucolic, post-*Anschluss* Thal, only a few miles from the Styrian capital of Graz but to all intents and purposes a world away from the city, the juvenile Arnold Schwarzenegger (his peculiarly local family moniker translates approximately to 'black ploughman') did not have access to a television set, the instrument through which he would eventually assume mandatory power. He remembers the time his authoritarian father, Gustav – a policeman and one-time member of the Nazi Party's paramilitary *Sturmabteilung,* the Brownshirts – brought home a refrigerator, and how the Schwarzeneggers marvelled at its technologically miraculous coolness, repeatedly opening and shutting the door to confirm this phenomenon's veracity. Life was thus frugal, but lived amongst forest-dappled vistas befitting a Wagnerian opera and the humble origins of most imminent heroes, whose fabulous labours of log-cabin-to-White House-style ascendance usually begin early in life.

Arnold started competitive bodybuilding when still a teenager, partly as a potential route of escape from Thal's comfortable if stultifying prospects, and partly, according to most biographers, in order to secure approval from his father (paternal endorsements were apparently scarce, and more often lavished on Arnold's brother, the handsome Meinhard, who was a year older). As a distraction from uncomfortable realities, Schwarzenegger looked to boys' adventure comic-books featuring *Nibelungenlied* strongman Sigurd, and to the folk giants that supposedly dwelt in the Black Forest, performing feats of supernatural vigour. Gaidorf Kino in Graz became another, more engrossing means by which Arnold indulged his grandiose adolescent fantasies through an obsession with powerfully masculine characters. He immersed himself in the 'violence and hanky-panky'-filled[3] adventures of well-built actors such as Mark Forest, Johnny Weissmuller, Brad Harris, Gordon Mitchell, Steve Reeves and Reg Park, frequently watching their cinematic escapades several times over. With each exposure, Arnold grew increasingly certain that he was somehow being shown his own *raison d'être* as an over-endowed 'superman' in excess of both Gustav's entreaties (which were then for Arnold to become a champion curler, soldier and provincial virility symbol) and Reg Park's exemplar: 'He was rugged, everything I thought a man should be . . . I was transfixed.'[4] It was, though, the American Reeves who was 'the right man in the right place at the right time,'[5] a catalyst Joseph Campbell would identify as the 'figure of the herald in the psyche that is ripe for transformation . . . marking a new period, a new stage in the biography.'[6]

The six-schilling movie outings 'released a kind of desire of violence in me,' said Arnold, who was known in youth to exert himself cruelly upon weaker individuals, 'and I could let it go through fantasy by seeing it on the screen.'[7] Moreover, the taut flesh, epic scenarios and general excess on display suggested a bigness that rural, neutral Austria could not accommodate; late-1950s Hollywood and its Mediterranean counterparts – via their cheap but spectacular imagery and television-baiting splendour – represented a luridly exciting world where the gigantism of the classical past was brought animatedly into the modern. Although Italy and Spain produced a great deal of Arnold's favourite films, it was Hollywood that, for Schwarzenegger, bespoke true greatness, and only the Californian Mecca of thrilling entertainment would suffice as a professional destination. Arnold hated the literature and high arts his father forced him to study, but saw in the recapitulated heroes of popular cinema an opportunity for fun and adventure on a global scale.

As Laurence Leamer explains, Arnold was geographically frustrated not simply by his teenage isolation in a farming village, but in a much broader respect:

He was a citizen of an Austria that before defeat in World War I had been the centre of the Austro-Hungarian Empire, overseeing the destinies of 67 million Europeans. In the late 1930s, many Austrians had hoped to restore their nation's greatness in an alliance with Nazi Germany, but the Austrian-born Adolf Hitler led them into a disaster unprecedented in their history. The Austria that Arnold was born into on July 30, 1947, was a despairing, defeated country occupied by the Americans, British and Russians.[8]

The United States was rebuilding an indebted, humbled and beholden Europe, a continent tainted by deep-rooted guilt and common assumptions of moral shortfall by comparison with the vanquisher America. Exalting the proud nation that he had partly shaped in the pages of *Life* magazine, Henry Luce declared that the 'American experience is the key to the future . . . America must be the elder brother of nations in the brotherhood of man.'[9] The 'culture of size to which Arnold was subscribing,' notes Nigel Andrews, 'existed spiritually and scenically over there.'[10] America, self-contained victor over poverty and tyranny, was bounteous, efficient and in the middle of the biggest consumer boom in history (a surge largely propelled by suburbanites' credit-funded expenditure on televisions and fridges – a 'technology for a better living');[11] Arnold, aware of the Stateside limitations of his own provenance, and cognisant of Reg Park's similarly atypical origins (Park was British South African), knew that his acceptance into the fraternity depicted in J.K. Galbraith's *Affluent Society* lay in becoming a superior Maciste, or even better a Hercules, whom Park had played in innumerable, multinationally populated low-budget sword-and-sandal epics that had found cult success on both sides of the Atlantic.

In point of fact, Arnold looked more like the 'perfect representative [of the Hitlerian] Aryan ideal'[12] than the 'softer' Graeco-Roman archetype of classical antiquity, and shared many of the Führer's less pernicious ideas about the importance of health and fitness as outlined in the notorious *Hausbuch für die deutsch Familie*.[13] Arnold's burgeoning, globally defined ethos, though, was not stymied by any definite affiliation with hard-line ideology. His was indeed the ideal, mythically invested Aryan body (descended in legend from a spurious 'pan-German' ancestry of 'supermen, destined to dominate the world with the ruthlessness of ancient savagery' and co-opted by the National Socialists in their quest to build a *Herrenvolk*).[14] However, the mind was adapted in the aftermath of the sins of the father, to fit with the absurd conscientious malaise afflicting a revisionist state that had 'shamelessly milked its status as Hitler's first victim and erected memorials to its anti-Nazi fighters for Austrian freedom. These were the foundation myths of a Europe liberated from history; they expunged awkward memories and asserted the inevitability of freedom's triumph.'[15]

Such cultural forgetfulness, a symptom of the 'profound shudder which follows on the regime of any one of history's magnetic tyrants,'[16] also affected the Americans, whose prominent Theodore Roosevelt-era activist Margaret Sanger thus advocated the 'science' of eugenics: 'More children from the fit, less from the unfit – that is the chief issue of birth control,' she pronounced.[17] What is more, articulates Susan Sontag in a 1975 essay on the dubious allure of the Third Reich's formal prescriptions:

> The same aesthetic responsible for the bronze colossi of Arno Breker – Hitler's (and, briefly, Cocteau's) favourite sculptor – and of Josef Thorak also produced the musclebound Atlas [1936, by German Lee Lawrie] in front of Manhattan's Rockefeller Center and the faintly lewd monument to the fallen doughboys of World War I in Philadelphia's Thirtieth Street railroad station.[18]

The vigorous and sublimely mechanised male body, as traditionally deified by totalitarianism and the bodybuilding cult alike, held honourable charm for both Europe's and America's patriots – until epochal shifts relegated such nationalistically redolent fetishisms to the pages of minority-interest magazines and forwarded the ersatz, tempered forms and physiognomies of Weissmuller, Reeves and Park et al. by way of surrogates.[19]

Undoubtedly, whilst his idols sit comfortably within the post-war cultural scheme, Arnold harks back to the conceptual chimera of the Nazi master-race fantasy: the state-manipulated apparition of a 'new man' (born of the co-optation of myth) who is as flawless as a machine yet as resourceful as a warrior-leader. Serving to 'unite Americans as Americans against an alien order,' Arnold, as J. Hoberman writes, *'embraces and embodies the covertly admired Teutonic virtues.'*[20] Thilo von Trotha, writing in 1936, stressed that:

> The beauty of the Nordic race includes heroism. Here lies a difference to Hellenic art, which often shows a Southern softness, which does not belong to the harshness of the Nordic-Germanic character. Heroic matter-of-factness, together with a Nordic ideal of beauty, must become the basis of a new age of art in Germany – otherwise art will continue to oscillate between Southern formalism and Asiatic chaos.[21]

The United States, however, has never entirely rejected this historically and morally pregnant archetype, an ideal made widespread not by the Nazis, but by the American racial purists to whom Hitler looked for inspiration. 'It is clear,' opined the American Breeders Association's Charles Woodruff in 1910, 'that the types of human beings from northeast Europe are our best citizens and have, therefore, to be conserved.'[22] The truest manifestation of human heroism, then, according to such mindsets – or the 'best' a man can be in terms of aesthetic, biological and mental status – is *homo Europaeus* rendered muscularly hard.

During bodybuilding's first heyday, in the late nineteenth century, promoter Bernarr 'Body Love' Macfadden, the first to stage a physique competition, concocted a slogan that recruited many to his cause, and whose rhetoric sounds appalling to a post-Nazism ear: 'Weakness is a crime. Don't be a criminal.'[23] Applying the same logic and playing to the fears of culturally indoctrinated, less-than-Herculean adolescents who dreaded a lifetime of sexual failure, Charles Atlas's ubiquitous magazine adverts for his 'Dynamic Tension' system followed suit, inspiring a legion of similar programmes that promised to turn previously 'soft, frail, skinny' adherents into 'real men,' who 'look like winners.'[24] Comic-book strongmen and related psychological exploitation pitched at young adults are indeed revealing modern manifestations of an age-old somatic creed; but, it is those civilly funded, solid tributes to genetic cathexes that represent America's most regressive, misguided public symbols of its own insecurity. Located close to the heart of American government, Washington DC's famous Boy Scout Memorial (by Donald DeLue) demonstrates a clear resurgence of the von Trotha-endorsed aesthetic. A shrine to 'physical, mental and moral fitness [the three are always equated in fascist lore], love of country, good citizenship, loyalty, honor, courage and clean living,'[25] it was erected in 1964, the year of the first Vietnam draft-card burnings, the shutting down of the University of California's Berkeley site by the Free Speech Movement, and the Mississippi Summer Project (of which three members were slain by the Ku Klux Klan) to register new black voters.

Schwarzenegger, according to Manfred Thellig, who accompanied him on an early bodybuilding excursion to Munich, loathed political correctness, however justifiable, and 'just loved those leftover relics of the Third Reich . . . those Teutonic statues.'[26] Though never an anti-Semite, Arnold – the young hero-trickster with a physique worthy of Thorak or Breker – seemingly knew how to tease by traversing the fine line between edgy humour and almost pantomimic villainy; he was 'just playing Tarzan'[27] with people's sensitivities, says Thellig, or playfully evoking his repressed cultural lineage whilst insinuating the unthinkable and unmentionable. It appears that Schwarzenegger, rightly or wrongly, bore little shame regarding his heritage's aesthetic values, and utilised an awareness of discursive potency to emphasise precariously anachronistic links to Nazi concepts of a putative biological elite. Blanket repudiations, in Arnold's mind, were perhaps damaging and unnecessary concessions to a worldview that would not accept unchangeable truths about his inherent nationality.

Since his earliest foreign successes, Arnold has not had much need of pretence or the adoption of a de-Europeanised personality; rather, he astutely discerned early on that his nature as a Germanic émigré (and those inferred associations that go with that status) might be an essential factor in his paradoxical charms. Nietzsche's 'children of the future' ('the self-overcomers of morality,' who are 'beyond good and evil'), notes Keith Ansell-Pearson, are those, like Schwarzenegger, 'who refuse to be "reconciled," "compromised," or "castrated" by the present age.'[28] With a single-mindedness that precluded, pro tem, any thoughts of committed romance or academic education, Arnold set out to prove himself by adopting an extreme extension of his father's egocentric, (semi-)Nietzschean philosophy: 'that the pursuit of strength, competition and victory should supersede all else, and that some men are superior and others eminently inferior.'[29] Again and again, between strenuously punishing bouts of muscle-engorging 'repetitions' in the gymnasium ('Only great pain is the ultimate liberator of the spirit'),[30] he sat watching films, inculcating a mantra of strident ambition: 'When I saw great people, I said to myself: "I can be there . . . You have to be hungry. You have to want to conquer."'[31] Bodybuilding, however, would remain Arnold's *sine qua non* for the next several years – he could wait to be a film star until he was ready, and indeed wait with the comforting certainty of total self-belief. Sure in his admiration not only of Park and Reeves, but also of inspirational leaders from Charlemagne to (allegedly) Hitler, Arnold told his vicarious but realistic father: 'I want to be the best-built man in the world, then I want to go to America and be in movies.'[32]

In the midst of post-war crises pertaining to the role of the American male (and especially in the 1980s, as tropes of maleness were both politically and culturally redefined during the 'Reagan Revolution' as symbolically replete, 'hard-body'[33] attributes), Arnold, visually and aurally perhaps the *'absolute image of the Fascist human being,'*[34] resonated deeply within his chosen heartland. He would popularly embody heroic, timely traits that Nixon, Ford, Carter, Reagan and most of their constituents could not, whether by dint of guilt, perceived ineffectuality or old age. As Blitz and Krasniewicz point out, 'We have animated the perfectly sculpted man and made him a living statue of the American Dream.'[35] What seems equally pertinent, though, is that we have in addition gradually but surely apprehended him from the superseded, vanquished 'demon' of his Old European roots and turned these qualities to our advantage: we have, principally by means of our cherished silver screen, made him a recycled totem of victory with which to contain the *entartete Kunst* of protest, intellectualism, elitism, cultural experimentation and artistic sedition. Much like comic-book creators Jerry Siegel and Joe Shuster's infant saviour, brought to an America of the 1930s from Krypton ('a distant planet so far advanced in evolution that it bears a civilization of *supermen* – beings which represent the human race at its ultimate peak of perfect development'), Arnold had arrived thirty years later to fight the 'good' fight as a living paladin of somatic exceptionalism.[36] 'It is the victors [of the Second World War],' said Winston Churchill in May 1945, 'who must search their hearts in their glowing hours, and be worthy by their nobility of the immense forces they wield.'[37] The nebulous soul of America, 'defined by the common history, traditions, culture, heroes and villains, enemies and wars, defeats and victories enshrined

in its "mystic chords of memory,"' would hence find purpose and identity in subsuming Schwarzenegger:[38] *Possunt quia posse videntur* ('They
can because they think they can'). Arnold, Hoberman remarks (though
he sadly never dilates), is a 'strategic asset'[39] for the post-war era. As for
Arnold's moral ambiguity, Antonia Fraser contends astutely that:

> [T]he private weaknesses which in themselves constitute evidence of
> humanity, are, however, a far cry from evil. It is surely by definition
> impossible for a hero to be totally evil. It is true that, as Lucifer
> was the fairest of the archangels before he fell, 'outshining myriads
> through bright,' traces of this attraction remain in evil's face . . . What
> our heroes and heroines do have in common, beyond some form of
> virtue, however masked, is an ability to capture the imagination.[40]

'Mythology,' writes Campbell, 'does not hold as its greatest hero the
merely virtuous man.'[41]

Arnold was never destined to be another Conrad Veidt, a victim of the
Nazis forced by fate to play Nazi villains: he was simply too 'good'; too
useful. Fascism as both an idea and a reality was not dead after the fall of
Berlin. Its 'essential elements – militarism, racism, imperialism,' argues
historian Howard Zinn, were 'absorbed into the already poisoned bones
of the victors.'[42]

Having taken myriad major bodybuilding titles (including four
NABBA Mr Universe wins, the 1966 award of Best Built Man of Europe,
the 1968 German Powerlifting Championship and the 1970 Mr World)
by his early twenties, Arnold was naturally coming to the attention
of those outside the still relatively esoteric sphere of muscle-fitness.
'People could relate to hugeness, to the animal spectacle of a big guy,' he
wrote in his autobiography. 'They called me "The Giant of Austria" and
"The Austrian Oak." Articles read: "If Hercules were to be born today,
his name would be Arnold Schwarzenegger."'[43] His sport, plus the
tutelage of Reg Park, had taken him to California in 1968, and America
was proving a dream come true. The Kennedy–Johnson era was coming
to a close, for which the conservatively inclined Arnold was thankful;
the sunny climate, fast cars and beach-loving, figure-conscious women
were agreeable; and he was becoming wealthy through a combination
of product endorsements, property investments, ghost-written articles
and cash prizes. Apparently disregarding the intellectual worries of an

overwhelmingly negative year (Vietnam, Biafran starvation, the crushing of Polish and Czechoslovakian idealism, the massacre in Mexico, the worldwide brutalisation of dissenters, and the murders of Robert Kennedy and Martin Luther King), Schwarzenegger was at the peak of his bodybuilding powers and eager to test the waters of a possible Hollywood career in any way feasible. His accent was still heavy, and he was at this stage correct in assuming this to be a barrier; Arnold began taking English lessons from his pedagogic girlfriend Barbara Outland while waiting on advice from mentors and friends, some of whom had film industry connections.

The first film project to come Arnold's way, thanks to bodybuilding periodical magnate Joe Weider (who had audaciously pitched the stolid Schwarzenegger as a 'Shakespearean actor' from Vienna)[44] was Arthur Allan Seidelman's *Hercules in New York*, a 1970 update of the sword-and-sandal genre piece with a fish-out-of-water twist that brings its legendary protagonist to the modern-day East Coast. (This is not especially novel, as such variations on a theme were common at the time. *Hercules in New York*, sometimes known by the suitably unserious title *Hercules Goes Bananas*, was only one of many similar attempts to revivify the rather dated Reeves/Park 'peplum' formula by transposing the action to an incongruous locale.) Working (but not for Italian television, as many accounts claim) on an inauspicious budget of around $300,000, Seidelman easily secured Schwarzenegger, an acting tyro with a desire to emulate and outshine his teenage idols. Billed as 'Arnold Strong,' and a mildly humiliating second to his near-identically named co-star Arnold Stang (recognisable as the voice of Chunky Chocolate and *Top Cat*), the soon-to-be-overdubbed Austrian nonetheless arrived in New York exuding typical bravado and enthusiasm for the thematically apt commencement of his cinematic mythos. Arnold's peculiarly American 'perfection of iconography' was underway: the 'intelligible spectacle' had begun.[45]

Arnold in the Land of Trials: Or, A Hero Re-spun

The key to modern myths is in the banality (taken seriously) of kitsch success and the popularity of triviality – final traces of worlds gone under.[46]

Following screenwriter Aubrey Wisberg's portentously intoned, half-serious voiceover on the subject of 'antique Greece' and a putative 'time when myth and history merged into mystery,' *Hercules in New York* establishes its unfussy plotline with an earnest scene set on Mount Olympus (during which traffic noises can clearly be heard). Aesthetically, the prologue crystallises Seidelman's low-budget, high-camp approach, something evidently born as much of monetary considerations as deliberation. Concomitantly, the dialogue is sub-Aristophanean, even if a casual mishmash of Greek and Roman nomenclature is applied throughout. (In fact, it would appear that characters from *any* well-known ancient schema are permissible – at one point Samson intervenes in a confrontation.) The naïve Hercules, dissatisfied with life in the clouds, longs to descend to the realm of mortality and make play amongst a humanity awe-struck by his prowess. 'I've been here thousands of years,' says Arnold – who wears only a sash and loincloth – to his forbidding father, Zeus; 'I'm bored. I only want to browse around . . . I'm tired of the same old faces, the same old things.' Zeus (Ernest Graves) proscribes such folly: 'You wouldn't like it down there.' 'Let me be the judge of that,' retorts Arnold, and, on the soundtrack, the first of the film's incessant taverna-style bouzouki dances heralds the titles. 'Total-immersion costume kitsch,' is how Nigel Andrews accurately describes the actor-athlete's first film, 'made on a wing and a prayer.'[47]

Though a bland, all-purpose actor dubs his voice, it is Schwarzenegger's vast bronzed physique that is striking, displayed from the beginning at every opportunity for our delectation or stupefaction. Indeed, the spectator may share the incredulity of the middle-aged, hysterically overcome female airplane passenger that witnesses, via her window, Hercules's grinning descent to Earth (an obvious, part-accidental metaphor for Arnold's real-life, avatar-like arrival from Old Europe): 'He was very handsome, and he had big muscles, and he was practically *naked!*' Her companion, by way of explanation to the stewardess (who is administering oxygen), says that she 'shouldn't have taken Agatha to see all those Greek statues – she's so impressionable!' As would become more or less routine for the rest of his cinematic career, Arnold's superhuman body, and his body's historical, mythical significance, is henceforth centralised in terms of explicit dramaturgical impetus and simultaneously fixed in paradoxical apposition. Hercules, we are told, is coming to Earth; he is not, however, merely a curious strongman, but also a bearer of bestial, sexual potency that must somehow be controlled or contained within a familiar, essentially emasculating discourse.

Schwarzenegger's physical sexuality is thus rendered analogous to that of a Greek statue (or at least the popular conception of such as are commonly exhibited – Arnold is no Satyr), its erogeneity disavowed by the pursuit of joyous athleticism as sublimation, its flaccid (or implicitly absent, unaesthetic) genitalia very much secondary in sensual purpose to the muscular male frame – the phallus displaced to an 'erotic numbness,'[48] or made metaphoric. 'To equip the muscular body with too visibly intrusive a genital endowment,' Kenneth Dutton explains of Hellenic depictions of Apollonian man, 'would be to replace the universal suggestiveness of symbolism with a restrictively literal and particular meaning, to substitute mere sexual prowess for the universality of divine potency . . . there is a curiously asexual quality discernable in the advanced muscularity of the bodybuilder's physique, and it could be argued that this is a central element in the symbolic language of the developed body.'[49] Arnold, therefore, is hereafter cinematically freighted with the cultural burden of both classical and contemporary representations of the muscled yet non-arousing hero-figure, for whom bigger is not necessarily better in every respect, and for whom power is located in the aura, rather than the act, of genetic influence. The Apollonian archetype, writes John Boardman, represented man 'at his idealised best, indistinguishable from the gods, whom [the Greek realist artist] conceived in man's likeness.'[50] If Arnold's earliest pro-filmic identity is indistinguishable from a god, then it is a god of co-existent chastity and virility, whose playfulness hints at phallic possibility, yet whose neotenic, Elysian spirit likewise makes the thought of erotic reality seem anachronistic or absurd: 'cartoon innocence mixed with caricature strongman contour; Desperate Dan meets Peter Pan,' comments Andrews.[51]

For a film made almost contemporaneously with Woodstock (both the festival and Michael Wadleigh's epochal film), the contrapuntal terror at Altamont, *The Wild Bunch*, *Easy Rider* and *Midnight Cowboy*[52] in cinemas and the hippies' Dionysian impulse at its absolute apogee, *Hercules in New York* is a cautiously neutered, sexless antidote to authentic concerns. 'I was King Kong,' said Arnold of his prowess in 1970, evoking an icon of animalistic, unbridled hypersexuality;[53] yet this atavism is not transposed to celluloid. Seidelman's film instead constitutes a ninety-minute assertion that Schwarzenegger's waxed, restricted libido embodies only feats of old-fashioned, clean-living strength and romantic stalwartness, rather than the emergent (if commercially subdued) counter-cultural themes, ambiguous morality, eroto- and ballisto-mania prevalent in the post-Hays Code film industry. When not tempered by humour, it would seem that evocations of actual, mechanical sex might ruin the metaphorical and literal line of Arnold's erect body, confront his many nominally heterosexual male admirers with problematic specifics, or generally despoil the contrived, comfortable illusion that Hercules's/ Arnold's intentions are avuncular. More so than Reeves's or Park's, Arnold's Olympian is an anti-pubescent *puer aeternus* (Jung's 'eternal child,' the boy hero unable to grow up) suspended in limbo between boyhood and maturity.

Even whilst the resurgent concept of 'free love' permeated the mainstream (getting as far as Broadway and the musical *Hair*), Schwarzenegger and sincerely expressed sexuality did not, and to this day do not, easily combine. Hercules, whose legendary attributes include comprehensive bisexual prowess, had been rendered eternally juvenile; by extension, Schwarzenegger has never mastered (or been especially keen to embrace) truly adult roles, every subsequent cinematic sexual encounter being in some sense either a humorous replay of the airplane-window fly-past or an emotionless, perfunctory anticlimax. 'The Third Reich,' according to George Mosse's study of Germanic racial representations, 'sought to strip nudity of its sexuality by drawing a sharp distinction between the private and the representational . . . the seminude body remained abstract, very much like a sculpture.'[54] Arnold's filmic persona, smooth, hairless and bronzed, in the same way continually transcends biology ('mere sexual prowess') as a contemporary American – via ancient Greece and the usually unmentionable but very significant influence of Nazi Germany – icon of unspoilt and protracted youth. His virility, or any hint of such, is acceptable only when cloistered within either his character's inherent reticence or an institutional archetype.

Back on the walled-garden set of Mount Olympus, ignoring several nubile goddesses' shrill pleas, Hercules's fairytale wicked stepmother Juno (Hera in Greek mythology) decides that it is better all round that the mischievous youngster is gone for eternity: 'Let Hercules suffer the consequences of his own obstinacy.' Zeus is more circumspect. 'Let us see what he is doing now,' he solemnly declares, consulting, strangely for an omniscient god, a crystal ball. We cut to a seascape, on which sails a beaten-up American freighter, and therein to a cabin and the sight of Arnold topless and towelling himself dry. The captain questions Hercules, who refuses to defer to authority, saying that he is 'democratic'; the demigod, however, soon qualifies this by adding that 'no mortal is superior to Hercules.' Seemingly unaware of the precipitous situation regarding his illegal-alien status, Hercules, now sporting a docker's jeans and furry hat, starts (bloodless) fights with the easily subdued sailors, until the ship reaches New York. The city's nature as a portal to opportunity is announced by a metonymic shot of the Statue of Liberty, which efficiently recalls the testimonies of all comers to Ellis Island, and its famous motto: 'The cowards never came, and the weak died on the way.'[55] Not for the last time, Arnold's art was uncannily imitating his life. America, an adventure-filled land of milk and honey for the far-from-weak Schwarzenegger, would logically prove a playground for his Hercules.

After excitedly disembarking to engage in another rapidly edited scene of improbable confrontation (this time with some dockhands who are promised 'Twenty bucks for the first person who flattens him!' by the ship's aggrieved bosun),[56] Hercules meets his timelessly comedic, physically inferior helper-companion. Having looked on with exaggerated, wide-eyed marvel at the ease with which the new arrival had despatched his assailants, the chinless, comparatively emaciated-looking Pretzie (Stang) – so named, he explains, because he 'sells pretzels on the waterfront' – urges Hercules into a taxi to avoid danger. Clearly, this incongruous pairing is 'the type of duo,' as reviewer Danny Peary noted, 'that would appear in *Mad Magazine* movie-poster parodies,'[57] as well as several previous Hercules films, in turn inspired by ancient stories. Jon Solomon observes that:

> The hero himself has the pleasure of his male companion's devotion. This companion can be of two sorts: either a mighty, meaty specimen like the hero himself, or a wimpy comedian who cannot lift stones or wine casks but who can instead poke soldiers in the behind with his dagger or bonk them over the head with ceramic jugs.[58]

On a morphological level, then, the film unsurprisingly adheres to narrative customs old and new. In addition, however, it also routinely (if reflexively) endorses eugenic creeds via somewhat brutal characterisations and a thematically malodorous interplay.

Pretzie, our 'wimpy comedian,' is a New York nebbish, a crudely stereotypical, cowering, money-oriented Mr Malaprop who is neurotic and fearful – the very object of the National Socialists' hate campaigns against 'degeneracy personified'[59] and a trope for what American industrialist Henry Ford, whose framed portrait hung on Hitler's wall, called 'ugly, indissoluble lumps.'[60] Juxtaposing Schwarzenegger with Stang, or Hercules with Pretzie, is therefore more than superficially impish; it reminds us of their contrasting somatic traits and those traits' inherent potential for comedy. However, in addition to this, it is an apposition that evokes a credo of 'manliness' – something 'at best paternalistic,' remarks Kevin White, 'at worst genocidal' – based on genetics and social Darwinism, locating once more in the American subconscience doctrines that had only recently been suppressed after they had been taken to logical extremes.[61] The disparity between the flaxen, nubile gods of Olympus and the 'typical' nebbish is apparent, whether we choose to scrutinise it or not: it is the physically weak yet scheming Jew who is ultimately grateful in subservience to those 'superior' beings and their representative on Earth.

Hercules and Pretzie predictably find friendship in this relatively liberal film, but the very unlikelihood of such a duo existing, in any historical reality and regardless of race or religion, frames the comedic situation squarely within a normalising contemporary mythology, working in vain against its own momentum to achieve an idealistically desirable but possibly irreconcilable marriage between differing mindsets: the mighty 'winner' and the enfeebled 'loser'; the 'enlightened' towering giant and the downtrodden '*Untermensch*' flung together by circumstances quite outside probability. Cornell professor Andrew Hacker distilled the truth about the national mood in 1970 in a *Newsweek* essay. 'We can no longer be a single nation, possessed of a common spirit,' wrote Hacker. 'Neither "class struggle" nor "civil war" entirely describes the contours of this discord. Suffice it to say that increasingly we will encounter one another as enemies.'[62] America's on-going quest for a 'national purpose' had yielded up no all-embracing heroes since the cruelly curtailed 'Camelot' of John Kennedy; *Hercules in New York,* uninterested in specific political comment or rumination, sees Seidel-man set out a stall around more universal comforts.

'If there is a perfect example of a hero,' claims Michael Senior, 'it is Heracles. Demi-god, monster-slayer, lone traveller on tremendous journeys, he is the doom-driven, task-achieving superhuman who occupies a central spot in the imaginations of all periods and peoples.'[63] By the same logic, if there is a contemporary exemplar of a persecuted converse, it is Pretzie. As Daniel Jonah Goldhagen notes in his ominous tome delineating the essence of anti-Jewish sentiment in Europe, '[T]he *Volk* . . . was conceptually linked to, and partly dependent upon, a definition of Jews as the *Volk*'s antithesis.'[64] Whilst *Hercules in New York* should in no way be construed as a rhetorically or ideologically anti-Semitic tract, it nonetheless draws on (ostensibly) anachronistic comparisons that parallel those at work within the tenets of bipolar, twentieth-century racialism.

It becomes increasingly clear that Pretzie has found new purpose in his association with the powerful 'Herc,' who, due to Arnold's captivatingly wooden performance, exudes a confounding duality – of callow bewilderment and strident machismo – that befits the part well. Having irrationally demonstrated his strength by stopping a fork-lift truck ('Fine chariot, but where are the horses?') and tipping over the taxi when confronted about what Pretzie hysterically calls 'the bread, the shekels, the long green, the money: *dough*,' Hercules encounters some student athletes in training, who are soundly outclassed by the son of Zeus whilst Pretzie looks on in dumbstruck admiration. Throwing the javelin and discus, and intercut with the awed expressions of both Pretzie and the students, Schwarzenegger takes part in a celebratory spectacle that constitutes Seidelman's cut-price, perverse (when one takes into account the director's ethnicity) distillation of Leni Riefenstahl's notorious *Olympia* (1938), a work obsessed with 'the magnificence of the body in action,' as the torch of humankind's healthful, 'pure' destiny is passed literally and figuratively from ancient Greece's explicitly homo-erotic culture to Nazi Germany's appropriated, kitsch revival.[65] (One may also sense Wagnerian aspirations in *Hercules in New York*'s misty-mountaintop opening, an echo of Riefenstahl's mythical imagery in *Olympia*.) Shot from low angles to accentuate his musculature, Arnold astonishes his audience, and especially his diminutive companion: 'That's my buddy! Greek fella – he's just come over!' he proclaims, and places a bet (having earlier demured from paying for the cab) on Herc to win the long jump. Naturally, Hercules indeed wins, and Pretzie, now firmly established as a one-dimensional antithesis to Arnold's brawny master, furtively checks his prize, stuffing the notes into his pockets.

De rigueur 'intellectual' and love interests materialise when Hercules and Pretzie are approached on the playing field by an inquisitive professor of classics and his mini-skirted daughter, Helen, who invite the pair for tea ('The conventional social beverage,' rather than what the paranoid Pretzie thinks means marijuana, even though this term was, even in 1969, outdated for all but the uninitiated). Upon arrival at the academic's apartment, Pretzie demonstrates his social ineptitude and boorishness, not only, as Hercules repeatedly does, by his ignorance of modern-day discursive *politesse*, but also by scratching his back with a stag's horn and stealing a cheap paperback on mythology, surely not the kind of book a learned professor would in reality own, yet one that succinctly reflects the film's hotchpotch, undernourished production values. Hercules goes on accidentally to insult Helen by asking if her other guest, Rod, is 'her lover,' at which the equally gauche Pretzie bristles, 'That's no way to talk to a broad!' A protracted wrestle commences between Hercules and Rod, offering an opportunity for Helen and Pretzie to mug their protestations and Hercules to amuse himself by doing what comes easily – lifting weights and causing amazement. Yet Helen, we learn, as she later informs her surprisingly tolerant father, has nonetheless accepted a dinner date with 'Hercules Zeus,' whose hefty magnetism, suppressed biology and incredulous smile, thanks to Schwarzenegger's innate joy at simply being in a film, was (almost) understandably too much to resist.

Several scenes of increasingly cheaply produced and poorly choreographed action ensue, including Arnold wrestling and punching a man in an absurdly unrealistic bear suit (the only one of Hercules's fabled labours to feature literally) as the infatuated Helen looks on, gasping; the introduction of some stereotyped hyphenate gangsters, who extort money from Pretzie – now the manager of Hercules ('The New Wrestling Wonder') in his new career as professional combatant – with asinine threats whose barely credible nature stretches any remaining inherent verisimilitude to its limits; a pause by Hercules and Helen outside the Rockefeller Center to admire and photograph the fascistic Atlas statue, before they go to a takeaway and Hercules, clearly impressed by American abundance, extols 'this fine food, for only a few coins'; an ill-fated weight-lifting contest between a newly mortal (he has been poisoned by Nemesis after a failed attempt by Mercury to bring him back to Olympus via persuasion) Hercules and the film's only black character, the coarsely named, mute 'Monstro'; and Arnold stripping to the waist, fighting and/or flexing for compliments whenever the script will allow, which is often. Despite all these caveats, and despite the combined efforts of the director, producers and screenwriter (who clashed over the humorous content, resulting in a noncommittal, unsatisfying blend of slapstick and sternness), Arnold's undeniable qualities shine through even the heavy-handed dubbing and the Styrian's ostensible inability to act, at least in the orthodox sense. Stang and the rest offer compensatory, over-the-top performances, but it is through-and-through the young Arnold's film, even though he would subsequently attempt, in somewhat untypical shame, to buy out all prints of what in many ways represents a benchmark: the birth of a hero, and the first, little-seen cinematic 'trial' of Arnold on his road to mythic potency.

Martin Flanagan asserts that '[p]lot in the contemporary action film is deployed as a series of narrative hurdles the hero must overcome, a structure that parallels the trope of "testing" identified by Bakhtin in the Greek romance.'[66] Further to this insight, Thomas Sobchack notes that such generic films are:

> based on the structure of the romance of medieval literature; a protagonist either has or develops great and special skills and overcomes insurmountable obstacles in extraordinary situations to successfully achieve some desired goal, usually the restitution of order to the human world invoked by the narrative. The protagonists confront the human, natural, or supernatural powers that have improperly assumed control over the world and eventually defeat them.[67]

True to formal prescription, we have witnessed Hercules bringing hope to the weak, innocuous love to the lonely, and, ironically, inspiration to the amateurs of an eerily ahistorical New York that seems distanced from and despondent with actuality. The only light in this drab, regressive city of intellectual darkness is Arnold: when all around is failing desperately, his presence lends a natural-born hero's hand.

Sobchack's dramaturgical scheme, of course, would recur time and again in Arnold's second career, and applies equally to his 'hurdles' in life and overriding aspirations to superhuman greatness. Seidelman's film, though divorced from *au courant* concerns, speaks volumes of its star as subject. In words that unerringly pertain to Schwarzenegger, Joseph L. Henderson dilates:

> The myth of the hero is the most common and the best known myth in the world. We find it in the classical mythology of Greece and Rome, in the Middle Ages, in the Far East, and among contemporary primitive tribes. It also appears in our dreams. It has an obvious dramatic appeal, and a less obvious, but nonetheless profound psychological importance . . . Over and over again one hears a tale describing a hero's miraculous but humble birth, his early proof of superhuman strength, his rapid rise to prominence or power, his triumphant struggle with the forces of evil, his fallibility to the sin of pride . . . these godlike figures are in fact representations of the whole psyche, the larger and more comprehensive identity that supplies the strength that the personal ego lacks. Their special role suggests that the essential function of the heroic myth is the development of the individual's ego-consciousness – his awareness of his own strengths and weaknesses – in a manner that will equip him for the arduous tasks with which life confronts him.[68]

Arnold would in due course take on all comers, whether human competitors, fabulous beasts or established notions of artistry or aesthetics, and (usually) win. At *Hercules in New York*'s climax, Hercules races with Pretzie in a chariot through Broadway and Central Park (during which, in a curious underscoring of *Hercules in New York*'s own cultural dissonance, we see a cinema showing *Easy Rider*). This visual superimposition of Arnold's syncretistic, high-kitsch contemporary monomyth against the most obvious mythical symbols of 1970s metropolitan America (its adverts and skyscrapers – themselves over-endowed temples to 'free-world' excess) serves as a useful if inchoate metonym: Upton Sinclair's 'urban jungle' has superseded the bush and scrub of the virgin land, formerly the testing ground for immigrant heroes.

Schwarzenegger – and his mysterious essence – had arrived to make play in America, that 'mythical place of rebirth for those strong enough

1. Hercules and Pretzie commandeer a chariot in Hercules in New York

to survive the rite of passage,'[69]and largely on his own cultural terms; he indeed much later attempted, obliquely yet appreciably, the 'restitution of order to the human world' by choosing and shaping his on-screen persona in symbiotic acuity to the popular taste of 'Joe Six-Pack,' the demographically conceptual, swing-voting denominator of the 'regular guy' whose own aspirations are limited, but whose predilections in the way of entertainment are for easily understood, preternaturally vigorous protagonists.[70] Germanely, Victor Burgin et al. describe action films as 'fantasies of omnipotence, heroism and salvation . . . a counterpoint to the experience of oppression and powerlessness';[71] audiences perhaps not only want to *be* Arnold: they also want to be rescued.

At the height of his fame, Schwarzenegger would appreciate and exploit the production/consumption dialectic like few others, embodying the democratic myth of opportunity for all who truly want it, whilst elevated to stardom in part by a rare, epochal 'charisma,' 'a certain quality . . . by virtue of which [a star] is set apart from ordinary men.'[72] As Richard Dyer outlines in his groundbreaking 1980 study, *Stars*, 'The signification of a given performance sign is determined by its place within culturally and historically specific codes';[73] Arnold's temporality and psychic function in 1970 had yet to dovetail, but *Hercules in New York* all the same assayed his signifying vocabulary within a phenomenon Dyer labels 'structured polysemy,' or the shifting semantic relationship between a star's meaningful performative attributes, premeditated and unplanned, and audience perception (or 'reading') thereof. Pretzie, after Hercules's odd change of heart and decision to return to the land of the gods,[74] hence speaks presciently when he laments, wallowing in Kafkaesque loneliness, his friend's departure: 'The strongest guy in the world, joining up with a nothing like me. Boy, he really made me feel like something, a half-pint like me. I ain't never gonna forget him.' Over a slow-motion montage of Arnold's previous feats of strength (overturning the taxi, pushing apart enormous pillars of rolled paper), we hear Hercules communicate with Pretzie over the latter's transistor radio, reaching across the status divide – using the broadcast media – from the remote pantheon of Olympus, where he remains out of reach, having touched and changed the lives of the ordinary, only for a fleeting moment. 'It wasn't what the headshrinkers call "wishful thinking," was it, Herc?' 'Any time you wish me to be with you, all you need do is think of me, and I will be with you,' replies Hercules, signifying Pretzie's means of escape from freedom into wilful submission.

Almost needless to say, *Hercules in New York*, in many respects a prevaricatory and peripheral oddity whose content seems disengaged from both Nixonian rhetoric and its counter-cultural rejoinders, was not a critical or commercial success; it would thus be a full six years before Arnold again found a principal film role and continued on his journey to a personal Olympus. Minor parts in Robert Altman's *The Long Goodbye* (1973) and the made-for-television *Happy Anniversary and Goodbye* (Jack Donohue, 1974) followed, in which Arnold played poorly considered stereotypes: clichéd, taciturn heavies. (The former is described by John L. Flynn, perhaps a little unfairly, as an 'ugly, boring, film travesty'; the latter starred Lucille Ball, who for a while took Arnold under her aegis and gave him acting tips.)[75] Having more than proved his worth as an athlete, and evinced considerable charisma even when pitted against Seidelman's budgetary dearth, Arnold was cast in 1976 by renowned *Five Easy Pieces* (1970) director Bob Rafelson to act alongside Jeff Bridges and Sally Field – two young but nevertheless respected performers – in *Stay Hungry*. Schwarzenegger's part was not a great digression in terms of repertoire, yet it seemed a natural fit: Arnold would portray a laconic bodybuilder in a film whose tagline read, 'If you've got an appetite for life . . .'

Arnold in the New New South: Pumping Dixie

> Southern history, unlike American, includes large components of frustration, failure, and defeat. It includes not only an overwhelming military defeat but long decades of defeat in the provinces of economic, social and political life. Such a heritage affords the Southern people no basis for the delusion that there is nothing whatever that is beyond their power to accomplish.[76]

By the mid-1970s Arnold had built an empire as the chief representative of his ilk. He crowned his achievements by taking part in something of a cultural vindication for the bodybuilding profession: a well-attended seminar at New York's Whitney Museum entitled 'The Articulate Muscle: The Male Body in Art.' When queried by a reporter about how it felt to be 'reduced' to a sex symbol, Arnold replied, 'I'm in Heaven. I feel like a king.'[77] 'I was born to be a leader,' Schwarzenegger informed the *Sunday Times* shortly thereafter; he would either find fulfilment as a dictator, or a saviour, 'like Jesus.' On Arnold's apartment wall hung a plaque that summarised its occupant's worldview: 'Without bodybuilding, there's no NATION-BUILDING.'[78] Fitness for the consolidatory establishment of psychic nationalities, collective self-definitions that Benedict Anderson memorably labelled 'imagined communities,'[79] was thus firmly established in Arnold's mind as something equated harmoniously with the pain-hewn (masculine) 'body beautiful' and its power as a restorative. 'All of us are faced at some time or another with the task of performing the labour of redemption, first on ourselves, then on others,' mused Joseph Goebbels in his 1929 *roman-à-clef*, *Michael*. 'If we are to be strong enough to form the life of our era, it is our own lives that must first be mastered.'[80] Echoing the sentiments of *Twilight of the Idols*, Nietzsche's 'grand declaration of war' on equality, Schwarzenegger likewise considered it 'decisive for the fortune of a people and of humanity, that civilisation begins in the right *place* . . . the right place is body, demeanour, regimen, physiology; the *rest* follows therefrom.'[81]

Charles Gaines's Alabama-set novel *Stay Hungry* had in 1975 been piquing Bob Rafelson's interest for some time. He had, however, been hampered by an inability to find the right actor to play champion bodybuilder Joe Santo – until the effortlessly confident Schwarzenegger's endearing screen-test. It mattered not that the part had to be rewritten to accommodate Schwarzenegger's thick accent (Santo was now Austrian, rather than American), or that Arnold's 240-pound physique was deemed 'just too godamn big'[82] even for a competitive, top-flight muscle-man: Arnold's charm as the (a)typical immigrant hero, combined once more with uncanny synchronicity, had won him over. Gaines, on whose suggestion Rafelson approached Schwarzenegger, was struck by Arnold's singular aptness, remarking that he 'had an eerie feeling that the fictional character was somehow based on Arnold.'[83] 'You can look all over the world, Bob,' Schwarzenegger apparently told Rafelson at an early meeting, 'but you will sooner or later turn to me.'[84]

Gaines's screenplay for *Stay Hungry* concerns Craig Blake (Bridges), a wealthy, prematurely jaded 'sonny-boy' and property heir who becomes embroiled in a real-estate deal worth millions of dollars to a Mafia family. To make good on the arrangement, Blake has to persuade an elderly alcoholic gym-owner, Thor Erickson (R.G. Armstrong), to sell up his 'Olympic Spa' in order that a high-rise can be erected on that site. Upon visiting the gymnasium, moral complications arise as the recently orphaned Blake finds himself enamoured of the bodybuilders and their karate-kicking female cohorts. He meets and befriends Mr Austria, Joe Santo (who likes to work out wearing a bizarre, Zorro-like costume), and the Olympic Spa's down-to-earth receptionist, Mary Tate Farnsworth (Field). Mary Tate and Blake find sex and love, but their plans are ruined by Blake's nouveau riche cousins, who disparage the unfettered Mary Tate for her naïve manners. Uncle Albert (Woodrow Parfrey) dismays at his nephew's newfound interests, especially warning him away from girls of low breeding. Meanwhile, the Mafiosi attempt to encroach upon the gymnasium's hitherto stable microcosm by destroying the air-conditioning equipment; in response, the multi-racial bodybuilders fight it out with their counterparts from the world of organised crime, having first paraded through the streets of Birmingham (one of the most race-fixated and bigoted cities in America)[85] in a rather camply orchestrated, and strangely tolerantly received, consciousness-raising exercise. Santo, a bastion of healthy morality in clear apposition to the dissolute Thor, then takes the Mr Universe title. Forsaking a life of privilege, Blake makes his own life complete by setting up house with Mary Tate, and finally all is restored to Capra-esque equilibrium as Blake and Santo acquire the Spa following Erickson's ignominious arrest for assaulting (under the pernicious influence of drugs) Mary Tate.

In the majority of Arnold's scenes, and in contrast to *Hercules in New York*, the actor is conspicuously clothed; indeed, Schwarzenegger is usually more covered than Bridges or Field, whose tight-fitting outfits are provocatively minimalist. The rationale behind the Zorro costume, according to Rafelson, was to keep Arnold's torso hidden until the Mr Universe finale, whereupon the director at last relishes his subject's most apparent asset.[86] Arnold's body is thus, again, central, but as an object of implicitly forbidden cathexis whose purpose is in its climactic (if sexually under-endowed, by comparison with his co-stars) revelation. Amongst all the flesh on display, it is Arnold's that is under wraps, occupying a zone withheld from the spectatorial gaze, yet undoubtedly pregnant with self-possessed potential. Schwarzenegger, in *Stay Hungry*, brings his body to the New South – or the *New* New South, a place historically divorced not only from its once all-providing agricultural base, but also from the transgressions and misdeeds of its past – to offer a metaphorical buttress against which is posited the romanticised, elevated body politic comprising all the film's other characters: Schwarzenegger's body is rendered (almost) metaphysical, a giganticised helper-agent from a more dignified, imagined time and space.

Cinematic representations of sub-Mason–Dixon Line America were overwhelmingly negative in the 1970s. Bill Bryson generalises, though he does so accurately and speaks of a common perception, when he writes that, 'It surely is no coincidence that all those films you have ever seen about the South – *Easy Rider*, *In the Heat of the Night*, *Cool Hand Luke*, *Brubaker*, *Deliverance* – depict Southerners as murderous, incestuous, shitty-shoed rednecks.'[87] *Stay Hungry* hence constitutes an oblique but nonetheless hopeful antidote aimed at restoring faith in the South's best, secular values (solidarity, folk culture, loyalty, charity to the deserving), and by extension a remedial, therapeutic statement determined by circumstance. The undistinguished, default presidency of Gerald Ford, who had pardoned the great 'sinner' Nixon for Watergate ('an American tragedy in which we all have played a part'),[88] was about to give way to the 'soft-body,' 'ineffectual' tenure of humanitarian Jimmy Carter. In 1976, Carter campaigned for the Democratic nomination on a promise that he would 'never lie to you [the voters],' and bestow egalitarian principles on an America tired of internecine strife. 'It is time for our governmental leaders to respect the law no less than the humblest citizen,' he said, 'so that we can end the double standard of justice in America. I see no reason why big-shot crooks [by implication, Nixon included] should go free while the poor ones go to jail.'[89] The erstwhile peanut farmer from Georgia would go on, based on this rhetoric of ostensibly natural law, to beat Ford; America's wounds clearly needed healing with a soft, anti-Beltway touch – a caring hand to accentuate the positive in the national character and draw out those qualities of diverse nationhood that behoved a time of gentle transition from the pain of Watergate and Vietnam to the pride in vigour and renewal offered by Reagan's ideological statesmanship. Canvassing for the presidency, Carter had spoken of a 'time for America to move and to speak not with boasting and belligerence but with *quiet strength*, to depend in world affairs not merely on the size of an arsenal but on the *nobility of ideas*, and to govern at home not by confusion and crisis but with grace and imagination and common sense.'[90] *Stay Hungry*, to be sure, reflects these desires, both broadly in its narrative scope and more acutely through its use of Arnold, his carefully deployed body, and his character's paradoxical, idealised nature.

The first we see of Schwarzenegger is his famous, competition-posed silhouette on the Olympic Spa's sign, a noble and mysterious advert of his mythic presence. Santo is introduced in person as a gentle, inspirational guru, thoughtful and ruminative in deportment and speech. As opposed to Blake's family, he shows both humanity, when helping Blake clean up his injuries after a bar brawl with some thugs, and unexpected refinement, commenting on Blake's collection of cut-glass antiques that they 'ought to be in a museum,' at which Mary Tate smiles, simultaneously confounded and beguiled by his depths. Nor does Santo appear interested in wealth, having gone not to California, but to the culturally peripheral, recession-hit Birmingham; when Thor, the money-oriented but psychologically troubled impresario, promises that Santo will be 'as rich as cream and feeling fine' after winning Mr Universe, Santo replies that he is 'feeling fine already,' and it is obvious that the bodybuilder places loyalty above financial necessity (why else would he stay in the 'tutelage' of such a shambling character?).

Against a backdrop of the Confederate flag on the wall of the gymnasium, here signifying not slavery and rebellion but old-fashioned community, Santo continues to train, in the reassuring (for the spectator), liberal-endorsed company of a jive-talking, adoring black man, Newton (Roger E. Mosely). The legacies of 'Jim Crow,' George Wallace (poised to make another presidential bid in 1976) and Commissioner 'Bull' Connor brushed aside but not entirely forgotten, Santo, the Aryan 'king,' is the hub around which Gaines's and Rafelson's Olympic Spa turns, a nexus for communality through endeavour in a locale that blacks, until recently, had called the 'Johannesburg of the South.'[91] 'A truly appropriate representation of the southern black experience,' affirms James C. Cobb, 'must incorporate not only tributes to those who overcame, but reminders of what they had to overcome as well.'[92] As parking lots across the Southern states replaced former slave quarters, and older locals sought to 'de-emphasise' the importance of slavery to their heritage, *Stay Hungry* seconded the notion that such discomfiting realities were best 'paved over.'[93] Newton, and especially Blake's gracious old manservant, played by Scatman Crothers, are in many ways positive (if typecast) depictions of blacks; yet, there is a disavowal – a therapeutic whitewash – of their shared past. Blake's antique cut glass, as a piece out of aristocratic history, indeed belongs in a museum: by the same logic, the horrors of pre-war and civil-rights-era Alabama should be memorialised and placed in full view, so that its citizens might truly reconcile themselves with what once was.

Santo becomes a hero/mentor, swimming partner, squash opponent and trainer to Blake, offering sporting aphorisms that apply equally to inter-personal relationships and, germanely, a rethinking of the South's bloody history: 'Names don't mean anything more to me than titles'; 'You can't grow without burning.' ('A new body to be got,' wrote Carlyle in *Past and Present*'s advocation of 'Hero-Worship,' 'not without travail throes . . . all birth and new-birth presupposes travail!')[94] We learn that Santo's father was a 'sculptor and a teacher,' and it would seem that these talents have been passed on (though the actual lineage may well be via Breker rather than Michelangelo). We learn also that Santo is 'not homosexual,' but he is never, unlike Blake and Mary Tate, seen to make any intimate contact, despite offering to 'prove' his heterosexual credentials when challenged by a shallow female member of Blake's entourage. Santo's sexuality remains diegetically off limits, superfluous or even a danger to the narrative's coherence, which might fracture if Arnold's superman is anything less than ascetically transcendent: a leader-godhead beyond temptation, powerful enough to develop his vast body – as an icon of stalwart determination – by sheer force of will, and humble enough (that is to say, sufficiently brought down to earth) to keep it judiciously hidden. That Arnold/Santo is taciturn also coincides with Arnold's self-confessed messianic objective, and is a partial harking back, diegetically and industrially, to simpler times of star-as-divinity spectacle. Richard Schickel, with reference to the silent era, claims: 'A godhead is supposed to be inscrutable. It is not expected that he speaks directly to us.'[95] This nostalgia is, of course, mediated through a coastal, bourgeois sensibility evident in the film's social themes: 'Realism, psychologism, the "happy end" and humour reveal precisely the bourgeois transformation of [the "plebeian"] imagination,' opines anthropologist Edgar Morin.[96] *Stay Hungry* was Schwarzenegger's first such exercise in social-realist unification, and it would prove to be the last and most subtle example of the star performing this artistic function within a realistic premise or a naturalistic ethos.

Santo again demonstrates his healing powers when he takes Blake on a sojourn into the forested mountains, to reacquaint him with the old-time Southern culture and bonding rituals with which he has lost touch. The pair meet with some affable, inter-generational bluegrass musicians, with whom Santo (his enlightened, New Southern machismo to the fore) plays the fiddle. Blake subsequently gets drunk on moonshine, losing his inhibitions and building a bridge to 'authentic' community by dancing in imitation of the quaintly hospitable village elders. Rafelson shoots the dance sequence in a wide, high-angle shot, further accentuating the all-subsuming folk ritual's shamanistic power over Blake by using a lengthy, continuous take. This is persuasive, primal stuff, as captivating for the spectator as for the enraptured aristocrat; the director cites it as the one scene, among his entire corpus, by which he would like to be remembered.[97] Memories of John Boorman's *Deliverance* (1972), and its menacing, perverted Appalachians, are temporarily forgotten under the influence of this joyous celebration. Moreover Arnold, the god-like mediator, stands head-and-shoulders above the native mountain men, his violin hypnotically rousing Blake's spiritual conversion to the cause of true camaraderie. Santo's smiling response when an intoxicated Blake apologises for 'stealing' Mary Tate's affections is magnanimous in the extreme, but perhaps not surprising given Santo's transcendental, quasi-divinity: 'That's cool . . . I've never seen her happier, that's terrific.' If Blake is willingly lost in the jamboree, Santo is conversely elevated from total abandon, his virtual omniscience granted by both an unearthly stature and a deific mental repose.

Rafelson contrasts, by editorial apposition, the free-spirited jamboree with a social gathering held at a tasteless, modern mansion owned by Blake's family. 'Look at these people,' says Santo, above sarcasm and still smiling: 'This is what you call class.' The implication, for the viewer and for Blake, is that 'class' is what is found on the bayou or in the woods, with the auratically endowed folk and their music and magical moonshine. The new-moneyed guests mock Santo for his physique, calling him a 'freak,' and do not appreciate the rusticity of the bluegrass music his band plays to entertain the soirée. 'What happens to bodybuilders when they get old?' asks the dissipated Uncle Albert. 'They die,' replies Blake after some consideration, although, within *Stay Hungry*'s narrative, at least, there is a sense of untouchable immortality around Santo, the avatar who has opened a gateway to a better future based on recapitulating the past without revisiting its horrors. If Santo were to get old, or so Blake suggests (he does not say that old bodybuilders 'wither,' or 'give up'), he would thus be reborn anew in a different guise, his bodybuilder's skin sloughed to make way for a renaissance. To acquiesce to burdensome decay, then, would be a fate worse than death for the dignified Santo and his gallant disciples.

Backstage at the Mr Universe contest, Santo (as did Arnold in real-life pageants) sits serenely composed when all around him are posing and panicking in a rush to prepare. He remains the only contestant not flexing, and is clothed in a shirt until the last minute before his curtain-call. When finally Rafelson strips him down, Schwarzenegger's body is shocking in its voluminous bulk. Away from the other competitors, in a separate, Spartan room, Arnold silently lifts weights in total dedication to 'stay hungry' for the prizes (both in sport and in life) that are inevitably his. 'I told you a while back: you can't grow without burning,' he tells Blake, who has chosen an injudicious moment to confront him anew about Mary Tate. Curiously, with respect to the fascistic undertones inherent to bodybuilding, Ernest Gold's theme from *Exodus* (Otto Preminger's 1960 film about the foundation of Israel, or, more saliently, America's imperial guarantee to the historically deserving) announces Santo's arrival on stage for the final. The audience is conspicuously pan-racial and equally male and female, as Santo poses, bathed in bronze light, to great adoration: this is, in sympathy, what Schwarzenegger adored, and what Rafelson saved for his denouement – the worship of a leader by his disparate but united followers. As Blitz and Krasniewicz imperatively declare:

> [T]he theme of the film has been one of the philosophies driving Arnold's career: stay hungry – for success, fame, wealth, and power. Even more significant, the movie echoes an effect that Arnold's career has had on the culture at large: America (and much of the rest of the world as well) long ago developed a powerful appetite for each of Arnold's incarnations, and the culture has *stayed* hungry for more than three decades.[98]

Stay Hungry, though, is about more than Arnold's lust for material glory; it is about truth claims, tradition and historicity, and about asserting the New New South's validity as a functioning part of the United States during the mid–late 1970s.

In 1978, *Time* magazine declared that the 1970s were, for most, 'elusive, unfocussed, a patchwork of dramatics awaiting a drama' – all in all, a 'historical pause not worth remembering.'[99] Hence, note Pauline Maier et al., the bicentenary festivals of 1976:

> were marked less by high expectations of marvellous tomorrows than by wistful nostalgia for a mythic past . . . The nostalgia bespoke discontent with the present and apprehension about the future . . . the country remained divided over the claims of minority groups and, increasingly, of women and homosexuals. Resentments lingered over Vietnam.[100]

The government's *Bicentennial Report to the People* was not much more positive: 'We entered the bicentennial year having survived some of the bitterest times in our brief history. We longed for something to draw us together again.'[101] Arnold's purpose – and he always has a purpose, something that partly explains the public's 'powerful appetite' for him – in Rafelson's fable is to coalesce the Olympic Spa, and, by force of example, the wider macrocosm. A society needs heroes, said Joseph Campbell, for precisely this reason; cultures generate 'constellating images to pull together all these tendencies to separation . . . The nation has to have an intention to somehow operate as a single power.'[102] *Stay*

Hungry had allowed Arnold to inhabit (albeit fleetingly and somewhat spuriously) the Jesus role he coveted. His symbolically and literally strong body is *Stay Hungry*'s religious subject, just as is his inspirational attitude, and the two are, as always, symbiotically entwined:

> In the earliest times, kings and queens were deified, gods and goddesses humanised, given earthly habitation in temples, offered food and drink and their *intervention sought in human affairs* . . . Though modern religion has been intellectualised and refined and science has fostered disbelief, such elements survive in popular form today . . . as descendants of the saints of popular legend.[103]

Though it is in several respects a progressive film (as is apparent, for instance, via its wilful female characters, frank account of male-on-female abuse and positive treatment of a profession commonly assumed to be entirely homosexual), *Stay Hungry*'s 'incoherent text'[104] nonetheless sees essentially conservative values and psychology as paramount institutions. This is not to say that Rafelson's surrogate-family canvas is quite akin to that of the saccharine *Waltons,* or that it constitutes a Rockwell-esque vision of absolute togetherness, but rather that it strives to make an optimistic, realistic case for a more integrated, organic national identity encompassing 'healthily' inclined, civic-minded folk of all classes and colours. The female characters, though relatively independent and involved in atypical activities, are all conventionally sexy and prioritise relationships and nurturing; the bodybuilders, though sometimes engaged in implicitly gay self-parody, are resolutely straight, as Arnold/ Santo, their alpha-male Aryan mentor, makes clear. This is, perhaps, a necessary, prevaricatory approach to big-tent liberalism as dictated by Hollywood's fundamental needs: '[I]n order to justify its claim to being democratic, [bourgeois ideology] has to accommodate so much,' notes Robin Wood, 'that contradiction and complexity are its ineradicable qualities.'[105] Contradiction and complexity, cognitive difficulties inherent to the interpretation of Arnold's films (and to the often confounding discursive slippage between film and reality that persists in relation to Schwarzenegger), are notably at play in *Stay Hungry*; the intra-textual dissonance largely arises from a well-intentioned desire, apposed with Arnold's pro-filmic infallibility, to reconcile the disparate and seek out commonalities. Rafelson and company – here very much operating from the more frivolous end of the New Hollywood's liberal-left political spectrum – are too enamoured of Santo's/Arnold's nobility to allow him free rein or to introduce sufficient impudence. Arnold's charisma was not fully exploited or as centralised as it might have been, though this is (in hindsight) easily recognised in the tentative, early use of the Austrian in a role that required a toning-down of his trickster persona and a concomitant accentuation of noble purity. However, given the star's contemporaneous metamorphosis from bodybuilder to bona fide actor, *Stay Hungry* nevertheless served its purpose as a stepping stone, earning Schwarzenegger a rare critical plaudit: the Golden Globe for Best Newcomer.

One of Arnold's ambitions in 1976, as he neared retirement, was to promote bodybuilding and de-stigmatise it, in the process freeing it from popular (though often, correct) assumptions about its stars' 'deviant' social proclivities. *Stay Hungry*, Rafelson's 'incoherent' dose of melioration for the *pars pro toto* Deep South, had provided an interim outlet for Arnold's ambassadorial advertising; he would succeed more fully in this endeavour through his most important early film role (this time explicitly as himself) in *Pumping Iron*, the cinematic, pseudo-*vérité* amplification of Schwarzenegger as 'Schwarzenegger' that permanently and securely embedded him within American culture.

Pumping Arnold: A Pageant of Marvels

> There are men who may look to a leader to guide them for they fear they will lose themselves on, across, within their own bodies or in the far greater mysteries of other bodies – the body of the people (*der Volkskörper*), the body to which in some strange way . . . men who require an external 'extended' self to achieve 'wholeness' feel bound.[106]

> I don't care how many times you've seen something like him [Arnold] – it's an experience.[107]

Charles Gaines's second book on bodybuilding, *Pumping Iron: The Art and Sport of Bodybuilding* (1974), was a mostly factual account of the sport, undertaken with photographer George Butler. Appropriating the thematically succinct, high-concept title of Gaines's book as inspiration, Butler set out to record the 1975 Mr Olympia contest using a combination of the Robert Drew/Richard Leacock-originated 'direct cinema' approach and the kind of interventional, dramaturgical tactics previously employed by documentary filmmakers such as Robert Flaherty, all those under Briton John Grierson's aegis at the GPO Film Unit and, latterly, brothers Albert and David Maysles (former Drew associates, whose *Salesman* (1968) and *Grey Gardens* (1976) are definitive classics in the 'reality-fiction' mould from which *Pumping Iron* is cast). Butler, with co-director Robert Fiore, pieced together a story – and shaped the film's characters according to narrative convention – by mixing high-fidelity reactive observation with set-up situations, scripted interviews and judicious editing.

Schwarzenegger, as the chief focus of Gaines's manuscript, was involved in a creative capacity from the start, offering suggestions as to how he might best convey his essence and appear, on camera, as the most appropriate condensation of himself. Naturally, the Austrian Oak relished the process. The original *Pumping Iron*, a self-admittedly 'respectful report,' had unabashedly trumpeted Schwarzenegger, calling him 'the most perfectly developed man in history,' and 'one of the most magnetic men in the Western world . . . *an idea made fact*.'[108] In the book's introduction, Gaines and Butler proclaimed their objective: to rehabilitate bodybuilding in the national consciousness, bring it out of 'the shadowy corners occupied by dildos and raincoat exhibitionists' and dispel conceptions of 'narcissistic, coordinatively helpless muscleheads with suspect sexual preferences.'[109] Eventually finding theatrical release in 1977, after a prolonged period of post-production funding difficulties, the film would be no different in extolling Arnold as a figurehead or its evangelical feel. Both signalling, and contributing to, the burgeoning fitness craze stemming from middle-class Americans' quest for a 'sound spirit led through the healthy body,'[110] Arnold – a guru for the religiously confused, post-1960s 'me decade' – was advocating fashionable, palliative concepts of vain 'self-realisation' fused with a morally compensatory (if ultimately specious) form of group therapy.[111]

A pre-title scene immediately sets out *Pumping Iron*'s stall around notions of cultural authenticity and 'respectable' creativity. Arnold and fellow competitor Franco Columbu are being instructed in how to pose by petite ballet tutor Marianne Claire; thus, these men are clearly not working-class stereotypes: they are engaged in *art*, in displays of grace, and are confident enough in their heterosexuality to display sensibilities more usually associated with femininity. The titles themselves are juxtaposed with an assemblage of footage featuring archaic strongmen, whose bathing-suited physiques and stiff, almost reticent postures seem unimpressive when compared to the modern-day bodybuilders depicted in the subsequent montage. Shown in competition over a song that intones, 'Everybody wants to be a hero . . . Everybody wants to live forever,' the men on display are oiled behemoths. It is Arnold, though, who is saved for last, blowing kisses to the crowd and flashing a gap-toothed smile that would remain untouched by cosmetic surgery into late middle age; the stage belongs to him. Butler and Fiore waste no time in introducing Arnold's affable, magnetic personality: he walks into Gold's Gym, California – 'a kind of dream factory for bodybuilders'[112] – as if he were a homecoming Knight Templar fresh from the crusades on a tour of honour, and his 'subjects' display fitting reverence. Joking, as always, Arnold nonetheless commands all about him. 'I want to see about gaining some muscles,' he says upon eventually reaching the reception desk after a follow-shot that recalls Albert Maysles's famous tracking of similarly upcoming hero Senator John F. Kennedy in Robert Drew's *Primary* (1960). When Arnold ludicrously compares 'the pump'

*2. Bodybuilding as artistic practice (*Pumping Iron*)*

(the rush of oxygenated blood to the muscles) experienced during working out to 'having sex with a woman and coming,' the analogy is delivered with such effervescent self-assurance that it is momentarily plausible. 'Can you believe how much I am in Heaven? I am getting the feeling of coming in the gym . . . backstage when I pump up . . . I'm getting the feeling of coming day and night – so that's terrific, right?'

Repeatedly, we see and hear Arnold reiterating this exuberant yet non-threatening sex appeal and absolute heterosexuality: a 'general sign of "normality,"' notes Yvonne Tasker, 'denying the supposed perversity of a man's interest in the male flesh.'[113] He poses for a faintly comedic photo-shoot with back-combed female bathing beauties, who drape themselves over his enormous thighs; his 'beautiful body' impresses both male and female convicts at an arranged Terminal Island appearance; he frolics childlike in the ocean; and, against the sunlit Californian mountains, he flexes (again to the anthemic, upbeat title song), a blissful symbol of natural, healthy virility at one with the ancient, massive rocks. As Samuel W. Fussell confides, here was masculinity as a discrete, human completeness:

> There he stood on a mountain top in Southern California, every muscle bulging to the world as he flexed and smiled and posed . . . A human fortress – a perfect defence to keep the enemy host at bay. What fool would dare storm these foundations? . . . I knew it in an instant, my prayers were answered.[114]

Fussell's quest for identity through the veneration of a leader figure is illustrative of personal crises in many societies, not least in liberal democracies. Weimar may have uniquely sown the seeds of National Socialist power, yet to mid-1970s America, struggling to find renewal after deposing its criminal president and caught between abandon and reaction, Erich Fromm's warnings nevertheless pertain:

> The loss of the self and its substitution by a pseudo self leave the individual in an intense state of insecurity . . . The automatization of the individual in modern society has increased the helplessness and insecurity of the average individual. Thus, he is ready to submit to new authorities which offer him security and relief from doubt.[115]

Though the camera never settles on Arnold's or any of the other men's crotches (presumably out of a fear of prurience or revealing a certain relative lack), the male body – of which Arnold's is the supremely hypertrophied example – is throughout an ersatz, 'anthropomorphised phallus'[116] representing, as Christine Anne Holmlund states, 'the search for the ultimate meaning of generic "man" . . . [and Arnold] is the most muscular, most articulate, most virile, and most Aryan man around.'[117]

One thing the filmmakers left out of their 'respectful report,' however, was an interview that shed light on Arnold's idea of what the 'ultimate meaning of generic "man"' might be. 'Arnold sought power,' writes Laurence Leamer, 'and the physical power of bodybuilding was only the beginning, the first training ground. When he stepped out of the gym, he saw the world no differently than when inside.'[118] Schwarzenegger told Butler that, 'People need somebody to watch over them and tell them what to do. Ninety-five percent of the people in the world need to be told what to do and how to behave . . . I admired Hitler, for instance, because he came from being a little man with almost no formal education, up to power.'[119] Arnold was not the only aspirant young man to have praised the Führer from Stateside. JFK, another of Arnold's role models, conceded in his diary that 'Hitler will emerge from the hatred that surrounds him as one of the most significant figures who ever lived . . . He had in him the stuff of which legends are made.'[120] Arnold's American *Übermensch* – somebody whose ambition was to 'watch over' the '95 percent' in his view set adrift without a meaningful rudder – was running amok in the 'training ground' for power, much to the amusement of Butler and Fiore. For the purposes of the film, trainees other than Arnold are depicted as contrapuntal types under his sway. The good-natured, insecure Mike Katz is a respectable young family man, if also a definite non-threat to Arnold's 'super-masculinity';[121] Franco Columbu is an amiable, cartoonish 'child' (an outwitted Alviss to Arnold's Thor), who cannot escape either the social shadow or the de facto rule of his untouchable friend; and Lou Ferrigno – swarthy, 280-pound, East Coast challenger – is the diffident, eminently repressible, flip-side of the Schwarzenegger 'legend' (a perceptibly authoritarian legend, maybe, but unsullied – for which Schwarzenegger must now be thankful – herein by references to Hitler).

Pumping Iron, as is increasingly obvious, depends greatly on such appositions and oppositions against its primary star. Arnold's 'nemesis,' far from being in a permanent state of self-confident, orgasmic delight, is instead depicted as wallowing in a purgatorial ordeal. Twenty-four-year-old rival, Ferrigno, dramatically speaking, is posited as a darkly brooding yin to Schwarzenegger's dazzling yang. Shown training in a dimly lit basement gymnasium in Brooklyn, which could not offer a more pleasing filmic contrast to the Venice Beach Schwarzenegger had made his playground, Italian-American Ferrigno seems huge, but somehow destined to lose. His father, Matty, has appointed himself (at the filmmakers' behest) his son's trainer, but for all the Burgess Meredith-style bluster, his is a pathetic lot: shouting commands at Lou – partially deaf from childhood – who in turn grunts 'Arnold, Arnold, Arnold,' as he lifts weights amongst flaccid, chubby co-subscribers. Impaired by an obsession with the unstoppable force of nature that is clearly destined to eclipse him as he had eclipsed others before him who sought to strip him of the Mr Olympia title, Ferrigno's thickset, tormented face says it all: mounting a challenge to Arnold's golden king – 'a god enshrined on Mount Olympus'[122] – is tantamount to hubris, and all resistance will end in Sisyphean frustration. Arnold, observes Leamer, projected the 'tough, impregnable core of a victor . . . Lou was a loser, and both men realised it.'[123] Still living at home, defined by an all-consuming need to displace Arnold ('I'm gonna *beat* 'im, I'm, I'm gonna *beat* 'im!') and surrounded not by bikini-clad women but by his father and plain-looking siblings, Lou, at least when regarded alongside Schwarzenegger in *Pumping Iron*, could not be a more natural-born disappointment.

Matty Ferrigno recounts, over a series of still photographs from the family archive, the sad story of Lou's debilitating ear infection, and the boy's fervent adoration of Schwarzenegger, the inspiration for his bodybuilding endeavour. Predictably, Arnold evinces no concern about the Ferrignos' threat. We cut to the Austrian, lounging on a Californian beach; when asked if he has any message for Lou, the reply is nonchalant: 'Tell Lou I said hi. Tell his dad I said hi . . . Be very nice to him; he needs a lot of help.' Arnold is then seen performing press-ups with two giggling women on his back (who give a tally in German), chewing gum whilst admiring his *latissimus dorsi* development, and almost silently lifting immense dumb-bells before comparing biceps in the shower with Franco. Lou, meanwhile, incessantly roars and glowers his apparently lonely way to competition form. Even if Ferrigno does reach his peak, says Arnold, he will be psyched out by the mischievous charmer: Arnold will book into a hotel with him, stay the night and simply brainwash him into losing.

After we have witnessed Columbu's quaint Sardinian home and his slightly embarrassed-looking sideshow feats of blowing up a hot-water bottle until it bursts and lifting a car's rear end (feats Arnold had abandoned after the indignity of *Hercules in New York*), the film relocates to Pretoria for its final act. Upon arriving, Schwarzenegger is asked by a journalist about his ideal woman (he likes them all: 'big breasts, little breasts, big ass, little ass'); Ferrigno stays close to his father and poses awkwardly with a leopard, who licks the oil from his thighs. Arnold's archetypal 'trickster' persona is exemplified again during two remarkable scenes.[124]

In the first, a story is told to a bookish, thickly bespectacled reporter who, sitting opposite Schwarzenegger, looks like the '97-pound weakling' from the Charles Atlas adverts. Disinforming an inadequately developed German trainee about a 'new routine from America,' Arnold apparently coached the gullible competitor in screaming loudly while he posed, with the result that 'they carried him off the stage . . . They thought he was crazy!' In the second, Arnold sits down to breakfast with the Ferrignos. Beginning his assault by patronising the polite, already beguiled family, Schwarzenegger segues into an effortless psychological game:

> He isn't even in shape yet [pointing to Lou], he didn't get the timing right, I'm telling you. A month from now would have been perfect for you . . . Can you imagine the feeling I have: *six times* Mr Olympia. I called my mother yesterday and told her I won! She said, 'Congratulations!' Calm him [Lou] down. Help him. Don't screw him up this time!

So Lou's winning has been pre-empted; the younger man cannot respond – he does not have the chutzpah or social resources to fight Arnold on his own terms, instead walking away smiling from an act of quiet hostility. Yet Arnold is endearing even here, likeable even when the trickster in him is working to confound and thwart others not possessing his 'semi-divine or semi-magical powers.'[125] Indeed, as Alexander Eliot points out, 'numerous heroes . . . possess a rather dangerous magnet-ism.'[126] It is, perhaps, not quite high time for Arnold to grow up fully, or to abandon forever the juvenile qualities that would be sidelined in the second phase of his cinematic career. His filmic 'rogue's progress'[127] was nearing its end, but had a little space left to blossom. 'I have no weak points,' intones Arnold over footage of his pre-judging routine, and in effect he is right. 'From the USA, via Austria,' Arnold naturally wins Mr Olympia for the sixth time (Lou comes third, Frenchman Serge Nubret second), and casually announces his retirement from the 'greatest sport' immediately thereafter. He was 28 years old. 'Your day will come, Lou,' says Matty.

Wearing a T-shirt emblazoned with the legend, 'ARNOLD IS NUMERO UNO,' Schwarzenegger finds merriment in an ostentatiously brandished joint and a glass of champagne. Unlike the Hitler remark, Butler and Fiore felt comfortable integrating this indiscretion; after all, intoxication (the Bacchic ritual) is the conqueror-god's prerogative: 'The lustful and quarrelsome family of the Greek god Zeus, upon Mount Olympus, drank nectar by day and by night. Kings of Greece in Homeric times were reported to "tipple like the gods." The Norse gods and heroes at Valhalla made much of intoxicating mead.'[128] Arnold calls for a speech, but Lou just wants to eat his cake. By way of an epilogue, Schwarzenegger and a weary-looking Ferrigno family are seen riding in the back seat of a bus, returning from the contest. Arnold says that he will come over to Lou's house for a 'nice meal.' Lou's mother will cook 'spaghetti, meat balls, cheesecake, apple strudel – the whole business.'

3. Arnold's conqueror-god makes play in Pumping Iron

Then, declares Arnold, smiling his disarming smile, she will 'fix me up with your sister.' *Pumping Iron*, in its final moments, has driven home its message of Arnold's 'immense superiority and brilliance.'[129] 'He isn't satisfied with just screwing Lou,' comments Wendy Leigh: 'Lou's sister is next on his agenda.'[130]

Audiences loved Schwarzenegger, as did the critics. *Time* magazine's Richard Schickel appreciated Arnold's 'cool, shrewd and boyish charmer,' noting that 'he exudes the easy confidence of a man who has always known he will be a star of some kind. Arnold has a gift that cannot be acquired no matter how hard an athlete trains.'[131] Gary Arnold at the *Washington Post* lauded an 'amusing, buoyant documentary about competitive body building, dominated by the humorous though awesomely proportioned star presence of champion of champions Arnold Schwarzenegger.'[132] *Pumping Iron*, its January 1977 premiere attended by celebrated musicians and artists, was invaluable, un-buyable publicity that conveyed something of the real Schwarzenegger to the urbane world. Evidently, here was a man who could enchant, inspire and bedevil in equal measure. Many observers presciently saw a great media career for Arnold, though they were excusably unsure as to what exact form it might take. The implicit question was, how might such a man best utilise his atypical talents – how might he best bring his gifts to the service of art? The answer was a long time in coming, and may not have been what everyone expected of the 'boyish charmer.' Another five crucial years would elapse before Arnold would find the mainstream film role for which he was indubitably born.[133] During this period – a time when, stimulated by numerous economic, industrial and social factors, the New Hollywood's left-leaning critical sensibilities mostly yielded to a glut of spectacular, simpler excesses – American politics and society underwent significant transformation.[134] It was these changes, wrought upwards from grass roots, which paved the way for Schwarzenegger's far-reaching pop-cultural conquest.

Colossus
Arnold's Hollywood Putsch

If the deeds of an actual historical figure proclaim him to have been a hero, the builders of his legend will invent for him appropriate adventures in depth. These will be pictured as journeys into miraculous realms, and are to be interpreted as symbolic, on the one hand, of descents into the night-sea of the psyche, and on the other, of the realms or aspects of man's destiny that are made manifest in the respective lives.[1]

If we didn't have Arnold, we'd have to build him.[2]

Scholar Howard Zinn's hope for a 'Revolt of the Guards,' or a peaceful uprising of the 'slightly privileged and slightly uneasy,' never materialised.[3] In its place came a reflexive resumption of conservatism that, in the recent era of Goldwater against the Great Society, would have been unthinkable. President Carter had pledged much, but had not delivered on his rhetoric's promises. As Andrew Sinclair puts it, succinctly and acutely:

Rarely has a President worked harder in office for less result. His human rights crusade that led to the Helsinki accords with Russia was honoured in their breach, not in their observance. The Camp David agreements which appeared to create a peace between Israel and Egypt proved no more than an extended truce that bore no relation to the torments of the Middle East. And the aborted attempt to rescue the American hostages from the revolutionary regime in Tehran showed the President's impotence in the face of force. He seemed ineffectual, a man who meant well, not big enough for the Oval Office. Even his one act of statesmanship, reaching accords with Panama over the Canal Zone, appeared to American conservatives to be appeasement rather than a necessary recognition that Central America was no longer the barnyard of the United States.[4]

Paternal Republican Ronald Reagan, who had run a campaign under the slogan 'Let's make America great again,' trounced Carter in the 1980 election. His 'New Right' platform advocated across-the-board tax cuts, school prayer, pro-life religiosity, small government (though by 'big' celebrity and Hollywood glamour) and laissez-faire, 'trickle-down' fiscal proposals – a controversial, supply-side theory that even Reagan's future running-mate, George Bush, had ridiculed as 'voodoo economics.' He addressed commonly held frustrations regarding foreign affairs, domestic pride and national defence, promising to galvanise America's global standing and offer assertiveness where Carter had looked weak. The staunchly conservative, erstwhile actor's victory hence demonstrated not only a clear need amongst constituents for a renewal of past glories, pride and certainty, but also widespread disillusionment with liberalism's failings and the unfocused Democratic Party. Reagan, though ultimately an unwilling agitator, distrusted (and, later, publicly denounced) Russia as an 'empire of evil,' implementing massive budgetary inflation for rearmament of the USA in order that this might act as a warning to such territories. The economy was eventually stimulated, out of necessity, by working up a debt against the future. But, with the 'misery index' high (20 compared to 14 in 1977), 1980 campaign audiences relished Reagan's way with a sound bite and looked hopefully to an empowered future: 'A recession is when your neighbour loses his job. A depression is when you lose yours. And recovery is when Jimmy Carter loses his,'[5] said the 'Great Communicator.'

Those on the left viewed the Republican resurgence with remarkable apprehension. Writing in the *Nation*, intellectuals lamented the 'economic stagnation, declining international strength, and social anxiety . . . selfishness, resentment, [and] paranoia' that was 'replacing freedom with a combination of McCarthyism, militarism, and cultural regimentation.'[6] Radical journalist Andrew Kopkind, however, admitted that the 'left today is dispersed, fragmented and isolated': in other words, it had no practicable rejoinder, damaged as it still was by Cold War liberal antipathy toward its principles.[7] Perhaps most pertinently, Reagan's elevation was a symptom of the increasingly self-centred 1970s, which, as Pauline Maier et al. attest, 'helped lay the groundwork for a politics less concerned with an overarching public interest than with a self-absorbed individualism.'[8] Such attitudes resonated precisely with Arnold's somatically centred, power-fixated ethos, and found voice at the helm of a US body politic injured by Watergate, Indochina, the hostage crisis in Iran and an 'economic affliction of great proportions.'[9] Reagan, seemingly 'an image without a body, a projection on a screen'[10] – who had entitled his 1965 autobiography *Where's the Rest of Me?* in an allusion to a line spoken as amputee Drake McHugh in *King's Row* (1942) – needed to shore up his realm via symbolic association, or by melding this disembodied image of elderly leadership with a resilient, surrogate mass. America would be reborn, thought Reagan, to pursue its 'manifest destiny' afresh, finding ascendance through a concerted performance of physical wholeness: 'countless American bodies unified by the same American spirit, one glorious body politic repeating in unison an old actor's favourite lines.'[11] 'Strength,' emphasised the 73-year-old President in a globally broadcast speech to the nation, 'is essential to negotiate successfully and protect our interests . . . If we're weak we can do neither.'[12]

Reassertion of national 'muscle' became the leitmotif of Reagan's tenure, the military his favoured instrument of dominion. Schwarzenegger would thus be put to the test, as a proxy fighter and as a symbol of potency, like never before. His primed, mature body, hewn by pain, trial and epic voyage, was about to get *really* tough on 'Carterian wimpishness.'[13] Reagan's inaugural address exhorted the nation to 'dream heroic dreams';[14] Schwarzenegger, if he wished to realise his own dream, now faced a heroic tour of duty in the emblematic service of his adopted country and symbolic father:[15] 'The original departure into the land of trials represented only the beginning of the long and really perilous path of initiatory conquests and moments of illumination. Dragons have now to be slain and surprising barriers passed – again, again, and again.'[16]

Adventures in the West: Life's School of War

[I]n the late seventies [we] were living in some political equivalent
of biblical end times . . . For a kid who had been raised on tales of
the GI generation's heroic accomplishments, it was obvious that our
civilization was in decay, that we had gotten too far away from the
natural order of things.[17]

In 1981, Arnold began filming John Milius's brutal, proto-samurai
epic *Conan the Barbarian*. John Milius was an alumnus of Roger
Corman, NRA member and military history enthusiast; an ambitious
adaptation of Robert E. Howard's Depression-era sword-and-sorcery
stories featuring the eponymous hero of the mythical Hyborian Age,
Conan was an expensive ($17 million), brash production that required
a fittingly sizeable star to flesh out Howard's Cimmerian warrior.
Having written memorably abrasive dialogue for *Dirty Harry*, *Jaws*
and *Apocalypse Now* (all of which have entered cinematic lore at least
partly for their verbal exposition of Milius's heartfelt motifs: 'violence,
outlaw glory, and a loner's self-contained code of chivalry and integrity
in a world of hypocrisy'),[18] Milius was clearly at home taking charge
of Schwarzenegger's pre-Enlightenment muscle-man. Revising a script
first drafted by anti-war veteran Oliver Stone, the self-proclaimed 'Zen
fascist' was in no doubt as to the intentions of this artistic exercise,
beginning his screenplay with an epigram paraphrased from Nietzsche's
Twilight of the Idols: 'That which does not destroy us makes us stronger.'[19]
When Arnold was momentarily hurt on set, bleeding from his head after
a failed stunt, Milius set forth his own ideals (and pretensions) with
apt tyranny: 'Pain is momentary, film is eternal.'[20] As Laurence Leamer
recognises, this ethos was 'perfect not only for Conan but for Arnold
. . . out of weakness grows strength,'[21] or what critic David C. Mills
calls a 'fascist strongman . . . the embodiment of the greatest that can be
achieved: the survival of the fittest, a keen mind in a superlative body
. . . answerable to a supremely trained will.'[22] With typical hyperbole,
Arnold promoted the film by declaring that 'this wasn't a movie, this
was a battle';[23] Conan, a noble, white swordsman and defender of family
honour against dark, alien forces from the realm of Emerson's 'Dreams
and beasts . . . the two keys by which we are to find the secrets of our

nature,' was in addition an apposite emblem of the nation's psychic preoccupations.[24]

An invasion, led by marauding, foreign snake-cult chieftain Thulsa Doom (James Earl Jones, George Lucas's preference for the voice of universal evil), provides motivation for *Conan the Barbarian*'s revenge-quest storyline and sets the scene amply for all that follows. The despotically inclined Doom, established visually through John Bloomfield and Ron Cobb's production designs as an ethnic savage and pagan of the most unpleasant kind, violates the young Conan's village, contentedly decapitating his mother in front of the child's callow eyes. It is immediately clear who the villains of this piece are supposed to be: the tribe alone under the spell of an atavistic, bestially inclined black man, who worship the Edenic serpent (equated with original sin) as opposed to Conan's 'Crom,' a singular, anthropomorphic Norse-type deity willing to protect the 'valiant' and 'virtuous' as the Christian God, restorer of the 'natural order,' had always been invoked on the side of the Americans' crusades. Conan must fulfil his destiny, moreover, because of a collective dream – the self-defining story of bipolar 'otherness' – and its relevance to contemporaneous affairs of the American heart. 'Our world,' wrote Jung, 'is dissociated like a neurotic . . . forced to take extraordinary measures of defence, at the same time as he prides himself on his virtue and good intentions . . . It is the face of his own evil shadow that grins at Western man from the other side of the Iron Curtain.'[25] Or, as Campbell puts it: 'The whole purpose of the ubiquitous myth of the hero's passage is that it shall serve as a general pattern . . . Who and where are his ogres? Those are the reflections of the unsolved enigmas of his own humanity,'[26] a humanity always in need of deific purpose, and in search of the essential, elusive gallantry behind campaigns of anger. Conan's 'just' revenge, after all, is for an act of arguably lesser grotesqueness than the killings of 'Gooks' at My Lai, anti-war 'Peaceniks' at Kent State, or 'Redskins' at Wounded Knee.

During the film's title sequence (following a shot of some snowy mountaintops the like of which Nietzsche would have approved), Conan's father (former competitive bodybuilder William Smith) is seen casting a sword; it is, its maker tells Conan, the only thing the boy can trust. A sword – more so even than Dirty Harry's fetishised .44 Magnum – is a valiant weapon only for the skilled, a totem of honour in an age of ethical uncertainty. Unlike the M16-A1, the notoriously user-unfriendly 'black lickin' stick' of Vietnam that endlessly malfunctioned with fatal consequences, the sword connotes eye-to-eye justice – the fictitious American Way in contradistinction to the dishonourable reality of the Hotchkiss gun's overwhelming of the Indians' cavalries, the Rolling Thunder carpet-bombing exercise, mutually assured nuclear oblivion and covert operations culminating in primal murder by GIs.

Pre-bomb warfare and its supposedly pure motives (evoked in relation to the frontiersman ethos) resonated with Reagan and throughout his 'Doctrine,' hostile to Qaddafi's Libya, post-revolutionary Iran, Grenada (invaded in an exhibition of 'grotesquely excessive force' and 'stylised berserking'),[27] Panama, Nicaragua, and the Soviets in Afghanistan. In a revealing 1983 statement that the Alzheimer's-afflicted Reagan might have had sufficient acumen eventually to regret (and that has in hindsight proved supremely ironic), the 'gallant cowboy in the White House'[28] declared a love for the fervently Islamic Mujahideen, apparently due to their dignified, archaic ways:

> To watch the courageous Afghan freedom fighters battle modern arsenals with simple hand-held weapons is an inspiration to those who love freedom. Their courage teaches us a great lesson – that there are things in this world worth defending. To the Afghan people, I say on behalf of all Americans that we admire your heroism, your devotion to freedom, and your relentless struggle against your oppressors.[29]

Milius shared similar dreams:

> [E]verybody, I think, had that fantasy of what would happen if your home was invaded and you would fight the Russians and whatever . . . When I was a kid in the early '60s and '50s . . . The greatest fantasy of all was that we were going to go up to the mountains and resist the Russians with flint-lock rifles, cap-lock rifles, anyway.[30]

According to the President's near-sighted logic, anything was preferable to those 'international brigands' prosecuting the Brezhnev Doctrine. Soviet totalitarianism, the omnipresent, machinistic evil by implication projected onto the enigmatic hypnotist Thulsa Doom and his cult of homogenised idolators, was presented as anathema by Reagan's Brylcreemed old leader of the Great Colossus, Winthrop's 'City on a Hill' forever riddled with contradictions. To fight the good fight, at least in the public imagination, 'Ronbo' attempted to mould himself as a morally untouchable counsel to those who could and would risk death to clear the prairie – the armed forces – and the cultural sway effected by big-corporate, deregulated Hollywood.[31] ('[W]ise old men are essential to the hero's accomplishments. They represent forces in the unconscious . . . which guide and fortify the saviour in the midst of deadly struggles.')[32] Schwarzenegger, the tireless ethnocentric individualist on a mission of will, took up his simple weapon (what he thinks might be the sword of Crom: of God), wielded it with fearlessness, and went off, in *Conan the Barbarian*, to bring about superhuman restitution for the sins of the barely repressed, displaced 'dark double, the imaginary twin who sustains his (or her) brother's identity.'[33] Instead of unfeasibly fighting the Second World War anew, Arnold and Hollywood engaged with culturally vulnerable, surrogate stereotypes originating in the southern, Asian, Warsaw Pact and African lands (Doom, the cannibalistic heretic, connotes in a number of ways a hyper-neurosyphilitic Idi Amin, on whom the West has always been disproportionately fixated).[34] But, 'in some sense,' Vamik Volkan cautions, 'enemies have to be like us.' In other words, a fundamental part of humanity – and one that impacts upon Arnold's exaggeratedly Teutonic traits of pragmatism and strength, his peculiar donation to the cultural assertion of the 'new world order'– is perhaps the 'search for an enemy to embody temporarily or permanently disavowed aspects of our selves.'[35] No longer emblematic of a clearly defined, tangible villainy capable of world domination, Schwarzenegger – a paradoxical chimera of American ideology and Germanic 'will' – was nonetheless repaying his peoples' debt to the Free World, acting out the tribulations of a subdued, affectedly civilised American id. Hence, it was not only Thulsa Doom who embodied the return of the repressed, but also, to a significant degree, Arnold.

In a direct lift from Pastrone's *Cabiria* (1914), Conan, like Maciste, becomes a slave, forced to push a deceptively pointless 'Wheel of Pain' for many years until his fellow serfs have died: ergo, only the viable survive, a crypto-Reaganite trope par excellence – '*leaner*, more *efficient*, more *competitive*'[36] – of which Milius approved. 'Survival of the fittest . . . Everybody wants that. Everybody wants to push at their Wheel of Pain and become Arnold,'[37] he opines. Conan's stoicism and wilful deferment of gratification are remarkable; his indefatigable work ethic, 'a key element of what it means to be American,'[38] has hypertrophied his muscles, ready for the task ahead. Part of this task, not coincidentally, is celebrating 'the Aryan male physique with a single-mindedness that would have delighted Leni Riefenstahl,' Robin Wood reminds us;[39] for, 'muscles can function as both a naturalisation of 'male power and domination' and as evidence precisely of the labour that has gone into that effect,' avers Yvonne Tasker.[40]

Diverging from Thoreau's influential opinion that 'disobedience is the true foundation of liberty . . . Let your life be a counter-friction to stop the machine,'[41] Conan endures the drudge of slavery as if it were a character-building rite of passage ('You can't grow without burning,' one might recall), only to be sold into a life of pugilism as a pit fighter. Still, the Cimmerian does not complain, seeing it as his training for ultimate revenge and spiritual redemption in the eyes of Crom, inventor of vanquishing steel. 'What is best in life?' an elder asks the grim-faced Conan; his reply, delivered in Arnold's rapid-fire, staccato intonation, has gone down in cinematic legend for arguably worrying reasons: 'To crush your enemies, see them driven before you, and hear the lamentation of the women.' This, an anxious attitude to inter-tribal relations many mainstream leaders in the United States have mandatorily possessed (whether candidly or otherwise), from the hero of Milius's film – out of pain, comes forth truth. '*That*, is *good*,' responds the elder, in a reiteration of Nietzsche's salient view on 'the importance of having enemies . . . People are productive only at the cost of having abundant opposition.'[42]

This overcoming of torment, and the seeking of potent meaning from such, is Conan's reason for being. For the maintenance of these desirable qualities he is 'bred to the finest stock,' becoming an Aryan stud; this being Arnold, orthodox romance is out of the question, the ersatz, phallic sword's 'discipline of steel' taking its place as an extension of his body. He finds spiritual emancipation not through rationally articulated protest, but via killing a great many people in consensual combat and adopting an uncompromising attitude toward adversity. Much of the time virtually mute, Conan prefers actions to dialogue: 'The only thing that counts,' said Arnold, 'the only way he gets rid of problems, is by getting physical';[43] 'I wanted to let [the Russians] know that . . . We wanted deeds, not words,' echoed the President.[44] Physical freedom, 'a long and unremembered dream,' is finally realised when Conan, superfluous by virtue of too-predictable superiority, is spontaneously let loose by his owner to make a man of himself on the tundra, a harsh *tabula rasa* on which independent personal development can thrive. The wilderness will forge Conan's warrior identity, as his father's symbolic weapon was forged from flame, and as American patriots blithely imagine their heritage was originally rendered – from the necessary hardships of the strong-hearted founding settlers rather than a desire to make-over the continent in the image of the superiorly equipped white man and the indispensable industry of kidnapped, black labour. 'We need the tonic of the wildness,' explained Thoreau during his brief experiment on Walden Pond. 'We need to witness our own limits transgressed.'[45]

For America's slaves, who made possible the transgression of natural barriers, there was no such honest poetry as the Wheel of Pain, only the stultifying indignity of cotton fields and chain gangs followed by the tardily instituted Thirteenth Amendment and more than 100 years of second-class citizenship. Conrad's statement in *Heart of Darkness* (1902), an ambivalent, essentially Eurocentric examination of the 'savage within' upon which Milius drew for Coppola's *Apocalypse Now* (1979), is pertinent and, as always, axiomatic: 'The conquest of the earth, which mostly means the taking it away from those who have a different complexion or slightly flatter noses than ourselves, is not a pretty thing when you look into it too much.'[46] A myth parallel to Thoreau's pseudo-transcendentalism, articulated by James Fenimore Cooper and espoused in *Conan the Barbarian*, is that the paleface, former European is able to defeat his rivals only by accommodating the wilderness within him, in so doing becoming neither brutish nor civilised, but something new: a conquistador perfectly adapted to the fabric and equilibrium of the world; an *American*.[47]

Conan wanders the russet and grey mountains, which seem aesthetically to exist in harmony with his physique, temperament and costume (contrary to Thoreau, he seems master of the wild) in search of like-minded adventurers and clues to the whereabouts of Doom. Along the way he meets a comedic Mongol helper-companion, Subotai (Gerry Lopez), a meagrely clothed female thief, Valeria (ex-dancer Sandahl Bergman), and a sultry woman who offers him sex. Again, Arnold's diegetic libido is frustrated – she turns out to be a succubus who bleeds Conan's power while he is inside her, and who must be purged by fire for her counter-cultural willingness to immerse herself in feminine bodily pleasure and 'embrace the holiness of sin.'[48] Entering a Middle Eastern-styled village, Subotai and Conan learn of Doom's sect and its insidious, quasi-un-American ways from a frightened local: 'Two or three years ago it was just another snake cult; now, everywhere. It is said that they are deceivers; they murder people in the night. I know nothing.' Talking of the 'evil men in the Kremlin,' Reagan said:

> I had been told that Lenin once said, 'First, we will take Eastern Europe, then we will organise the hordes of Asia . . . then we will move on to Latin America; once we have Latin America, we won't have to take the United States, the last bastion of capitalism, because it will fall into our outstretched hands like overripe fruit.' His heart was warmed, though, by what he saw as a 'moral fiber running through our people.'[49]

Conan's quest, correspondingly, is thus established not merely as primarily reciprocal; he has a mandate to execute Doom, his 'apparatchiks' and his beguiling serpents – they are spreading doctrines to the easily assimilated and weak of spirit, who topple like Truman's 'dominoes.'

After grappling and killing a somewhat stolid giant snake – straightforwardly readable as a symbol of Conan's/Arnold's on-screen penile sexuality, which usually must be controlled at the pre-production stage – Schwarzenegger and Bergman, a Hitlerian eugenicist's superlative Adam and Eve, share a love scene, during which Arnold seems to temper his own erotic potential. The pair look awkward and unmoved, prompting the derision of reviewers such as Peter Rainer, who not inaccurately complains that Arnold is 'about as emotive as a tree trunk. When he's supposed to show love for Valeria, he might as well be staring at a hunk of burlap.'[50] 'Given Arnold's legendary boldness with women and his ability to literally embarrass them into bed,' ponders Wendy Leigh, 'his sudden reticence is difficult to explain.'[51] Schwarzenegger was a carnally rapacious film star, wealthy businessman and fitness icon, yet unaccountably was and is incapable of conveying realistic lust. It may be that Arnold has always been aware, as a consummate self-salesman, that cinematic sex – especially of the earnest kind – is, despite an eagerness to please John Milius's 'troubadour of lost traditional manhood,'[52] ultimately not his forte. Moreover, it is perhaps not congruent with what we want to see of Arnold's soldier-hero unbound, a semiotic epitome of the '"tirelessly forward-striving, restlessly toiling German" – the man who strives to escape woman, the mass, and himself,'[53] existing within the filmic discourse of sublimated joy in muscularity, mountains and otherwise towering endeavour. Arnold losing himself to the emotional complications of women, thereby in addition sullying his unconscious relationship to both the prudish, elderly patriarch in the White House and a largely conservative fan-base, would be a step too far towards psychic corruption for an icon standing on higher ground, watching a lesser humanity 'stretched between the animal and the Superman – a rope over an abyss.'[54] Nietzsche's thoughts on 'Dionysian currents' in tension with the Apollonian likewise pertain. Arnold may have sensed the irreconcilable Marcusian 'contradiction of modern society . . . that it perpetuates the traditional "performance" ethos instead of transforming work into play and redeeming sexual pleasure,'[55] a revolution in consciousness sought by anti-establishment forces threatening to the Right with which Schwarzenegger was basically aligned. Our hero could not, therefore, subsume himself entirely to the Dionysian impulse, 'rest in innocence' with Campbell's 'Woman as Temptress' ('goddess of the flesh . . . the queen of sin'),[56] or abandon himself to the kind of ecstasy, instinct or chaos beloved by 'deracinated intelligentsia and dropouts . . . mixing the barricades and the dance floor.'[57]

Guided by the 'Children of Doom,' who are a scarcely veiled troupe of just such late-1960s, Manson Family-type hippies, and spurred on by the entreaty of the aged King Osric (Max von Sydow) that Conan rescue his daughter from their clutches, Conan rides to Doom's province: the Mountain of Power, a proxy Kremlin. While disguising himself as a pilgrim by contemptuously holding flowers – the emblem of Haight-Ashbury and all its vague, permissive sentiments – Conan thuggishly sees off a priest (doubtless enervated into committing licentious acts, so the film suggests, by an overly liberal milieu) who attempts to seduce him.[58] Uncovered as an interloper amongst what looks like the Altamont Festival of the Bronze Age, Conan is eventually taken captive and brought before Doom, who, in an overload of banal Christian symbolism that Nietzsche would have scorned, crucifies him on the Tree of Woe. He dies, is brought back to life by Valeria in a ghostly ceremony, and goes on to decapitate Doom at a rally in front of his followers: quid pro quo, the ritual slaying of the black villain by the white champion, a regression to the depths not of the putatively 'barbaric' soul, but of the imperialist mind. 'I found myself thinking,' mused Roger Ebert of the film's closing scenes set atop a Speer-esque edifice, 'that Goebbels might have approved.'[59] Valeria's posthumous reappearance as a valkyrie, *deus ex machina*, does little to offset this opinion.

In killing the Other, as Doom rightly says, Conan is killing his own reason to live; he was born when his mother was slain. Having no option but to kill Doom (this is the equal and opposite, 'natural' reaction), Conan must then take for himself kingdoms, *ad infinitum*, based on a need to demarcate his concept of self. Without opposition, there was no conceptual Third Reich; without the 'Ruskies,' no conceptual America; without America, no Schwarzenegger. Over a shot of the 60-year-old King Conan atop a throne, the film's closing narration is prescient of Arnold's future and redolent of his function:

> So did Conan return the wayward daughter of King Ozric to her home. And having no further concern, he and his companions sought Adventure in the West. Many wars and feuds did Conan fight. Honour and fear were heaped upon his name. In time he became a king by his own hand, but that is another story.

Though it is sometimes confused in its outlook, arguably overlong, often 'ostentatiously stupid,'[60] as the *Washington Post* concluded, and frustratingly ponderous, *Conan the Barbarian* was a commercial success, producing a sequel and a spin-off: *Conan the Destroyer* (1984) and *Red Sonja* (1985), both directed by Richard Fleisher and both inferior in many respects. Where *Conan the Barbarian* is atmospherically charged, *Destroyer* merely looks pantomimic, relying on a more child-friendly, comic-book sensibility to bring in custom excluded by the first film's 'Kong-sized celebration of violence' played earnestly.[61] *Red Sonja* stars Brigitte Nielson as its eponymous heroine, aided by Schwarzenegger's contractually obliged (to Dino De Laurentiis), extremely Conan-like warrior. Milius's influential original, however (cf. any of the sword-and-sorcery films that comprised a brief vogue in the mid-1980s), was consummate for Arnold, and he was right in thinking it would open doors to greater things. 'Arnold knew that his place in the scheme of things had been vindicated by *Conan the Barbarian*,' writes John L. Flynn, 'though he realised it was only one stop along a successful journey.' 'Look where Ronald Reagan is today,' he said. 'I call that achievement. There's a long, long way to go. I'm only at the beginning.'[62] As 'beginnings' go – Arnold was already twelve years into his film career and at an improbable age to become a major star – *Conan* could not have been more propitious.

Whilst America looked for an efficacious combination of soma and mentality and sought vainly to purge its global identity of the misdeeds and hypocrisy of the past, barely tenable notions of 'chivalry and integrity' became paramount in revising, excusing and repainting a *modus operandi* cast from an aggressively xenophobic mould. Leaders of the United States, Michael Rogin argues, have perpetually marshalled white Protestant males against a succession of 'monsters': 'the Indian cannibal, the black rapist, the papal whore of Babylon, the monster-hydra United States Bank, the demon rum, the bomb-throwing anarchist, the many-tentacled Communist conspiracy.'[63] President Taft spoke presciently when he observed that 'the day is not far distant [when] the whole hemisphere will be ours in fact as, by virtue of our superiority of race, it already is ours morally.' Wilson likewise denigrated 'naughty children' who need 'an authoritative hand.'[64] 'Freedom,' the chief mantra of the American spirit, has thus always been linked, in the minds of conventional jingoists, to expansion into nature rather than social togetherness, to self-interested victory rather than harmony, and to fear of what Klaus Theweleit describes as a 'threatening confrontation with the interior,'[65] whence the Schwarzenegger effect doubly comes. Nationalistic sentiment began to fade in the 1960s, hitting a low in the decades that followed; Robert Kaplan bemoaned an 'eclipse of nationhood'; Peter Schuck deplored 'the devaluation of American citizenship.'[66] Arnold rouses both the memory of conquered Second World War enemies, racially acceptable ghosts from a time when the 'identification of Americans with their country reached its highest point in history,'[67] and the pernicious, distasteful but inarguably human drives that gave rise to such desolation in the first place.

'God, guts and guns, now as then, are the combo that makes America great,' asserts Thomas Frank of the recent conservative movement.[68] Reagan summed up his plans to:

> recapture our dreams, our pride in ourselves and our country, and regain that unique sense of destiny and optimism that had always

made America different from any other country in the world. If I could be elected President, I wanted to do what I could do to bring about a spiritual revival in America. I believed – and intended to make it a theme of my campaign – that America's greatest years were ahead of it, that we had to look at the things that had made it the greatest, richest, and most progressive country on earth in the first place, decide what had gone wrong, and then put it back on course.[69]

President Reagan, an erstwhile 'New Dealer', frequently 'remembered' his childhood as it could not have been: an invented Midwest of robust individualists occupying a fictional hinterland beyond the influence of canal-building schemes, farm assistance, federal protection and everything redolent of the demonised collectivism, the crypto-socialist agenda behind what had 'gone wrong.' 'He is,' wrote Garry Wills, 'the sincerest claimant to a heritage that never existed,'[70] a man who discovered his own identity, frontier rhetoric and political appeal largely through cinematic roles; for Reagan, 'Hollywood turned dreams into reality.'[71] 'The Gipper' was, though, in his films and life as 'head of state,' often on the reserve bench, on crutches, truncated, bed-ridden or dependently domesticated, a 'sanitised Disney version of the union between Hollywood and Washington'[72] unable to transmit visceral charisma or instil in the public a belief that he had 'saddled up,' as Kennedy had, in the good, actual war. 'I did wish Jack Warner would think of me on the back of a horse wearing a cowboy hat,' confessed Reagan in his 1989 memoir. 'I was hungry to do action pictures . . . But when I'd ask Jack to put me in a western, he'd cast me in another movie in which I'd wear a gray-flannel suit.'[73] Spending the war stationed in California, Reagan eagerly viewed the conflict on celluloid; when he resumed his studio contract, he was not allowed, by dint of a countenance deemed unsuitable, to be the kind of hero he truly admired. His political attitudes transmogrified by a creeping fear of Communist Party infiltration of labour organisations, Reagan instead looked to become a figurehead.

Reagan's elected superman was effectively neutered from the neck down, existing as an incomplete signifier to the degree that he was shot, not as Martin Luther King or John Kennedy had been shot, but by a socially inadequate marksman acting out a movie-based fantasy on the night of the Oscars. Commander-in-Chief Reagan, or the signified

'Reagan' who loved to quote Harry Callaghan ('Make my day!'), came from the movies – but the movies were not enough without the dimension Arnold (and, to a transiently very popular but politically mechanical extent, the obtuse-looking, victimised Rocky and Rambo characters proffered by Sylvester Stallone) could provide when called upon to incarnate the Reaganite mythos of 'natural' American ambition, personal faith and solemn valour. As Carol S. Pearson notes:

> Conservatives . . . are more comfortable slaying dragons than are progressives, for whom battle is complicated both by unresolved identity questions and by the desire to reconcile their own values and concerns with the needs of others . . . The Warrior's approach to spirituality is to identify evil and eliminate it or make it illegal. It is the impetus behind the campaign to get prayer back in schools, to wipe out pornography, to get rid of sex education, and to deny jobs to homosexuals . . . It is critical to remember here that in our culture the Warrior hero has been envisioned most often as a white man . . . [Concerning] pull-yourself-up-by-the-bootstraps capitalism, warriors take the truth that enabled them to develop some sense of hope and meaning to their life and go out to convert the world.[74]

Moreover, according to Vincent Pecora:

> In the era of *pax reaganensis* . . . policed by Conan the American – the 'new world order,' a phrase whose historical resonance alone demands the keenest suspicion of all that it attempts to name – in the face of all this, it may not be inappropriate to keep Nietzsche's fractured mirror around.[75]

Reagan was an ageing material prospect without sufficient brawn, his wounded-soldier film routines all but forgotten; Schwarzenegger, conversely, was a vital new Nazi-bushido prosthetic for the 'new world order' dictated by late-Cold War dialectic, the invincible means to a corporeal expression of a purely human, 'righteous' struggle for 'freedom' in ostensible divorce from the specifics of modernity and attendant intellectual complications. Charles Bronson, Chuck Norris and Sylvester Stallone – the latter often trouncing Arnold's box office performance in the early–middle 1980s – may have offered audiences similarly visceral excitements, but all were too perceptibly cynical, charmless, exploitative or po-faced in their jingoism to inspire the type of enduring, insidious personality cult ('a different order of magnitude to that of all but a few politicians,' writes Gary Indiana in 2005) of which Arnold is still the object.[76] Linguist Robin Lakoff notes that Americans 'want a daddy, a king, a god, a hero . . . a champion who will carry that lance and that sword into the field and fight for us.'[77] Nobody fitted this need better than Arnold, the 'natural' hero endowed with both mythical and clearly cut historical potency, and his 'daddy,' Reagan. Schwarzenegger, equates Niall Ferguson, 'is to the human frame what the United States is to the capitalist economy':[78] the fittest, biggest, and most ruthless, confidently 'repeating the same brutal dance'[79] as if the City on the Hill might never crumble. 'Film is forever,' said Reagan. 'It is the motion picture that shows all of us not only how we look and sound but – more importantly – how we feel.'[80] Arnold, was over-developed, avowedly Stateside, and reading from a well-worn script.

Schwarzenegger's next choice of role, however, challenged his star image and accentuated his uniqueness: he would, for an unknown director in a low-budget science-fiction parable, play the villain.

Rendezvous with Destiny: Or, a Post-Modern Prometheus

'The Great Brain was sort of an accident,' replied the old man . . . 'When they lumped up all the factories, of course, they lumped up all the robots in one place for convenience, and when they got through, blessed if they didn't come to find out the dratted thing could think, just like they could.' . . . 'War!' yells the Brain. 'The machines have gone and declared war on their oppressors. Democracy is in peril; insidious forces is undermin' the sacred liberties! We're a-going to civilize you!'[81]

In the great science-fiction stories, we stare into the monster, and it is ourselves that we always find staring back.[82]

Like Mary Shelley's *Frankenstein*, James Cameron's *The Terminator* (1984) was born of a propitious, unshakeable dream. While bed-ridden with a fever during post-production on *Piranha II*, former New World Pictures effects supervisor Cameron imagined a menacing, humanoid skeleton of steel, determinedly pursuing its victims across a war-ravaged vista. With the help of producer-partner Gale Anne Hurd, the filmmaker developed a tortuous story involving a robot assassin sent back in time from a totalitarian, machine-run future to kill the mother of a messianic resistance leader; in turn, the resistance sends back a warrior to counter the machines' endeavour and protect the *Mater Dei*. Owing, to various degrees, heavy thematic debts to a multitude of prior tales, including works by Herman Melville, H.A. Highstone, H.G. Wells, Harlan Ellison,[83] Fritz Lang, Michael Chrichton and – most obviously – Shelley, *The Terminator*'s screenplay essayed a contemporary, ambiguous meditation on technology's eventual consequences, and the Promethean, Babel-like hubris of man-made creation gone too far.

In casting his morally untroubled, inexorable monster, Cameron initially considered Lance Henriksen (later to play humane android Bishop in Cameron's *Aliens* [1986]); Schwarzenegger, however, thought differently. Turning up to lunch with a sceptical Cameron, Arnold lobbied through force of charm for his chance to play the emotionless robot, and not audition, as had been suggested, for the part of the ostensible hero, Reese. Winning the role originally meant for Henriksen, with the character actor's wiry physique, inconspicuous air and gnarled physiognomy, was a coup: Cameron had been persuaded, in a total reversal, to employ a 220-pound-plus, six-foot-two Austrian bodybuilder – hardly the kind of character to blend into a crowd, even amongst the preening luminaries of 1980s Los Angeles. Schwarzenegger, as Adrian Wright observes, made a 'devastatingly astute choice,' sensing perspicaciously that he could bring to the killer cyborg qualities the cinema-going public would not abhor, but vicariously admire.[84] 'In our private fantasy world we'd all like to walk in and shoot somebody we don't like,' said Cameron in hindsight, and all the better to do this in the brazen shape of a 'perfect male figure,' the converse of Henriksen's jaded-looking interloper.[85] That afternoon, following a three-hour conversation, during which Cameron and Schwarzenegger bonded over a shared love of motorbikes, the deal was completed.

Despite coolly dismissing the project to friends as 'some shit movie I'm doing,'[86] Schwarzenegger knew that this was a shrewd, lateral career move away from the danger of prehistoric stereotyping: *The Terminator*, assesses Nigel Andrews, is 'two hours of crunching violence and bio-mechanical ingenuity that defines Homo Reaganus as a semi-berserk automaton warrior-visionary, trying to sort out the next millennium while the current one lies twitching for attention.'[87] Moreover, it was perhaps more suited to Arnold's taciturn essence than even *Conan*, placing him in a chiliastic context of conventional heroes made strangely inadequate, of old worlds reaching their deserved terminus at the hands of peculiarly familiar forces, and of shifted moral sands. Sean French notes, in his accomplished pocket-book on the film, that 'there is nothing as potent on the giant cinema screen as the blank face on to which the audience can project their fantasies and desires . . . the audience gravitates towards the character who has the aura of a hero';[88] no matter, apparently, if this 'hero' is a jackbooted Germanic harbinger of the coming American apocalypse – a hulking symbol of the millennial myth's enduring function as a 'floating framework for explaining the "big picture."'[89] From Columbus's discovery of the New World, through political demonology, nationalist ideology and the on-going quest for a new world order, these notions have played a significant part in rendering America a sacred realm and its people the chosen. As Eugen Weber writes:

> Articulate the unspeakable and you begin to exorcise it. Even as we suffer, everyday reality is commonplace and trite . . . The darkness of men, displaced, becomes the darkness of the world . . . Endism is in fashion once more because it provides a context: an ideology of catastrophe.[90]

The 1980s, dubbed the 'Doomsday Decade' by critic James Besser, were, as Philip Lamy explains, 'especially steeped in apocalyptic thought and millennial themes. The conservative morality of the "Reagan Revolution" was aided in part by the prophetic and evangelical fervour of the religious right . . . Current global unrest, environmental pollution, and arms proliferation imparted a macabre reality,' and an epochal impression of ultimate, purgatorial destrudo.[91] (By 1992, 53 per cent of adult US citizens, interpreting reality for themselves, hoped for the literal, imminent return of Jesus Christ and a subsequent cataclysmic confrontation with evil.)[92] Cameron's pop-millennial employment of the apocalypse trope is thus an appropriation of the fire and brimstone of Revelation, updated for a more secular audience whose perceptions of the shape the end might take were altered by Reaganite rhetoric, America's 'obsession with recovering unvulnerability'[93] and the mooted SDI (or 'Star Wars') space-based defence programme that threatened, at least in the public imagination, to push the boundaries of war-craft into the cosmos.

Nonetheless, Cameron utilises customary mythological devices in what is a politically dark tale loaded with uncomfortable implications pertaining to our deepest desires for order, the beauty of pure functionality, and how history eternally recurs. *The Terminator* invokes not only the Madonna and her gun-wielding Saviour-to-be, but also the Devil in all of us who find ourselves, against any logical judgement, sympathising with Schwarzenegger – the bringer of the end, an emissary of the Beast – over his targets. As John Gray has argued, 'The freest human being is not one who acts on reasons he has chosen for himself, but one who never has to choose. Such a human being has the perfect freedom of a wild animal – or a machine.'[94] A pre-ordained function, therefore, is perhaps what many who feel divorced from active warfare and traditional archetypes unconsciously crave: an unwavering genetic (or binary-encoded) mission, and a tangible role in securing the future of their kind. To make a difference, then, a person must be driven by a contradiction that the Terminator, and *The Terminator*, need never resolve: 'We cannot escape the dread that in a factory all the products are alike,' David Thompson writes. 'But at the same time we hound ourselves with all kinds of imperatives of efficiency . . . The grind goes on, an everyday fascism.'[95]

Arnold first materialises in detritus-strewn 1984 Los Angeles from a matrix of lightning, a stranger at the end of yet another long crossing, naked and crouched in the foetal position, his muscles coiled (one might recall Rodin's *The Thinker*, a somewhat playful association). The Terminator is hence an 'immaculate' soldier-manhood reborn (Reese [Michael Biehn] will later describe the process of time-travel as like 'being born'), free of remorse, love and decay, a battle-primed ideal straight from the Third Reich's 'conservative utopia of the mechanized body,'[96] and a living echo of Arno Breker's inspirational, 'machine-like'

4. *Schwarzenegger's memorable arrival in* The Terminator

figures, 'striking contrived poses of unbridled menace':[97] 'a new type of man, physically perfect and ready for violent action.'[98] He obtains his clothes – a modified SS NCO-style coat, jackboots and studded, fingerless gloves, all post-modern, Tom of Finland-tinged hijackings of storm-trooper chic – by stealing them from some punks. Aimlessly hedonistic, jobless representatives of the thriving underclass, they seem almost to deserve purging by Arnold's purpose-driven, factory-made monster who will paradoxically take on their ineffectually fetishised emblems of separation and make them real. (Schwarzenegger's leathers hint daringly at a penchant for sadomasochist homosexuality; as Larry Townsend wrote in the 1980s: 'Big man . . . Big man in leather . . . You gotta earn the right to wear it . . . Can you take what you like to give?')[99] By contrast, when Reese arrives, wincing in pain and furrowed with all-too-human worry, he purloins his shabby, grey mackintosh and ill-fitting trousers from a derelict: there is no sartorial competition between Arnold's rebel with a cause and Reese's tired special agent.[100]

Whilst the disoriented, surreptitious and persecuted-looking Reese/ Biehn attempts to locate Sarah Connor (the waitressing *Mater Dei*, played by Linda Hamilton), Arnold simultaneously goes about his mission with a *Kristallnacht*-like disregard for property, collateral killing or detection by the police: he resembles nothing so much as a rogue SA trooper bent on pragmatic genocide, obliterating all those listed in the phone book under the requisite name. Reese steals a shotgun by cover of darkness; Arnold obtains his weapons (a 'twelve-gauge auto-loader,' laser-sighted pistol and Uzi 9mm) with the brazen illegality of a Western outlaw, simply shooting dead the shopkeeper when asked for money. 'You know your weapons, buddy – any one of these is ideal for home defence,' says the shop owner; the Terminator certainly knows his guns, and it is difficult to argue with Arnold's persuasive, measured performance or Cameron's skewering of pretensions. As David Thompson observes:

> When foreigners marvel at so many guns in American households they are given answers that refer to colonial history, the perilous frontier, and the second amendment to the Constitution. Those answers seldom admit that guns also represent adventure, and the country's own reluctance to give up its own romance. The great role of the Western, in Hollywood history and America's uncertain maturation, is as a parable of excitement, action, prowess becoming law.[101]

There are many dualities at the core of *The Terminator*, and one of the most apparent concerns not right and wrong, but 'natural' prowess, a battle for survival in which the fittest will survive and to which Arnold, the ostensible favourite in this struggle, is perfectly adapted. When

5. Making a 'purchase' (The Terminator)

Schwarzenegger delivers his laconic, tough-guy 'zingers' ('Wrong,' in the gun shop, or, most famously, 'I'll be back') – perhaps *The Terminator*'s most crucial innovation in terms of Arnold's acting career – there is undoubtedly a gleeful blackness to be appreciated and shared in this anticipation or celebration of homicidal *élan*. It is at moments like these, notes Tom Shone, that the phenomenology of cinematic carnage becomes thrilling in a new and disconcerting way: 'Something seemed to have sprung up between the screen and the auditorium – some change in air valence, a static charge, switching the moral current of the movie. The villain was playing like the hero.'[102]

Despite Reese's several flashbacks (to the future battlefield of Los Angeles), which attempt to invest his character with ruggedly masculine, selflessly militaristic traits, he is never a convincing foil for Arnold. He is undermined by emotion, falls prey to the diversion of love, constantly needs helping by Sarah ('On your feet, soldier!'), 'blabs to the police like a stoolie'[103] and seems gratingly aware of his own imminent martyrdom. 'These complicated emotions which should make him more sympathetic actually make him seem weak and neurotic,' comments Sean French. 'Pursuing a woman across time, which might seem impressive in a narrative novel or poem, appears on the big screen more like the behaviour of a stalker.'[104] Moreover, the denizens of Los Angeles, whom Reese is trying to save, exhibit a disregard for dangers inherent to the generic conventions of horror and science-fiction. Gadgets, troublesome though they are, already rule their lives, but, typically, the future will not be a golden realisation of the Eisenhower-era dream, wherein mankind is saved from toil by free-market expertise, but rather a vindication of D.H. Lawrence's opinion that 'America simply teems with mechanical inventions, because nobody wants to do anything. They are idealists. Let a machine do the thing.'[105] Even Jefferson loved labour-saving gadgets, but deplored the factories of Europe, unwilling to see any connection between this mode of production and an eventual bigger picture, in which even the USA's vistas and personal freedoms were compromised by the self-estranging repression (or so Marx, and later Herbert Marcuse, would argue) offered by big industry.

'The shortsightedness, and the selfishness, of the public's readiness to discount the future price to be paid for present well-being,' writes Steven Goldman in an essay on filmic treatments of technological themes, 'accounts for the way technologies are implemented and for their ultimate consequences.'[106] Sarah's *Jetsons* T-shirt is but one of several mischievous hints at such corollaries: Cameron's Angelenos wear personal stereos and cannot hear intruders over the brash, electronic music; they frivolously fornicate, eat junk food and go disco-dancing (in a club called Tech-Noir) after working dead-end service jobs for abusive customers; they ignore portents and disregard Reese's warnings because they do not fit with 'enlightened' values; and above all they foolishly trust in the police – an operation controlled by the state, a central apparatus 'hooked into everything,' like Skynet, and 'trusted to run it all' – to protect them when they should be protecting themselves against the coming atomic purge by taking up constitutionally sacrosanct arms and fighting back. The Terminator, Reese tells Sarah by way of necessary, if leaden, exposition, suffers no contention and is immune to distractions, qualities here inherent to Arnold's appeal that humankind might have to adopt – and that Sarah does indeed adopt – if it is to overcome fate and stay alert to dangers: 'It can't be bargained with, it can't be reasoned with, it doesn't feel pity, or remorse, or fear, and it absolutely will not stop, ever, until you are dead.' If Reese were as redolent of a true action hero, the film may have served Biehn's career as well as Arnold's.

These are, of course, mixed messages aimed at enthusiastic consumers of electronic goods, and there exists in the film an uneasy double-bind entailing the respective roles of Skynet/the Terminator and Sarah/ Reese.[107] Far from offering a comfortably left-wing tract against corporate weaponry and Star Wars-type militarism, *The Terminator* instead seems to suggest a solution based on what French calls:

> a right-wing anti-authoritarian tradition, an individualism which sees almost all forms of social organisation and control – police, army, federal government, tax collection, even printed money – as creeping forms of communism which are neutering the pioneering spirit that built America . . . Cameron's fable of a disastrous breakdown in society, a future conflict in which success will depend on the individual's will, bolstered by years of training and a personal armoury, owes more to survivalism than socialism.[108]

To destroy the Beast, John Connor, the inevitably Caucasian Christ figure, must eventually return, but this new JC will have guns blazing in a show of adaptation to the needs of the age, and he must become, in part, that which he must destroy – his 'individual's will' dictated by the greater, atavistic will of his genes. Ironically, Arnold's displaced Captain Ahab, in the 'past' of 1984 is the true individualist of the piece (a Melville-esque 'dark hero' replete with 'God, guts and guns,' although he is effectively attempting to commit deicide, to play God by killing his flawed creators), finds himself crusading on behalf of the same ethos. In what is perhaps the film's most iconic sequence, Arnold walks slowly and purposefully into the police station where Sarah is being held and obliterates every functionary therein. Sarah escapes with Reese, but not before Cameron has depicted a great many almost identical, very violent and percussive deaths, as officers are continually sent reeling and screaming by Arnold's deftly delivered shotgun blasts. The NRA would not vocally condone this behaviour, but, all the same, the robot, in performing his 'retroactive abortion' is only protecting his kin: the police, like the punks and the disbelieving intellectual Dr Silberman, are presented as deficient, weak, and endlessly expendable targets.

Repeatedly exposed to explosions, ground under a lorry and eventually denuded of his flesh, the stony-faced, ever-resilient Arnold is resurrected as a Ray Harryhausen-style stop-motion skeleton (like the Free Corps, *deutsch bis auf die Knochen* – 'German to the bone') for the film's final act. He is finally crushed to death by a hydraulic press operated by Sarah, the only character to have the necessary spirit of machismo and to notice that the Terminator, born of the production line, can only be destroyed by the forces of robotised mass-production that made him – the very same tools that take jobs from the hard-working, hard-swearing man: 'You're terminated, motherfucker!' It is a painful realisation, and one that courses through the film, that the cure – once the Machine has overrun the Garden – is the same as the disease. As his LED pupils flicker and expire, there is an undeniable sense of loss for this indomitable soldier, a feeling that he ought to have beaten such fallible humanity as Reese and his charge. In *The Terminator*, Arnold enters the City of Angels, naked and free, takes what he needs and makes it his domain; he shows outlaws what it means truly to live by one's own rules, be they from free will or determined; and he takes more from his existence, untroubled by vice or philosophy, than the organisms he mimics. In the future, suggests Cameron, there will be no place for cities, no need for the dirty battlegrounds of human folly, because humankind will rediscover its soul after the ultimate sin: expending resources on fighting ideological wars abroad whilst ignoring immediate neighbours and the imminence of a doomsday wrought from artificially coalesced civilisation.

The Terminator repeatedly and clearly conveys anxieties about the metropolis's role as a morally and literally polluted technological dystopia – and about the West Coast's nature as a modern-day Sodom, or 'the ultimate signifier of decadence and "unreality"'[109] – which have long abounded in both cinema and the wider culture. Agrarianism versus agglomeration is a dialectic running through American history since Jefferson: Josiah Strong deplored the 'perils' of 'wealth, its worship and its congestion, anarchism and lawlessness, intemperance and the liquor power . . . massed in the city'; 'Every city has been a Babylon,' proclaimed Lyman Abbot in the 1880s, assessing both sides of the story, 'and every city has been a New Jerusalem.'[110] Puritan ministers hopefully headed west, hoping to turn this last best prospect into another New England, yet found additional grist for their jeremiads: there would be no redemption just yet, and the newly born gold-fever, which had largely seeded the West Coast's powerful magnetism, lived on beyond its literal meaning to assume numerous appearances. Present-day California, and in particular the 'harlot Babylon' Los Angeles – birthplace of the cults of bodybuilding and ostentatious celebrity, the silicon chip, three-quarters of the hard-core pornography videos made in the United States, and, spiritually, Schwarzenegger himself – offers an eschatological gift to the cataclysmically inclined, or those who seek a coherent worldview via beliefs in either dispensationalism or simply a free will corrupted by knowledge, bound eventually to bring on a pre-ordained doomsday.[111] Kathleen Stewart and Susan Harding record a 'proliferation of contemporary apocalypticisms,' which:

> locate the enemy within Western institutions and Enlightenment ideals themselves. The horrors of modern warfare, economic depression, the Holocaust, experimentation on humans, and the atomic bomb were all, in part, precipitated by the application of rationality, science, and the offspring of science, technology, and effected in the name of liberty and equality.[112]

Reflecting an obsession shared by libertarians, religious fundamentalists, cultists, backwoods militia, New Age devotees and radical anti-federalists alike, *The Terminator* revels in millennial obliteration – in the end-times 'darkness of the world' caused by the fallible pursuit of universal reason, centralised governance, or simple hedonism. It is persuasive in its depiction of the fall of mankind, the sinners massed in an impersonal, dirty, electronically infused enclave perched on the brink of the world, pushing at the boundaries of hope and torn between possibly inextricable drives to preserve and exploit the environment. Americans have frequently travelled westward with optimism, a sense of adventure, and open minds, but, as Joan Didion warns, 'The mind is troubled by some buried but ineradicable suspicion that things had better work out here, because here, beneath that immense bleached sky, is where we run out of continent.'[113] Perhaps Ronald Reagan, one-time Californian governor, oneiromantic architect of SDI and a great believer in 'the land of our dreams and mankind's great hope,' was unconsciously willing on the end-times when he declared in 1981 his wish 'to renew ourselves in our own land,' now morally derelict and deserving of Armageddon.[114] 'Since the late 1950s,' notes Frank Ninkovich, 'nuclear war had been considered a strategically irrational course of action. The Reaganauts, however, decided to resume thinking about the unthinkable.'[115]

Unleashing everything 'unthinkable' from killer bees to atom bombs upon the precariously earthquake-prone City of Angels (the self-flagellating location of Hollywood's 'temple to permissive gods and easy ways'[116] and the Cold War-fuelled technologies that drive such films as Cameron's), the movies have always enjoyed testing by fire the United States' final frontier, the physical Outer Limit at which a once seemingly unlimited land expires, giving way to the unchangeable Pacific. 'Onto Los Angeles,' remarks Geoff King, 'can be projected what are perceived to be the most decadent and deplored tendencies of modern American life, in an act of ritual sacrifice.'[117] These forces, then, offer not solely annihilation, but also a thrilling purgation; the slate, it is usually suggested, can be usefully wiped clean, so that humanity may start anew after its inescapable clash with Nemesis, exemplified herein not by Arnold's 'cyber-punk' assassin, but by the blithe self-righteousness of a Promethean humanity, caught in an endless, international arms race, which allowed him to come into being in the first place. Diplomat George Kennan pointed out the obvious futility of 'this dangerous [nuclear] mess,' yet went further in identifying 'the measure of our own complicity in creating the situation we face today.'[118] It was the United States, Kennan remembered, that had pioneered research into bombs capable of worldwide immolation; *The Terminator* acknowledges that such culpability is a corollary of technological progress, and anticipates a time when a fear-struck, hypocritical America is hoist by its own petard and forced to review its vitiated nature.

Prior to the big-budget Bruckheimer/Bay/Emmerich revolution in selling 'front-row tickets at the end of the earth'[119]– a marketing broadside foreshadowed by Cameron's spectacular *Terminator 2* (1991) – the B-movie, of which *The Terminator* is a pristine example, was the cinematic vehicle of choice for venting millennial fears via the 'imagination of disaster,' as Susan Sontag has put it.[120] Moreover, in science-fiction films involving devastation as a direct consequence of hubris, avers Robert Torry, 'we often discover an element of almost impatient desire for what such apocalypticism has always imagined: the benefits to be obtained by massive destruction.'[121] Only by construing the appeal of such 'benefits' can we understand the T-101's significance; furthermore, we might then understand why such numbers clamoured to see Schwarzenegger reprise his signature role, but resurrected, via a virginal birth, as the paternal protector: at once an undying god from the machine, and a machine from and at one with God. ('[A] recognition of mortality,' states Joseph Campbell, 'and the requirement to transcend it, is the first great impulse to mythology.')[122] Arnold's robot – 'splendidly isolated from mere mortals'[123] – represents a paradoxical force for ultimate good, a more-than-worthy, individualist adversary ridding the world of all but the few who would rise above their blue-collar, city-bound lives, punish thy neighbour with an eye for an eye, or move out to the ranch and hole up with a precision-engineered shotgun, embracing the inconsistencies of the American dream without declared recourse to anything other than a sense of kinship, outlaw romance and self-preservation within the natural, 'holy' confines of the USA.

But all this, and indeed Schwarzenegger's appeal, may be merely another manifestation of our basest desires to seek the fittest, most efficient example and follow a precedent towards prosperity: 'We are,' argues Richard Dawkins of the unconscious purpose of DNA, 'survival machines programmed to propagate the digital database that did the programming.'[124] Around the time of *The Terminator*, powerful calculators, fascinatingly analogous to primitive life, entered homes for the first time and created new distractions, obsessions and syndromes. During the Reagan years, the founders of Microsoft, Apple and Dell would ensure that personal computers not only assisted in human endeavour, but also that their error-prone, age-alienating systems permeated our lives and consciousness to an unforeseeable degree, begetting into the bargain an IT-literate elite. So novel and pervasive were these appliances that *Time* magazine, in 1982, named the PC as 'the machine,' in place of the man, 'of the year.' Robot man-servants of the kind predicted by enthusiastic television programmes of the 1950s failed to appear; in their stead came an information revolution of parsing, processing and encoding that threatened to leave stranded anyone not willing or able to acculturate.[125] (John Connor, as depicted in *Terminator 2* and *Terminator 3*, by necessity grows to embrace technology and to deploy computers, the very things that attempt to kill him, against themselves: this vicious paradox loops ad infinitum, like so much in Cameron's films.) The renegade, unstoppable Nazi in Arnold's mass-produced-but-unique robot (the T-101 model, 'assembly-line killing' in a personal form) plainly signifies a very real antagonist from history, along with clear elements of Karloff's and Lugosi's bogeymen. Yet the Terminator is a recognisable product of his contemporary audience's innermost escapist fantasies nonetheless. He is the implacable führer/father who, unlike Reagan, does not fear corruption, ageing, weakness nor ridicule; more than a 'devil figure that carries the sins of humanity,'[126] the T-101 embodies an unrealisable reverie in which the post-nuclear spectator, aware that Pandora's Box was opened over Hiroshima, can fight blindly for what he (Arnold's fans are overwhelmingly male)[127] is programmed to love, one high-tech machine raging against another until the skies inevitably turn dark. 'We cannot go back to the prescientific past,' writes Toby Johnson. 'What we require is a guiding myth, free of polemic, that cuts right to the root of religion, recasting it.'[128] It is these roots of religion, as deadly as they are redemptive, with which Arnold's more deeply charged adventures connect. As Cameron admits, 'There's a little bit of the Terminator in everybody.'[129]

Fighting for Love: The Business in Hand

As good as our space-age technology was . . . as powerful as America was militarily, I learned, as had President Carter, how helpless the head of the most powerful nation on earth can feel when it comes to the seemingly simple task of trying to find and bring home an American citizen held against his will in a foreign land.[130]

We probably kill more people in *Commando* than Stallone did in *Rambo*, but the difference is that we don't pretend the violence is justified by patriotic pride. All that flag-waving is patriotic bull – we're all in the entertainment business. And if killing is done with good taste, it can be very entertaining indeed.[131]

The Terminator's box office takings were good, if not astounding ($30 million, although on video it would become a huge sleeper hit), but this was not as significant to Arnold as its potent effect on his influence within the film industry: from now on, Schwarzenegger had the power to pick, shape and inhabit his roles with discernment. He was a known quantity, now as much for villainy as heroics, and could be relied upon to bring a certain workman-like sheen – and a fair amount of prescribed charm – to almost anything. Mark L. Lester's *Commando* (1985) afforded Arnold an opportunity both explicitly to play a father for the first time, and to go up against arch-rival Sylvester Stallone's brief monopoly of the all-action type. The film is Schwarzenegger's breakaway, post-*Terminator* rejoinder to Stallone's epochal *Rambo: First Blood Part II*; it does not, however, concern itself openly with specific contemporary politics, seemingly out of a fear of triteness and the kind of challenging critical intellectuality espoused by Noam Chomsky's analysis of 'Vietnam syndrome,' one revealing corollary of which is film producers' urge to make sense of movements damaging to American military campaigns abroad. As Albert Auster and Leonard Quart note, 'Hollywood could neither fit the Vietnam War into any of its old formulas nor create new ones for it,'[132] but *Commando*'s sheer disingenuousness, irrespective of (or perhaps in addition to) Arnold's protestations that the film should be regarded as pure fantasy, nevertheless betrays a cool judgement and a keen sense of cultural jingoism:

[Stallone's] is a very politically oriented movie and mine is not at all. Mine is humour-oriented. You can laugh and you can have a good time with it and I don't take myself seriously in the film either. I believe in comic relief, otherwise the whole thing becomes too intense and too heavy.[133]

In terms of killing, *Commando* is certainly 'intense' and 'heavy,' but this, apparently, is all part of the fun; Stallone and director George P. Cosmatos's *Rambo* may have borne a message, perspicacious or otherwise, but Lester and Arnold, ever the trickster, were enjoying a sub-Ian Fleming-type tease of their intended audience, who should not, according to the Austrian, let complex affairs of either protest or government ('patriotic bull') interfere with their cinematic death-lust. Such promotional tactics aimed, as Thomas Docherty notes, 'to attract the prime 18- to 25-year-old moviegoers, a group whose historical consciousness extends no further than disco, and who have been targeted in their time only by market researchers, not draft officials.'[134] Whilst *Rambo* inculcated in its younger viewers false memories of a misguided liberal backlash spoiling the all-but-won Vietnam War, Schwarzenegger carved for himself a rival niche, hammering home his brand of viscerally motivated comic-book violence without recourse to touching any raw nerves. 'Somewhere, somehow, someone's going to pay,' ran *Commando*'s tagline: it mattered only that the payers fit vague preconceptions of international treachery and could be derided as comedic, Latin foils for Schwarzenegger's oversized Aryan master.

Humour itself, of course, can be an ideological and identificatory tool. Gerard Jones states that, 'The humour and excess of *Superman* made it possible to laugh along with the creators while still thrilling to the fantasy of power . . . You could want the invulnerability and the power, but you had to laugh to keep people from knowing how badly you wanted it.' (Orwell opined that *Superman* constituted a form of 'bully worship,' 'an American version of the same craving for a strongman that had raised Hitler and Mussolini to power.')[135] America, at the highest level, was having trouble abroad and finding unilateral adventurism a difficult course; explicitly dealing with the thorny issues of Central American intransigence, Lebanese hostage-taking and global terrorism was not – and Arnold would agree – in accordance with big-budget action cinema's artistic remit, not least because of the economic risks involved in polarising public opinion. The 'fantasy of power' had consequently to be transposed onto a revenge quest founded on more base justifications. Susanne Jonas sums up the prevailing sentiment:

> [I]n this post-Vietnam era, it is clear that the overwhelming majority of the American working class does not support aggressive US policies

even in the name of 'containing communism.' The so-called 'Cold War consensus' has been shattered. It is for this reason that the Reagan administration faces, even now, a significant and growing anti-interventionist movement within the United States, and widespread public opposition to intervention.[136]

Commando therefore occupies a semi-safe middle ground of familially justified actions and fictitious banana republics, stereotypes comfortably replayed, and murderous revenge made absurd by deliberately inappropriate jocularity. It is not, though, isolated from its context or purely a force for innocuous entertainment; *Commando*, whilst disavowing Cold War realities played out in America's 'backyard,' nonetheless addresses what the President called one of his 'greatest frustrations . . . my inability to communicate to the American people the seriousness of the threat we faced in Central America,'[137] and marks the beginning of Arnold as the meta-textually significant 'Arnie,' taking up his mischievous, proxy-paternalistic crusade against the fraternally minded, overly beleaguered warriors of Stallone, Norris and Bronson. All, including the latecomers Steven Seagal, Jean-Claude Van Damme and Dolph Lundgren, would appear pallid by comparison – this was Arnold's time to shine as the warrior-father fighting a just cause, and to render incarnate Reagan's 'rescue fantasies and preoccupation with autonomy.'[138]

Arnold's character, John Matrix, is a retired colonel and single parent (there is no need for troublesome matriarchs here),[139] living out his pension with a young daughter on an idyllic, mountainside ranch: 'the safety of our homeland' as repeatedly evoked by Reagan when illustrating the leftist 'menace,' yet here a simpler thing, one step distanced from ideological rhetoric into the territory of the heart.[140] Lester's introduction of Schwarzenegger's retreat is a virtual advert for the United States' conservatively inclined idea of utopian freedom, a joyous status quo bound to be spoiled only by foreign interference. His enormous muscles, greased and pumped up again after *The Terminator* demanded some shrinkage, once again are central to the notion of the body politic; they are a metonym for American vigour, bicep-by-bicep assembled in an introductory montage that fetishises and fragments Arnold's physique like never before, as Matrix, personally shaping his portion of the wilderness into a garden, carries a huge log to be axed. Over James Horner's schmaltzy score, Lester demonstrates the paradisical, healthy happiness of Matrix and his daughter Jenny (Alyssa Milano), who enjoy eating ice creams, feeding wild deer, learning martial arts, fishing and smiling incessantly at the wonder of their relationship.[141] If this were not enough, a pink cardboard heart stuck to the fridge declaims, 'I love you Dad!' 'I love you too,' responds Arnold, an amusingly out of touch, not-so-stuck-in-the-mud daddy. 'Why don't they just call him "Girl George," cut out all the confusion?' he muses (aghast in mock bewilderment at the pop singer's sexual ambiguousness), while sitting for breakfast in a rugged cabin resembling Ron Kirby's in Douglas Sirk's *All That Heaven Allows* (1955), the over-endowed, hyper-manly prefecture of Rock Hudson's retrospectively extremely camp icon. 'When I was a boy, and rock and roll came to East Germany,' ponders Matrix, admitting to some intellectual curiosity about America's sub-cultural attractions, 'the Communists said it was subversive . . . Maybe they were right.' No doubt intended as a throwaway piece of comic fluff, this line instead reveals much about *Commando*'s conflicted attitude to what West German paper *Der Spiegel*, in 1956, called 'collective erotic eruptions.'[142] Jenny, something of a tomboy, appears to have tailored her own general development in accordance with the hermetically pre-pubescent idyll of the ranch; any violation of the Matrixes' territory must therefore be seen partly as a threat to her chastity and devotion to her father/mentor. Though Matrix clearly wants to abandon himself to the 'subversive' attractions of pop music and expressive sexuality, he is essentially built only for killing – another form of primal release he unconsciously and

6. *John and Jenny enjoy the idyll of the ranch* (Commando)

innately seeks, fortifying his body and living in refractory retreat in a bastion so that he might one day be embattled and achieve ecstasy on his own terms.

The peace is disturbed by a helicopter, bearing Matrix's old unit leader, Kirby, who, after being play-ambushed by Arnold ('Silent and smooth, as always!') brings news that Matrix's colleagues have been systematically assassinated by an unknown force: 'Could have been the Syrians, the South Americans, the Russians, a terrorist group. They're going to find you.' Two bodyguards are assigned to protect John and Jenny, though they are clearly expendable and, as Kirby admits, 'not as good as you were.' Father and daughter embrace, in what is becoming sentimental overkill: 'Is it bad?' 'I'm not leaving you.' 'Then it can't be bad.' However, Matrix must, at the prompting of the call to action, be reluctantly regressed back to his default state: a totality machine; a cyborg, programmed to kill. As Arnold's acting coach, Jeff Corey, explains:

> What this guy wants is to cultivate his own garden, smell the lilacs and plant radishes . . . [Matrix] dreads becoming a robot, he doesn't want it to happen. It's all in Shakespeare, you know. 'The time is out of joint! O cursed spite, that ever I was born to set it right.'[143]

Arnold's gleaming muscles must, then, realise their potential, as surely as bombs must explode to fulfil theirs. Carrying and chopping logs is a 'waste' of such assets (it is hard to picture, as Nigel Andrews comments, Schwarzenegger tending to radishes); by now we know and expect of Arnold that this is merely biding time before the real purpose, the main event in which Schwarzenegger's 'steel and strength and will'[144] is uncoiled.

Machine-gun wielding guerrillas raid the ranch, and the carnage begins; the bodyguards are killed because they did not smell the enemy coming, as the preternaturally sensitised Matrix did; and we learn that the operatives have kidnapped Jenny in order to force Matrix to depose, by killing, the elected leader of 'Val Verde,' once ruled over by the despot General Arius (Dan Hedaya), who dislikes being a civilian. Clearly only Matrix would do for the mission, as he is the recommendation of Bennett (an improbably paunchy, moustached and chain-mail-vested Vernon Wells), once one of Matrix's soldiers, now, for reasons essentially unknown, his sworn enemy. From the beginning, it is made plain what kind of man Matrix, in soldier mode, is. Going by Schwarzenegger's obdurate facial clenching and precision-rehearsed combat, the almost exact replay of *The Terminator's* accidental catchphrases ('Wrong!'; 'I'll be back, Bennett!'), plus the arsenal of high-tech 'home-defence' weaponry kept on standby in his shed, the spectator familiar with Schwarzenegger's extant *oeuvre* is left in no doubt that here is someone capable of operating on a robotic, innately determined level of out-and-out functionality far beyond Rambo's embittered and confused veteran:

> We are presented with a robot that can tell the time, find the North, stand his ground over a red-hot machine-gun, or cut wire without a sound. In the moment of action he is as devoid of fear as any other emotion. His knowledge of being able to do what he does is his only consciousness of self.[145]

And this Teutonic New Man is now fighting on America's side: not, ostensibly, in the Cold War that only two decades previously had threatened to destroy mankind, but for his 'normal life,' his female child, and for the right to bear arms in defence of a convenient equilibrium. Matrix, a 'hero of the revolution' who helped remove General Arius, accepts without question that Arius must now be killed rather than El Presidente Velasquez, the 'democratically' endorsed leader. Never are Arius's political leanings elucidated, and never is the populace of Val Verde, or the wishes and interests thereof, mentioned: this is all about unleashing the hyperbolic Kirby's 'World War III,' but in the sanctifying, divinely endorsed name of family.

A wisecracking, diminutive henchman, Sully, puts Matrix on a plane destined for Val Verde and his appointed mission, the smaller man sealing his fate with a sexual joke about Jenny ('You're a funny guy, Sully. I like you. That's why I'm going to kill you last.'). The colonel, however, has other plans, and manages to escape, leaping from the plane and landing in marshland with barely a scratch. He sets the countdown function on his watch with Terminator-like concentration and sympathy with the machine, setting up some filmic tension in so doing: he has eleven hours before he is noted as absent and his daughter is killed. After propitiously meeting up with bystander Cindy (Rae Dawn Chong, who offers some sexless glamour and happens to know how to fly an amphibious plane), killing Sully by dropping him from a cliff ('I let him go'), and engaging in some impressively choreographed fight scenes in shopping malls and motel rooms that even excite some perceptive self-reflexivity ('I don't believe this macho bullshit!' says Chong – 'These guys eat too much red meat!'), Arnold arrives at Arius's island hideaway to rescue Jenny from Hedaya's comically darkened would-be tyrant and pursue a highly implausible course of action: he will wipe out an entire personal militia. As Matrix tells Cindy, 'All fucking hell is going to break loose.'

A montage shows a bronzed, near-naked Arnold preparing to do battle, donning his combat equipment and camouflage paint with the ritualistic care of a calm and certain warrior.[146] The rapidly rhythmic, Vertov-esque cadence conveys a microscopic appreciation of such accoutrements' importance to both the tempo and iconography of modern war cinema, as well as agreement with the *Iliad*'s ancient 'arming scenes.' As Jonathan Shay notes in relation to Homeric culture, 'the tools of the soldier's craft, his weapons and armour, are more richly invested with symbolism than any other material objects he is ever likely to use.'[147] Homer describes how Agamemnon 'clothed himself in armour of bright bronze,' and the timeless parallels become vivid:

> Upon his legs he fitted beautiful greaves
> with silver ankle straps. Around his chest
> he buckled a cuirass . . .
> Across his shoulder and chest he hung a sword
> whose hilt bore shining golden studs, and
> bands of silver glinted on the scabbard, hooked
> to a gilt baldric. Next he took his shield,
> a broad one and a work of art for battle,
> circled ten times with bronze . . .
> Last, two tough spears he took, with brazen spearheads
> whetted sharp, and that clear bronze reflected
> gleams of sunlight far into heaven.[148]

Lester frames the component parts, which slot into place to become one with the warrior Arnold, in close-up: Matrix – as his name suggests, a template or tissue base – assembles himself with metronomic exactitude, the New Man as cyborg coalesced and commingled with his equipment, built piece by high-tech piece. Finally, his pistol is cocked and he stands for a moment, revealed now in full-length against the backdrop of an instantly appeared Wagnerian mist, in contemplation of his technologically sympathetic perfection. Germanely, Doran Larson notes that 'whenever we witness American bodies in conflict (or combination) with technology, we witness figures of the body politic in an age where the "technological arts" are not only a means of national unity but are the only means that make any conception of a unified political body viable.'[149] From his bootlaces to his grenade belt, Schwarzenegger is a primed machine, made in the USA and ready to deploy: 'A technological rationale,' wrote Adorno and Horkheimer, 'is the rationale of domination itself.'[150]

Who better to unleash this rationale of domination upon than the insecure, little Arius and his doughy, sadomasochistic caricature of a right-hand man, Bennett ('Freddie Mercury on steroids' is how Wells memorably describes the character, though the steroids do not appear to have given him anything like Schwarzenegger's gym-hardened body).[151] Storming Arius's headquarters, while the ex-dictator paces amongst his opulent surrounds (a contrast to Matrix's functional frontier retreat), the superhuman Arnold has little difficulty in despatching dozens of incompetent troops, sustaining only a token flesh wound for his endeavour. As the *Soldier of Fortune*-style wish-fulfilment continues, we see Arnold utilise his plethora of weaponry – including some binoculars that, when illustrated with a subjective shot, evoke *The Terminator*'s

7. Ready for 'World War III' in Commando

'robo-vision' device – with expertise. Arnold invincibly lays Claymore mines, garrottes, strangles, slashes, shoots, explodes and decapitates, all the while Lester cross-cutting to Arius and Bennett, the gleeful would-be child-killer, who uneasily wait for their inevitable doom at the hands of the man they could never be: 'Welcome back, John,' says Bennett, whose relishing of Schwarzenegger's physical superiority seems to border on sexual, 'so glad you could make it.'

At the film's climax (an apt word in both senses), Matrix skewers (or penetrates) Bennett with a boiler pipe: 'Let off some steam!' The preceding dialogue and grunting between the two men, however, set amongst the broiling sweat of the mansion's bowels as they dance a tango of death, has been at the very least implicitly homo-erotic in nature:

> *Matrix*: Put the knife in me . . . Look me in the eye. See what's going on in there, when you turn it. Don't deprive yourself of some pleasure. Come on, Bennett: let's party.
> *Bennett*: [*letting go of Jenny*] I can beat you . . . I don't need the girl . . . *I don't need the girl!* [*Bennett now becomes crazed*] I don't need no gun! Damn it John I feel good! Just like old times! John . . . I'm not going to shoot you between the eyes . . . I'm gonna shoot you between the *balls*!

Never does Matrix lavish such attention on Cindy; Bennett, a ridiculous, quasi-infatuated model of 'constructed freakishness'[152] in apposition to Matrix's biological king, is, in the macho-man's world of *Commando*, accorded the moment of passion in her stead. After Kirby and company land on the beach – somewhat too late to be of any help – and ask the unimpressed John to re-start his army unit ('This was the last time'), Jenny and her blood-stained father are reunited to the strains of bombastic rock music, flying away with Cindy to some kind of idealised yet, one senses, unviable future as a family. 'I will protect you,' intone the lyrics, a useful summation of *Commando*'s story and ethos: 'nothing can hurt you . . . We fight for love.'

As Reagan notes in his memoir, 'large numbers of Americans cared little or not at all about what happened in Central America – in fact, a surprisingly large proportion didn't even know where Nicaragua and El Salvador were located.'[153] He goes on to attribute a public reluctance to recognise collectivist dangers due south to 'post-Vietnam syndrome,' and it remains true that many were not willing to see invasions or massive intervention for fear of walking the same treacherous path into a 'quagmire' as Kennedy and Johnson had in Indochina.[154] Although the *Rambo* films' general reception (at least in more right-wing and reactionary circles) suggests a market for revisionism along the lines of blaming protesters and liberals, this was not something Arnold and Lester considered their job; instead, they posited Arnold's Matrix as a crusader for universally recognised values, pitting him against nebulous but grounded stereotypes. Put simply, a man exuding such confidence and brio as Schwarzenegger – now a marquee name, and one pregnant with marketable specificities – could not portray a veteran damaged by intellectual pressure. He is self-sent into the 'field' as a mechanised operative, demonstrating a duality of paternal and military functions ingrained by training and enhanced by his genetic make-up. Matrix/Schwarzenegger excels at 'performing the masculine'; he is the epitome of Barbara Creed's hypothesised 'simulacra of an exaggerated masculinity, the original completely lost to sight, a casualty of the failure of the paternal signifier and the current crisis in master narratives.'[155] 'Better' than Kirby's rugged but institutionally constrained unit leader and fitter (and more hetero and fecund) than the risible Bennett, Matrix's act of subtle persuasion is to ignite anti-Latin sentiments – via Arius's pantomimic kidnapper – and evoke the hostage crises that had unfolded in Iran and were unfolding in Lebanon without stirring isolationism or any controversies thereof. Joseph Goebbels, a master of the requisite discipline, asserted that such techniques were the most effectual means of public permeation: '*Of course* propaganda has a purpose, but that purpose must be concealed with such cleverness and virtuosity that the person on whom this purpose is to be carried out doesn't notice it at all.'[156]

The situation in Central America was byzantine, and the source of a governmental dilemma as to whether the CIA should buy freedom fighters, or whether leftist regimes should be directly toppled using 'Big Stick' tactics.[157] By disturbing the peace of Matrix's ranch, by asking for retribution, the villains wake a sleeping giant with strong parental instincts and a 'natural' desire to recover his kin; as first essayed in *Commando*, 'the "good guy" provoked into violent action'[158] would become a thematic stalwart of Schwarzenegger's mid-period *oeuvre*, and, moreover, resound within the popular imagination. Kenneth Dutton asserts:

Though in part these films can be seen simply as examples of the American vogue of movie violence which characterised the 1980s and early 1990s, it is impossible to divorce them from the persona of their hero, from the fantasy of an iron-muscled prodigy who exists somewhere inside the ordinary citizen (or the peace-loving but sorely provoked country) and can, if necessary, be conjured into violent action.'[159]

In opposition to stark reality, 'iron-muscled' Arnold-as-industrial-panacea gets the job done with a minimum of repercussions: there are no sequels or reprisals, presumably because all Arius's sympathisers have been killed, the slate utterly wiped. America's delicate problems could not easily be solved by incursions, diplomacy, technocratic manoeuvrings, the atom or the microchip. Steering clear of obvious political commentary but happily inviting criticisms of absurdity and gratuitous violence (criticisms that are comparably much safer in terms of revenue for a genre piece), *Commando* sets its stall around gunplay for the sake of pragmatism and a pale yet recognisable endorsement of the Monroe Doctrine, by now dissipated into little more than an ahistorical pretext.[160]

If Marxist revolutions were not a good enough reason either to declare filmic war or to secure a mandate for a real one, Schwarzenegger, a deft politician, would find another *casus belli* to slot into this 'curious expression of political emotionalism's' tenuous historical logic.[161] 'All this,' remarks Terry L. Deibel, 'at a time when the American people neither want nor feel they need concrete achievements in foreign affairs. As citizens of a status quo power, they already have most of what they want from the world . . . Sights are set low. Success means avoiding serious defeats.'[162] Producer Joel Silver correctly saw Arnold's pseudo-disinterested, 'camp self-awareness'[163] as the chief factor behind *Commando*'s limited artistic success, but did not, apparently to prescription, appreciate the film's symptomatic subtext of alternative remedies to public apathy: 'Of course *Rambo* and *Commando* have a lot in common. They are both larger-than-life stories about cartoonlike characters that take on enormous odds and win. I think, because of Arnold's unique presence, *Commando* has a sense of humour that *Rambo* doesn't have.'[164] As Arnold says, 'We're all in the entertainment business,' and, as the closing song insists, 'We fight for love.'

After finishing work on *Commando*, Schwarzenegger took on *Raw Deal* (John Irvin, 1986), an equally hyperbolic tale of gangland retribution. One of Arnold's rare box office failures – a disappointment due in large part to its humourless recapitulation of the previous work's themes and set-pieces – *Raw Deal* sees Schwarzenegger as decommissioned FBI agent Mark Kaminsky, who is out to infiltrate the Mafia in order to clear his good name and ease his drunken wife's status anxiety. Lacking in sympathetic interest, replete with confusingly generic stereotypes whose dialogue is heavily clichéd, and burdened instead of blessed by Arnold's improbable turn as an interloper, Irvin's derivative assemblage fails to convince on either a narrative or spectacular level. Despite glimmers of humour (Arnold's one-and-only, half-effective zinger: 'You should not drink and bake') and violent action sequences whose genuinely shocking, gung-ho disregard for humanity verges on obscene (Arnold driving around a quarry to the tune of The Rolling Stones' 'Satisfaction,' picking off his enemies with a rifle), *Raw Deal* provides few moments of note other than its dubiously miraculous ending: Kaminsky healing his paralysed chief by sheer force of will, as if the overcoming of pain (the rationale of the gymnasium, magically extrapolated here into something that can defeat the science of medicine) is akin to mind over matter, a simple barrier to be hurdled under the guidance of Arnold's inspirational superman.

Notwithstanding *Red Sonja*, in which he was peripheral at most, Schwarzenegger, now centre-stage, was faced with his first personally resounding setback. Critics were surprisingly kind, noting especially Arnold's 'appealing presence'[165] in contrast to 'Slimy Sly' (whose *Cobra* had performed equally badly in the summer of 1986);[166] yet audience attendance was low, and bad public feeling prevalent. Compounding its overarchingly cynical air, everything in *Raw Deal*, from the Homeric arming-scene montage to the revenge-motivated final act of slaughter, is simply too familiar. Screenwriters Gary M. DeVore and Norman Wexler, abiding by Dino De Laurentiis's short-sightedly avaricious decree, had scrutinised *The Terminator* and *Commando*, hoping to replicate a winning formula: their diligence is apparent; they fail, nonetheless, to sketch anything novel beyond an already worn template, and neither add colour to Arnold's career nor imbue *Raw Deal*'s script with artistic pertinence.

But perhaps the film's biggest failing, as noted in Wendy Leigh's unauthorised biography, was its 'attempts to humanise Arnold's character by giving him an alcoholic wife and a subsequent romance with a gangster's moll . . .'

> He and Dino De Laurentiis argued over the affair throughout the filming. 'Ah! You bang-a de girl!' Dino insisted. 'You bang-a, and you make off! Fuck-a de wife!' But Arnold, with his intuition regarding the prevalent mood of the nation, was adamant: 'That is you, Dino. Not me. I want to be bigger in films than I am in life, not smaller.'[167]

Schwarzenegger, momentarily, was treading water in a lacklustre, culturally extraneous production that Anne Billson cruelly (but fairly) derided as 'surrogate Norris';[168] true to form, though, he would learn from experience, hone his 'intuition,' and return in a new setting and with renewed – and more apposite – discursive purpose: to participate once more in what Michel Foucault interpreted as the United States' hegemonic 'battle for and around history . . . to propose and impose on people a framework in which to interpret the present.'[169]

Playing Tarzan: Arnold of the Jungle

> [T]he connection between imperial politics and culture is astonishingly direct. American attitudes to American 'greatness,' to hierarchies of race . . . have remained constant, have dictated, have obscured, the realities of empire.[170]

> Muscle heroes are not indigenous. Tarzan, although he lives in the jungle, is not of the jungle . . . In all cases, the hero is up against foreignness, its treacherous terrain and inhabitants, animal and human . . . The colonialist structure of the heroes' relation to the native is aid as much as antagonism: he sorts out the problems of people who cannot sort things out for themselves.[171]

Although it is possessed of obvious universal (and elemental) pleasures, *Predator* (1987) – John McTiernan's science-fiction-meets-guerrilla-war conflation of *Beowulf*, The Epic of Gilgamesh[172] and the much-filmed *Most Dangerous Game* – deserves to be judged a culturally resonant, relatively sober-minded and accomplished entity amongst its action/adventure peers. Indeed, not only is this technically impressive film 'a strikingly literal manifestation of Cold War anxieties . . . charged with political metaphor,' as Stephen Prince notes,[173] it also tenders Schwarzenegger's most nuanced and assuredly convincing performance to date, indicating a productive affinity with director, cast, location, character and subject. 'Acting is like bodybuilding,' said Arnold in 1987, again equating artistic achievement with muscular hypertrophy: 'The more you do it, the better you get – and each time I see myself getting closer to the perfect delivery of a scene.'[174] Schwarzenegger, in *Predator*, is evidently taking his part entirely seriously; roused by the challenges of the sweltering setting, and of his almost equally brawny and spirited co-stars, he exhibits especial dedication to making McTiernan's vehicle work on a dramaturgical basis. Though verism (and self-deprecation) is not Arnold's domain, he visibly *believes* throughout in *Predator*'s value as a fiction warranting total dedication.

The story is that of a group of elite Special Forces men, led by Schwarzenegger's Major 'Dutch' Schaefer,[175] who are sent by deceitful CIA operative Dillon (Carl Weathers: Apollo Creed in the *Rocky* films) into the Central American jungle ostensibly to rescue hostages. In actuality, the team has been recruited to execute a revolutionary group funded by the KGB in order to pre-empt its planned attack on sympathisers.

8. Dillon and Dutch at odds in Predator

Dutch decides that he wants no part of this mission, but is drawn reluctantly into destroying the enemy camp; the fracas, however, is noticed by a visiting extra-terrestrial trophy-hunter – an apt adversary, given Schwarzenegger's aura of near-invulnerability at this time – who begins to pick off Dutch's men one by one. 'I suppose it had reached a point with these action films where one of the heroes would have to fight a creature from another world,' remarked Joel Silver. 'What other possible terror could Schwarzenegger take on in an action-adventure film?'[176]

Literally, the 'terror' is the age-old monster-as-Other, but figuratively the terrain is America's hearts and minds, groping for a means to comprehend Vietnam (the conflict that is most obviously signified by the use of 'a widely recognised "Vietnam" iconography (lush, glistening, dense jungle, camouflage gear, hi-tech hand weaponry, napalm-style fire)')[177] via Nicaragua and the correlated disavowal or abnegation of 'imperialist' motives without mandate. McTiernan commented that *Predator* is 'in essence a battle of Titans . . . a classic hero story and a horror story, like the Norse Myths';[178] in addition, it makes a case, through modern myth-making and well-orchestrated revisionism, for the justness of efficacious occupation, and for the nobility of warfare in which adept assimilation proves crucial to victory over an 'alien subversive presence' with which Central America is shown to be infected.[179] Arnold (our Aryan, 'heroic' ideal) must thus learn the dark arts of guerrilla war so that the hard lessons of defeat in Vietnam can be deeply inculcated without resort to *Rambo*-esque, divisive particulars. The phrase 'No more Vietnams,' writes Keith Beattie:

> is encoded with the implicit message that 'this time we'll get it right.' Far from the end of innocence and soldiery, the war in Vietnam is rewritten as a negative correlative against which future military action is measured. 'Getting it right' – which not only underwrote but in some sense legitimated the invasion of Grenada and support for the Contra rebels in Nicaragua – also resulted in an upsurge of Allied rhetoric . . . To the victorious, then, go the rights to assert innocence.[180]

Arnold, notes J. Hoberman, 'is not haunted by the failure of Vietnam'; he does not 'dramatise old grievances or wallow in self-pity,' unlike Stallone.[181] 'Whatever [Stallone] does,' said Arnold, talking about of the films of 'The Italian Stallion,' 'it always comes out wrong.'[182] Political commitment, recognised Schwarzenegger, could be a double-edged sword (as it had been for his rival). Aware that 'ideology works better when we cannot see it working,'[183] Arnold intuited that his most important roles had great discursive power, but that this power lay less in rhetoric than more basic insidiousness playing on public misgivings. To obviate the need for explicit commentary and to avoid anything 'coming out wrong,' Arnold inhabited a pro-filmic world of primal and old colonial fears re-worked in the light of present-day national crises; at one critical remove, he palliated the tenderness of America's psychic denial, and slew the dragons of Otherness:

> How was a country steeped in its own mythologies of national and cultural supremacy to come to terms with losing to an undeveloped nation of what some Americans thought of stereotypically as little yellow people? What kind of stories could it tell about the war? . . . Like primitive people without a history we had a gap to fill and we turned to myth.[184]

Predator opens with a shot of the alien's spaceship falling to earth, seeding the planet with insurrectionary, exotic evil; in the film's first clear evocation of Vietnam, a helicopter likewise descends, its landing on a dusky tropical beach constituting a semiotic aide-memoire: in effect the spectator is witnessing a retelling of the conflict most associated – especially via the cinema – with such aircraft. We are then introduced to the imperturbably cigar-smoking Dutch, as he is given his mission by the 'General' (an aged R.G. Armstrong), who disparages 'this charming little country' to which Arnold's dutiful hero has lent his presence. 'What do you need us for?' asks Dutch; 'Because some damn fool accused you of being the best,' responds a voice off-screen. It is Weathers's Dillon, a hard-bitten 'shadow' archetype similar in quintessence to Apollo Creed's crude caricature of Muhammad Ali.[185] The two old comrades perform a spontaneous, homo-erotically eye-to-eye, arm wrestle, McTiernan lingering on their tensed biceps and distended veins; Dillon, of course, loses – Dutch, a man not of problematic words but of pragmatic deeds, remarks that his opponent has been 'pushing too many pencils' due to CIA bureaucracy (the insinuation is that that Weathers's body has atrophied, as the body politic might atrophy under the stricture of officialdom). Asserting his decency, autonomy, and ostensible aloofness from aggressive policy, Dutch says he did not go to Libya because it was not his 'style': 'We're a rescue team, not assassins.' Distanced from Reagan's 'all the way to the hangar'[186] rhetoric concerning Qaddafi (and those would-be killers allegedly sent to the United States by the Libyan), Dutch's morality and professionalism are hence reconciled, albeit uneasily, and the character simultaneously defended from accusations of compromise and deference to the kind of Machiavellian federal authority represented by Dillon. Schwarzenegger and company, then, are principled aggressors under the leadership of a masterfully resolute warrior, come to 'this charming little country' to perform a 'one-day operation' and go home with honour.

As their gunship crosses the border into 'Indian country,'[187] McTiernan presents his incongruent yet adeptly coherent squad: Blain (former wrestler and Vietnam veteran Jesse Ventura) is a tobacco-chewing, gung-ho cowboy with a predilection for comedically macho ripostes; Billy (Sonny Landham) is a Native-American tracker, proud and in touch with nature; Mac (Bill Duke), a shaven-headed African American, is cogitative (if borderline psychotic); Poncho (Richard Chaves) is an enthusiastic Mexican; and Hawkins (Shane Black) embodies the naïve young rookie. Whilst this disproportionately multi-ethnic band of stereotypes approaches its destination, we hear Little Richard's 'Long Tall Sally,' a tape of which Blain has put in his portable stereo. Again, previous literary and filmic interpretations of the Vietnam War are intimated, the Indochinese campaign and rock and roll, according to David E. James, being:

> intertwined so thoroughly that their inter-dependence is an exemplary instance of the operationality of modern culture . . . The movies have no authority in neither the experience of Vietnam nor representations of it, neither practically nor textually. In both they have been replaced by rock and roll, which will solve the awkwardness of Vietnam.[188]

An additional way to address this discomfiture is to imagine, as does *Predator*, a cohort whose diversity reflects a certain nostalgic revisionism, rather than fact: the number of blacks who fought in Vietnam, often with resentment at fighting a 'white man's war,' was highly inconsistent with the racial demography of their homeland.[189] The team, as Little Richard sings, is going to 'have some fun'; this lyric's sentiment imparts obvious irony, yet also permits a distinct, simultaneous displacement of the spectatorial destrudo (our perhaps innate urge to destroy, as outlined by Freud) onto the libido, and an abjuration, by dint of rock and roll's creative associations, of the brutal realities of recent warfare upon which *Predator* is essentially based. Schwarzenegger, though, unlike his boyish charges, does not partake in the fraternal banter onboard the helicopter (or, like Mac/Duke, exhibit nervous tics): this is, after all, a re-fighting of a lost war, staged for our vicarious enjoyment;[190] its viability as a populist artefact depends equally on it constituting 'fun,' and on the continuance of audience alignment with Arnold's transcendently superior conscience: he understands the painful nature of war.

Dutch takes the team deep into the jungle, which, due to McTiernan's vertiginous camerawork, in itself appears to teem with endemic, foreign menace. 'Remember Afghanistan?' asks Poncho, recalling a not obviously similar terrain; 'I'm trying to forget it,' replies Dutch, in the first of many references to authentic conflicts that never cite Vietnam by name. ('Same kind of moon, same kind of jungle,' says Mac; 'Makes Cambodia look like Kansas,' reiterates Blain: clearly, these men are 'trying to forget' something, while concurrently hinting at that same unmentionable defeat.) Billy, as a Native-American type endowed with earthy yet spiritual acuity, senses trouble, and comes across the skinned corpses of American soldiers of whose mission Dutch's is a repeat. We are reminded of the 'savage' brutalities attributed to the Viet Cong – atrocities no less civilised than the 'ear-bagging' proclivities of US GIs, alien trophy-seekers of another hue – and a parallel is drawn between the as-yet-unidentified perpetrator/s of the flaying and the mysterious, 'inhuman' 'Gooks' who ran tunnels and ambushed unseen. Poncho, as if to emphasise our heroes' righteousness in contrast to the heretical, atavistic or atheistic ways of the locals, crosses himself: 'Holy Mother of God,' he declaims, before Dutch, putting battlefield dignity before expediency, orders the men cut down. As Mac laments, 'Ain't no way for no soldier to die.'

Blain declares it 'payback time,' and reveals an implausible, hand-held Gatling gun ('Old Painless'), with which he plays his part in decimating the guerrillas' camp. This scene is one of gratuitous devastation, though it is also expertly constructed and lends a thematically crucial dimension. The spectator's – and the film's protagonists' – faith in high-technology firepower to obliterate *known* adversaries is bolstered, though only tem-porarily. Narratively, those who do not know how best to use the envi-ronment to outwit their enemies are quickly dispatched and not worthy adversaries for either the Predator (incredibly, or so it is suggested, the creature now lurking in the trees has ignored them because they are easy prey) or Arnold et al. Thus begins what Stephen Prince appositely calls *Predator*'s 'discourse on the waging of counterinsurgency warfare [and] the rhetoric of the Reagan administration about outside intervention by alien powers.'[191] Though the film cursorily appears to be a fable strongly opposed to positive intervention, *Predator*, it becomes increasingly clear, warns only against over-confidence and ignorance of one's foe. As in war since time immemorial, but above all in the jungles of Vietnam (and by extension those of South America), notes Jonathan Shay, 'the enemy struck not only at the body but at the most basic functions of the sol-dier's mind, attacking his perceptions by concealment; his cognitions by camouflage and deception; his intentions by surprise, anticipations and ambush.'[192] Ambivalent less about interventional war per se than about shock-and-awe militarism, McTiernan depicts the United States' Big Stick at work and subsequently highlights its failings in an untried setting: like Operation Rolling Thunder, remote execution is cursorily impressive, but ultimate victory over the bestial, ethnic forces of antago-nism will demand insight, adaptability and perception, coupled with Schwarzenegger's strength of both body and resolve.

After Dutch confronts Dillon about his subterfuge ('So you cooked up a story and dropped the six of us in the meat-grinder,' a contrived line delivered by Schwarzenegger with persuasive earnestness), the cohorts, now with a young woman (Anna: Elpidia Carrillo) reluctantly in tow, retreat to the dark jungle to wait for an airlift. However, they cannot be picked up in 'this hole' and must go to the border, unaware that the near-invisible, Grendel-like monster is stalking them. In an inverted echo of *The Terminator*, subjective shots represent the alien's thermal-imaging vision, picking the humans out from the backdrop whilst it remains camouflaged, immersed in the usually suppressed foramina of untamed nature that terrified urbanite soldiers in Vietnam:

Forget the Cong, the *trees* would kill you, the elephant grass grew up homicidal, the ground you were walking over possessed malignant intelligence, your whole environment was a bath . . . The Puritan belief that Satan dwelt in nature could have been born here, where even on the coldest, freshest mountaintops you could smell jungle and that tension between rot and genesis that all jungles give off. It is ghost-story country, and for Americans it had been the scene of some of the war's vilest surprises.[193]

To the accompaniment of Alan Silvestri's taut score, Dutch and company, wary of ambush, push through the greenery – the 'bad-ass bush,' as Mac calls it, to which Blain responds, 'You lose it here, you're in a world of hurt.' Through it all, Arnold/Dutch remains composed and aloof, without recourse either to complaint or to protective pendants like Billy's; his angular face-paint, unlike the others', complements his features, making his already prominent cheekbones appear harder. 'There's something in those trees,' warns Billy, the noble 'Redskin' now on his conquerors' side. As with Matrix in *Commando,* super-sensory perception is needed, but the nationally microcosmic team is here allowed to hold a share of such attributes, good and bad: to Blain goes the posturing and misguided assurance; to Poncho the primal wrath; to Mac the stalwartness; to Hawkins the childish humour; and to Anna the conflated feminine role of Schwarzenegger's damsel in distress/Campbellian goddess of this 'world of hurt.'

Only the neo-colonial hero Dutch can properly understand Anna, and only he can guide her to safety, simultaneously guided by her local knowledge of legend and acuity to age-old recurrence – or to the strange mystique of regenerative nature, as Campbell asserts:

> Woman, in the picture language of mythology represents the totality of what can become known. The hero is the one who comes to know . . . She lures, she guides, she bids him burst his fetters . . . By deficient eyes [in *Predator,* the untrusting Dillon's, and the edgy Poncho's] she is reduced to inferior states . . . The hero who can take her as she is, without undue commotion but with the kindness and assurance she requires, is potentially the king, the incarnate god, of her created world.[194]

Anna's bid for freedom spurs the monster into murderous action; she is splashed by the symbolically menstrual blood of its first victim (the semi-adolescent Hawkins, whose crude jokes about 'pussy' have rendered him unable to connect with the mythically feminised, demonised jungle [Satan dwelling in nature] in which the non-attuned, overly sexual masculine ego becomes threatened).[195] She then reveals what she knows to the white man from across the sea – Schwarzenegger-cum-Quetzalcoatl – who would sever her from bondage, educe from her the truth, and who would hence, via his hard-won dominion over the natural world, be god: Anna has all along known of 'The Demon who makes Trophies of Men.'

At the end of a creeping, vertical crane shot, we see Hawkins's disembowelled corpse, hanging like game from the treetops. Blain is eviscerated alive by the monster's laser-gun, and Mac catches a glimpse of the hunter, now plainly using some kind of high-tech camouflage device. Panicked by the eerie distortion of the jungle, he opens fire, precipitating a full forty-five seconds of ballistic pandemonium during which all surviving Americans unload their every round of ammunition in the supposed direction of the enemy's flight. The smoke finally clears; the Gatling gun whirs on empty. 'Not a trace – no blood, no bodies,' assesses Poncho, dripping with sweat (as are all the cohorts except Dutch): 'We hit *nothing*.' For all its might, their big, loud, fiery weaponry has proven useless. ('He boasted of no triumphs then, the gold-friend of the Geats, for his good old sword bared in the battle, his blade, had failed him, as such iron should not do.')[196] It transpires, however, that the elusive creature *has* bled: its green, non-ferrous sap, along with Hawkins's human stain, is now on the doubly stigmatised Anna. 'If it bleeds,' reasons Dutch, 'we can kill it,' although he alone will possess the requisite ability to stay the course and kill the beast. Dillon, Poncho and Mac (after psychotically muttering the lyrics to 'Long Tall Sally') are slaughtered; Billy in effect commits suicide by divesting himself of firearms and challenging the monster, whom he wrongly sees as a kindred aboriginal spirit, to a knife duel; and Anna flees, instructed by Dutch to 'Run! Get to the chopper!' Act Three will be about Schwarzenegger/Dutch, his mettle and his performance alone and under pressure.

Arnold pushes fast through the undergrowth, with the Predator in pursuit; coming unexpectedly to a cliff-top, he falls, arms flailing, into a deep river far below. This is a ritual purgation, as Mircea Eliade explains, before battle proper can commence: '[I]n whatever complex we find them, the waters invariably retain their function: they disintegrate, abolish forms, "wash away sins"; they are at once purifying and regenerating.'[197]

Susan Jeffords claims that 'because this imagery has its own tradition outside these films, its force suggests a continuity and presence larger than these individual events . . . as with Rambo, there is a new soldier, a "new man," who is not so easily defeated or humiliated':

> Reaganology would have us see this rebirth as a sign of a 'new America,' one that, as Casper Weinberger stated in November 1984, would engage in another conflict like Vietnam only 'with the clear intention of winning.' But operating in close conjunction with a return to school prayer, a hard-line anti-abortionism, and an outdated reconstruction of the nuclear family, it becomes clear that such a position is grounded, not upon a 'new' America at all but on a surviving patriarchy . . . the reinstallation of the authority of the white male.[198]

Both Arnold's lone warrior-hero, an archetype 'envisioned most often as a white man,'[199] and his nemesis, who follows him down in a show of inter-species (and inter-masculine) respect, are cleansed by the waters. Subsequent to Dutch's purgation, is his moment of epiphany; accidentally smearing his whole body in the cold mud of the riverbank, he becomes invisible to – and akin to – his ethnicised, dreadlocked pursuer: 'He couldn't see me . . .' Arnold, 'purified,' 'regenerated,' the 'sins' of Vietnam washed away, must henceforth fight the creature by adopting its own methods, or by temporarily becoming one with the exotic heart of darkness in which he is immersed.

Night and miasma descend on the tropical forest. Dutch, gone superficially native by virtue of his carapace of mud, machinates; he will use the jungle to ensnare the Predator, whom we concomitantly see tearing out Billy's spine and heat-blasting his skull to add to a collection. Having laid a series of elaborate traps, improvised from vines, leaves and trunks, Dutch slathers on some war-paint, lights a torch, climbs up to a high perch, and emits a bestial roar: the fight to the death is on. Swinging from branch to branch, Dutch manoeuvres into a position of lofty advantage, and succeeds in disabling the creature's invisibility device by launching an explosive-tipped arrow; he is, though, badly shaken by the resulting display of pyrotechnics from his opponent, which fails, as had the Americans' earlier, to inflict any serious damage. Nonetheless, there is a palpable and exciting sense that Schwarzenegger, just possibly, may not come away from this encounter entirely unscathed.

As Eric Lichtenfeld dilates regarding Arnold's newfound dimension of humanness:

> [O]ne of the film's greatest strengths is McTiernan's ability to make the audience believe Dutch might lose. This is not merely a function of Schwarzenegger fighting a seven-foot-two-inch alien. *Predator* is the film in which Schwarzenegger begins to loosen up in front of the camera . . . McTiernan draws from Schwarzenegger the exertion, suffering, and even weariness that *Commando*'s Mark Lester could not and that *The Terminator*'s James Cameron sidestepped.'[200]

This therapeutic rematch will of course be won, but not without proper intellectual account, prompted by McTiernan, for the hero's emotional investment: to wage a propitious campaign, one must prepare for the inevitable distress. Certainly we feel Dutch recognises, unlike John Matrix or the T-101, that, rather than death being granted instantly and cleanly by a filmic bullet's magical gift of immediate oblivion, '[i]n reality, to die of war wounds is to usually to die in lingering agony and madness.'[201]

As usual, though, it is the supposed toughness and specialness of Arnold's body that ultimately arouses the most thematic attention. The hunter seems to think, however wily Dutch may be, that Schwarzenegger's Aryan physicality is his chief asset. The alien pins Arnold to a tree with its huge hands and carefully examines his cranial structure, deciding that Dutch is a prime specimen, his racial superiority (for a human) 'written in the skull,' as it has always been for advocates of the Caucasian race's 'great mission of civilising the earth.'[202] (McTiernan's Rastafarian-styled villain is here in curious agreement with Emile Durkheim, who approvingly cited the phrase 'one who has seen an aboriginal American has seen all aboriginal Americans.')[203] Keen to the kudos and significance of obtaining Schwarzenegger's head in a 'fair' fight, the monster, in a reversal of the ubiquitous arming scene, takes off his high-tech weapons and helmet to reveal a yellow, mottled face with a mandible jaw.[204] 'You're one ugly motherfucker,' says Dutch, providing another level of justification for our vilification of the Predator. 'Just as physical beauty is believed to symbolise inner moral or spiritual beauty or goodness,' notes Anthony Synnott, 'so too physical ugliness is believed to symbolise an inner ugliness or evil':

> [T]hose who are perceived as evil – i.e. enemies of one sort or another: military, ethnic, racial, political, etc. – are 'uglified' – portrayed as

9. The alien hunter admires Arnold's skull (Predator)

ugly: *propaganda* includes 'uglification.' In Germany, for instance, Hitler presented the Jews as both physically and morally ugly in *Mein Kampf* (1924); the Aryans, on the other hand, were physically and morally beautiful, and biologically and spiritually superior.[205]

Though Schwarzenegger is his enemy, the 'ugly' Predator seconds these beliefs via his cherishing of Arnold and what he represents – even, quite improbably, to an extra-terrestrial visitor presumably not familiar with the human discourses of eugenics and good looks.

After a prolonged fistfight that bloodies Dutch extensively yet must not damage his skull, Dutch manages to crush his foe by releasing a pre-set trap, which swings a log into the monster. Noble to the end, Dutch raises a rock over his head in order that he might administer a *coup de grâce* to the dying alien, but finds himself hesitating to ask, 'What the hell *are* you?' This reluctance to finish is almost costs Arnold dearly, for it would have been a pre-emptive measure – through humanitarian dithering at the battle's closing moments, he risks his life: the alien has a mini-nuclear bomb, counting down to detonation. Realising his mistake, Schwarzenegger runs for cover, diving into a ditch with no time to spare, as the blast radiates behind him. We cut to the evacuation helicopter, and R.G. Armstrong's general, who exclaims, 'My God!' at seeing the burgeoning mushroom cloud below. A wide shot, held while an aubade parodying 'Fanfare for the Common Man' heralds a new day dawning, depicts the devastation, amid which Arnold stands, tired but – remarkably – alive. The locale is immolated beyond recognition, though Dutch and Anna have survived. Indeed, as Steven Prince concludes, the film, in its final moments, apparently resonates with the:

> darkest impulses of the Cold War. At the end, the forests have been levelled and burned, the environment and the local region destroyed in the struggle. They are a fiery wasteland, but the enemy is defeated and the surviving American is airlifted to safety. The Central American threat is eradicated. The land has been destroyed in order to save it.[206]

Prince also, perspicaciously, writes of *Predator* that the 'anxieties of the film seem to have been mobilised by a general cultural fear in the first half of the decade that an American invasion of Central America, particularly of Nicaragua, might be a real possibility.'[207] McTiernan's film is certainly a timely, cautionary tale. Nonetheless, it does not condemn conflict but rather asserts the need for specialised approaches and instinctual perception. At its climax, it stresses the value of pragmatism over kindness when faced with a belligerent enemy who might unleash terrible forces; moreover, it is crucial to the film's moral stance that it is the alien – ultimately shown to be a cowardly suicide bomber – who is willing, even happy, to go nuclear for the sake of pride. But it is that American icon of subjectively interpreted misadventure and/or tactical error – the Vietnam War and its commonly perceived mistakes of military judgement – that are most consistently evoked. From the alien's devious use of the jungle setting, to McTiernan's shorthand inclusion of rock and roll music, sweat-drenched paranoia, and enervation of the troops to signify the Indochinese experience, this is clearly about redressing the ''Nam' situation as a template for future endeavours. Only by understanding the opposition's precise nature, and by taking on a 'primal' enemy at close-quarters and in sympathy with his dangerous, outlandish terrain, might the First World restore order to the Third, or wipe the slate clean of insidious manifestations. *Predator* employs Arnold, soberly and efficiently, to head up its trope: like numerous other cultural expressions of post-Vietnam trauma, it constitutes a 'symbolic effort to bring back home again what we hope can be recuperated in imagination if not in fact: a not ignoble part of as all squandered in an ignoble war.'[208]

Discipline and Punish: New Bad Futures/New Bad Friends

Revisiting the arenas of Rome after nearly 2,000 years of Christianity, we feel as if we are descending into the Hades of antiquity. The amphitheatre demands more than reproach. It is beyond our understanding that the Roman people should have made the human sacrifice, the munus, a festival joyously celebrated by the whole city.[209]

The public execution is to be understood not only as a judicial but also as a political ritual. It belongs, even in minor cases, to the ceremonies by which power is manifested.[210]

Filmed during a long hiatus from shooting *Predator*, Paul Michael Glaser's *The Running Man* (1987) is loosely based on an early novel by Stephen King (writing as Richard Bachman). More literally so than in McTiernan's film, Arnold's function is gladiatorial; the setting, however, is not classical, but rather that of what Fred Glass terms the 'New Bad Future' (NBF)[211] – a dystopic, bread-and-circuses America gone to seed, whose degeneracy nonetheless evokes chronicles of Rome in the tertiary stages of imperial decline:

NBF films tell stories about a future in the grip of feverish social decay . . . The NBF scenario typically embraces urban expansion on a monstrous scale, where real estate capital has realised its fondest dreams of cancerous growth . . . The heroes, by themselves or with rebellious groups, go up against the corruption and power of the ruling corporations, which exercise a media-based velvet glove/iron fist social control. This repressive structure of society provides the films' rationale for lots of bloodletting. Despite their penchant for gratuitous gore as well as other problems (poorly conceived women characters, dialogue generally less lofty than Shakespeare) many NBF films tilt toward an intelligent, leftish politics, leavened with a sense of (black) humour.[212]

In Glaser's version of the NBF, Schwarzenegger plays an innocent participant in the sadistic, titular game show: a near-future *munus* designed to punish convicted criminals in a televised arena in which they fight for their lives (and usually lose) against heavily armed 'stalkers.' A morally ambiguous production that both criticises and proffers blood-thirsty mass entertainment, *The Running Man* nevertheless enters into a dialogue *with* America, *about* America, concerning the potential dangers of unchecked media influence and totalitarian authority in an isolated, culturally syphilitic West devoid of sufficient natural resources. The film recognises, it would seem, that if an oil-hungry, corporate-centred Reaganite ethos were to extend too far beyond the limits of a broadly liberal consensus and become the basis of a police state, an ironically anti-libertarian America – one not so distinct from the 'empire of evil' – might be the eventual result.

As the Soviet Union crumbled under economic pressure and the Cold War looked to be nearly won, Arnold's roles began – albeit very cautiously – to reflect a desire to critique possible outcomes of an unyielding, hard-line US ideology against the late-1980s 'pervasive backdrop of economic gloom.' David D. Hale continued:

> With the country seemingly awash in a sea of red ink as the Reagan era ends, many Americans are convinced that a protracted period of austerity lies ahead . . . The international economic system is characterised by financial imbalances and trade tensions that bear striking similarities to those that laid the groundwork for the Great Depression of the 1930s.[213]

Though *The Running Man* in and of itself constitutes an example of the very circus of which it is derisive, the film allows Schwarzenegger's 'apolitical' hero a chance to examine the human costs of the American Colossus in freefall, with no Roosevelt, New Deal, war or apocalypse in sight to halt the decay. As the star commented in 1987:

> I really enjoy doing pictures like *The Running Man* because they are very sophisticated kinds of films. I like the whole idea of the modern gladiator, the government being in control of the [TV] network and fixing the contest, and the show being organised to prevent people from rioting and protesting by keeping them glued to the television set. But I also like the whole idea and challenge of injecting comedy into the picture to lighten tension.[214]

In knowing contrast to received conservative opinion about Soviet humourlessness regarding ideological intransigence, Arnold entered the New Bad Future so that he might demonstrate understanding of the dangers of his own philosophy and offer cultural reciprocation to Mikhail Gorbachev and foreign minister Eduard Shevardnadze's enforced openness apropos Russia's need to adapt. As Raymond Garthoff observed, America's nominal 'victory' in the Cold War 'came at a time when a new generation of Soviet leaders realised how badly their system at home and their policies abroad had failed';[215] acute, as always, to the timely commercial opportunities of allowably moderate dissent from within, Hollywood – via the latter New Bad Future cycle – promulgated a noncommittal but nontheless readable message of similar self-analysis aimed at exposing potential rather than long-conspicuous flaws in its own 'system.'

From *The Running Man*'s first scene, we learn of Arnold's character (morally decent military policeman Ben Richards) and his humanistic leanings that run contrary to the unfeeling callousness exhibited by the majority in this institutionalised dystopia. (How Richards got this far into a career that clearly demands compliance to authority is unclear.) Unwilling to quell a Californian 'food riot' by opening fire on civilians, Richards disobeys orders to 'eliminate anything moving,' is knocked unconscious with a rifle butt, framed as the perpetrator of what becomes a state-sanctioned massacre, and sent to a high-security gulag where all inmates are fitted with explosive collars that detonate upon the wearer leaving a designated zone. Weaker prisoners are seen to collapse and die from exhaustion, but Richards is able to formulate a plan for escape along with fellow captives William Laughlin (Yaphet Kotto) and Harold Weiss (Marvin McIntyre); they manage to disable the perimeter fence's electronic signal and make a break for resistance leader Mic's compound to have their collars removed. Mic, a lank-haired former musician (played, aptly if rather vacantly, by Mick Fleetwood), is trying to locate the all-pervasive television network's uplink so that he might 'broadcast the truth.' 'The truth? Hasn't been very popular lately,' replies Richards, who, as a policeman, had been an interloper, but one whose anti-intellectualism, pragmatism and apparent lack of interest in revolutionary schemes renders him less sequacious, and hence more individualistic, than the collectively minded, hippie-ish underground who will eventually need his help: 'All I have seen is a bunch of low foreheads who think they can change the world with dreams and talk. It's too late for that. If you're not ready to act, give me a break and shut up.'

Declaring that he is 'not into politics – I'm into survival,'[216] Richards unwisely goes to his brother's apartment, only to find it occupied by Amber Mendez (Maria Conchita Alonso), a musician and fitness fanatic who likes exercising to a television show called *Captain Freedom's Workout* (the Captain is an ex-*Running Man* stalker, portrayed by Jesse Ventura as a virtual clone of *Predator*'s Blain). Under duress, Maria tells Ben that his brother has been 'taken away for re-education'; meanwhile, the producers of *The Running Man*, at the request of its 'high-camp nastyboots'[217] host Damon Killian (real-life game show presenter Richard Dawson), plot to capture Ben Richards to put him to use as the ultimate contestant: 'Look at that mother move!' says Killian, while watching surveillance footage of Richards's escape (closed-circuit cameras, symbolic of anxieties about the compromise of personal liberties, are everywhere in *The Running Man* and indeed most New Bad Futures). Richards kidnaps Mendez as an aid to passage and attempts to take her abroad, but he is stopped at the airport and imprisoned, whereupon Killian makes him an offer: 'You've got talent, you've got charisma, and you've got balls . . . I'd like you to "volunteer" to appear on tomorrow's broadcast.' 'Fuck you,' answers Richards, although he is then told that Weiss and Laughlin, also now apprehended and seemingly less able to survive the show due to their inferior physiques, will appear in his place if he does not. Ben, valiantly offering self-sacrifice but perhaps not without faith in his extreme muscularity and 'balls,' agrees to save the hapless revolutionaries by participating in Killian's kitsch spectacle.

The *munus* opens on a note of cod-Broadway excess, which, character-istically, both sends up and celebrates luridly sexist displays of titillation, in so doing challenging almost beyond comprehension Glaser's mode of intra-textual representation. A (quasi-)satirical introductory sequence features some lithe female dancers in tight Lycra costumes, gyrating amidst dry ice and strobe lighting for the spectators' amusement, scorn and somewhat dubious erotic pleasure; it is, however, impossible to know whether the prurient close-ups are more inherent to Glaser's, or the titular television programme's, aesthetic, a filmic conundrum raised contingently to the inevitable representational dilemma posed by show-within-a-show conceits. Critic Dennis Fischer found much to deride in the film's paradoxical stance, calling it 'as contemptible as the wrestling and game shows it is satirising';[218] his complaint is seldom more valid than when considered in connection with *The Running Man*'s apparent lack of self-awareness regarding sexual politics. Whilst Arnold is being walked to his dressing room, he passes Amber (who works as a composer for the network) and her power-dressing female friend, Amy, in the corridor. Gazing vampishly and longingly at Schwarzenegger's vigorous frame, Amy vocalises an alarmingly off-colour submission fantasy: 'Good job he didn't rape you then kill you. Or kill you then rape you. I mean, a guy like that, what would stop him?' It is for her overt sexuality, though, that she is implicitly vilified, rather than for her perversion or regressive mockery of women's workplace emancipation. Amber, the more demure and hence conventionally, 'properly' feminine of the pair, reacts by momentarily considering herself both lucky to have escaped Arnold's manly clutches and not a little deprived: 'Yeah . . . what would?'

Fans gather outside the studio to herald the arrival of the stalkers and place bets with bookmakers on which of the celebrities will be the first executioner of the evening. Killian then introduces the show by broadcasting a re-edited video of the 'Bakersfield Massacre,' now cut to scapegoat Arnold as the murderous 'Butcher of Bakersfield' – 'tonight's guest runner!' Led onstage to a chorus of boos, Schwarzenegger appears wearing a spandex jumpsuit, and is told that he is competing for 'fabulous prizes like a trial by jury, a suspended sentence, or maybe even a full pardon!' like 'last season's winners: Whitman, Price, and Haddad!' (whose corpses are eventually found by Mendez, rotting in a corner of the game zone). The network's true mendaciousness is revealed, and Arnold given extra incentive to exact revenge, when Killian presents Weiss and Laughlin, now also taking part in order to handicap Richards; Mendez too, having been caught attempting to steal unedited tapes of the Bakersfield slaughter, is a 'surprise guest . . . She cheated on college exams, and had sexual relationships with two, sometimes three different men in a year! [Hence, she is a corrupted Vestal],' admonishes the announcer, highlighting again the essential meaninglessness of the film's censorious attitude to double standards in the media. Before being launched down a vertiginous slide into the game zone (a wasteland 'left over from the big quake of '97'), Richards tells Killian, 'I'll be back.'

Briefly stunned, Killian – a true professional – responds with his own zinger, 'Only in a re-run.'

The pursuers themselves are re-runs from the colonial id: ethnocentrically imagined demons from beyond the edge of the world. 'Professor Sub-Zero,' a sumo-weight Japanese stalker on ice-skates who wields a huge, sharpened hockey stick, is the pursuer initially chosen (by the baying, greedy audience of voracious consumers about which this gory, incoherent film is highly disdainful) to attack the runners. However, Arnold gets the better of the Oriental killer by garrotting him with barbed wire ('He was a real pain in the neck'), shocking the network producers, the Justice Department and the crowd: no stalker has ever been outwitted by a runner before. Indulging the game show's format, Richards declares, 'Here is Sub-Zero – now, plain *zero*.' The ratings, needless to say, soar; a slyly contrived yet somehow self-denigrating acknowledgement of graphic, vicarious violence's mass appeal follows: the film has Killian explain to his superiors that ratings are what matters, 'and you ain't gonna get that with re-runs of *Gilligan's Island*.' Two more overweight pantomime grotesques, the power-tool specialist Buzzsaw and the opera-singing Dynamo, enter the arena, and are respectively dispatched and invalided by Richards, of whom an old lady declares, 'He's one mean motherfucker!' (In an echo of *Predator*'s lesson on the folly of humaneness, Schwarzenegger's character refuses to kill Dynamo, 'a helpless human being.' Later, Dynamo will attempt to rape Mendez – her earlier molestation fantasy is thus nearly fulfilled, although not by the 'desirable,' masterful Arnold, but by a representative of the narrative's boorish sense of phallocentric 'justice' – who electrocutes him with the network's sprinkler system.) Bets are now on as to whether Richards, unhampered by heavy machinery and reliant only on his 'natural' muscle, will make the next kill. His unfortunate co-contenders, with the exception of his prize, Mendez, are too weak to get out alive: Arnold must continue onward with only Amber, now, like *Predator*'s Anna (and indeed King Minos's thread-providing daughter Ariadne, to cite only one analogue from classical myth) the bearer of secret knowledge – the network uplink code – through the underworld, finally shattering the state's media-controlled illusion by exposing the network's lies. Without Arnold, spurred on to action as usual via a pseudo-personal, superficially non-partisan aggression, the underground movement would have been ineffectual; with him as their hero, they save the day and restore a sense of moral worth to the New Bad Future's Caligulan societal decay.

Christine Gledhill's general observation that 'no artistic practice, realist or otherwise, can ensure either a conservative or radical reading on the part of the audience'[219] is certainly true of *The Running Man*, a work that is unable (and maybe unwilling) thematically to reconcile an undeniably left-leaning criticism of corporate power with a uneasily co-existing, capitalist desire to exploit garish spectacles of ritualistic punishment in order to generate sales. Nonetheless, Glaser's text propounds a hypothesis that the American organism, in particular its drives to create wealth and disregard for any kind of 'socialist' ideals, might one day bring about not only Dickensian disparity, but also the type of disarray amidst which any over-extended, globally super-powerful nation must eventually find itself: isolated, internecine, and unable to tolerate dissent. Though external threats ('barbarians' at the gates) of the kind made so manifest at Pearl Harbor, or on 11 September 2001, occasionally present themselves, 'decline,' notes Niall Ferguson in a book subtitled *The Rise and Fall of the American Empire,* 'in this case seems more likely to come, as it came to Gibbons' Rome, from within.'[220]

Almost irrespective of whether the United States' international ambitions represent true imperialism, what is pertinent to *The Running Man* is Ferguson's point about 'the way the political system militates against farsighted leadership.'[221] To stay the course in conflict and subsequent rebuilding operations – and make the world a 'healthier', bigger market place – Americans should not only be given a 'forward-leaning engagement strategy';[222] in addition, argues Ferguson, they need to learn from the mistakes of previous empires, admitting some humility, whilst at the same time committing to the deposing of tyrants like Killian, and to John Kennedy's expression of a duty to 'truly light the world.'[223] Widespread ignorance of endemic fault-lines in a society geared toward exponential consumption, 'coca-colonisation,' dependence on fossil resources, and Dionysian gratification, must, Glaser suggests, give way to an epiphanic enlightenment if the balance of humanity is to be restored. America, if it is to keep its place at the head of the geopolitical table, must accept its 'responsibilities,' recognise its deficiencies and govern as if with purpose and beneficence. As George Kennan mused, 'I sometimes wonder what use there is in trying to protect the West against external threats when the signs of disintegration within are so striking.'[224]

Delusions of God-bestowed American grandeur, or the total faith in American ability to bestride the world evermore without sufficient political will to effect such internal changes as make hegemony practicable, are indeed hubristic. After unipolar power – perhaps a transient entity (at least if the power elite pays no heed to shifting global dynamics) – slips away in the absence of an abruptly purgative catastrophe, then the self-summoned world of the New Bad Future is one possibility offered up by Hollywood to serve as a warning. Capitalism, in the NBF, can of course be maintained: this is seldom depicted as a curse in itself, but the blind tolerance of unbridled superstructural development at the cost of infrastructural integrity is. When the workers' (and consumers') lives are compromised, or made meaningless by subservience to a regime whose sole interest is the maintenance of a precarious domestic status quo, a resilient leader must arise who is aware of the need for physical action, and of the ideological insidiousness of verbally articulated sedition. Counter-cultures, for mainstream action cinema, have proven either not up to the task, dangerously adherent to Old Left principles, or liable to self-destruct; in the NBF, hard-body, white male figures such as Arnold assume mantles of symbolic, patriarchal power because they are men (or women, in the complicated case of *Aliens'* 'Company' employee Ellen Ripley) of deeds, of *action*, who are capable of pushing physically for a difficult, but, they suggest, achievable balance of free-market economics and pan-societal empathy that might serve as a template for effective global leadership – by example – into the twenty-first century and beyond. 'For all the distrust summoned by authority and the unchecked exercise of individual power,' notes William Fisher in a paper on the 'Terminal Genre' (his near-equivalent of the NBF):

> how much more unsettling its opposite – the prospect of surrender and release to something amorphous and collective in character. Although the Terminal Genre may be 'multinational' in geographical scope, narrative co-ordinates, and appeal, let us not forget that like other multinational organisms, it has its source in American values and traditions of free enterprise, expansion, and domination.[225]

Wealth, of course, drives Hollywood; thus, it does not become or benefit the commercial cinema to lose sight entirely of popular concerns held by any and all consumer demographics. Criticised as early as

1981 by AFL-CIO union chief Lane Kirkland as 'economic Darwinism: the survival of the richest,'[226] hard-line Reaganomics, by the end of its advocate's presidency, still convinced those without conscientious qualms or Democratic allegiances. Humankind's most propitious objective, asserted Reagan favourite George Gilder, was a semi-religious attitude to trade that excluded only those without sufficient morality to get rich: 'Faith in man, faith in the future, faith in the return of giving, faith in the mutual benefit of trade, faith in the providence of God are all essential to successful capitalism,' he opined.[227] Such uncompromising, uncaring attitudes to the accumulation of wealth were commonplace on Wall Street, but spawned few favourable analogues in the cinema:[228] even if the financial heroes of the high Reagan era – modern-day robber barons like Donald Trump and Michael Milken – inspired the 'yuppie revolution' and were venerated on television in programmes such as *Lifestyles of the Rich and Famous* and *Dynasty*, they were not extolled as consistently by the film studios. Production of ironically meretricious blockbusters like *The Running Man*, often featuring incongruous, self-renunciatory ideas in a bid for wide critical resonance, constituted one flank of the film industry's semi-articulate response to deregulation and the glorification of monetary excess (the flipside of *Top Gun* remains part of the same, valuable coin). Coinciding almost exactly with the financial crash of October 1987, *The Running Man*'s theatrical release neatly dovetails with a confession, from the editorial pages of the *Wall Street Journal*, that 'conspicuous consumption is passé.'[229] The Reagan era's out-and-out exultation of greed had plainly lost some of its allure; trickling through to mass entertainment, this increased ambivalence in popular judgement saw concomitance in Glaser and Schwarzenegger's frivolous pandering to public unease.

The 'Market Empire,' that 'great imperium with the outlook of a great emporium,'[230] was selling itself once more – this time on a point of dichotomous introspection coupled with explosive spectacle. Money, rather than burning the pockets of blindly greedy protagonists, was instead writ large in every frame, whose wholesale content seemed frowningly to caution against precisely the mechanisms that created Hollywood entertainment – the apparatus, though only partially, was in the process of deconstructing itself as a rite of globally decreed confessional. 'If archaeologists can infer something about the character of a society from a few shards,' wrote H. Bruce Franklin in 1981:

[C]ertainly visions of the future created by large groups of highly skilled people armed with advanced technology, financed by millions of dollars, on behalf of giant corporations, intended to make handsome profits by enticing the cost of expensive tickets from masses of consumers, must reveal something about the character of our own society . . . The only future that seems unimaginable in Hollywood is a better one.[231]

This is not to say that 'The White Man's Burden' has, according to the cinema industry's habitually down-beat soothsaying, been apathetically relinquished and all hope in the promise of American primacy abandoned: NBF films are not *merely* 'trashy infatuations with an equally trashy future.'[232] When Hollywood worried about impending doom from the headland of the latter 1980s, it did so because of the survival instinct, visiting upon itself the pessimistic ghosts of capitalism's future, yet by the same curious logic mounting a moral defence whose petition to the 'masses of consumers' spoke volumes. In 1985, Robert Bellah's team at the University of California, Berkeley, warned in a report on American values that 'American individualism may have grown cancerous . . . threatening the survival of freedom itself.' 'The citizen,' so the authors concluded, 'has been swallowed up by economic man.'[233] Within *The Running Man* lies a half-buried reassurance of the system's prognostic ability: like a vaccine, it provokes an autoimmune response whose deeper purpose is, contrary to immediate appearances, to avow – via the white, muscular, 'healthy' male form of Ben Richards's called-to-action curative – the Darwinistically adaptive nation's sanguine ideological health.

Schwarzenegger's place in the scheme of things was changing, as the prudence of unsubtly embodying economic or military bigness diminished in inverse proportion to relative American influence (and public resentment of the debts and deficits that helped achieve this). No longer required to act as a rudimentary totem expressive (and reflective) of purblind Stateside unease about international superiority, Arnold adapted and began choosing roles admitting degrees of ambivalence. In harmony with popular awareness, and attentive to the withering of a neatly defined external adversary – the big, old ideological bloc that had hitherto been the literal and metaphorical target of choice – 'Arnie' (since 'the public hero is always sensitive to the needs of his time')[234] would instead have to take in hand divisions of politics and class, mounting a nuanced defence of material pleasure. 'The American model of consumer society,' writes Victoria de Grazia, 'had thrived [until the late 1980s] by setting itself up as the democratic, comfortable, equitable alternative to repressive, goods-scarce, and unjust ways of life. With no enemy to challenge it, would it retain its irresistible power?'[235] As USSR General Secretary Gorbachev, near the end of Reagan's tenure, asked US national security adviser Colin Powell, 'What are you going to do now you've lost your best enemy?'[236] Gorbachev's rhetorical question has immense salience to Schwarzenegger's career trajectory: his hero-Golem, born of the collective unconscious, was being dexterously remoulded to fight another day afresh in the light of newly displaced concerns. The 'irresistible power' of Arnold's brand, as it entered its tertiary phase, sought a third way to affirm the benefits of a hegemonically Americanised world community.

By the late 1980s, American voters were primed for the ostensibly milder, avuncular stewardship of ex-CIA head George H.W. Bush (a nostalgic anti-communist but a man burdened by an unwanted inheritance: 'Gorbymania'), and even the White House felt safe enough to speak of putting aside 'little local differences' between the USSR and the USA for the sake of working together by summit and dialogue. Arnold, his very presence a signifier of the power of the American Dream and his faith in competition entirely implicit, was ready to step into the cultural breach and welcome not merely a gentle reassessment of the direction American ideology was potentially headed, but a timely re-evaluation of the United States' relationship with the faltering power against which it had measured its material success for decades. Evincing a remarkably backhanded concession to the spirit of *glasnost*, he would even deign to play, in Walter Hill's *Red Heat* (1988), a Russian himself.

'[T]he antipathy that had characterised Soviet–American exchanges in the early 1980s had been replaced by a relationship that was less acrimonious and much more cordial,' recorded Phil Williams in a 1989 paper. 'If *glasnost* continues, and if the Soviet system becomes less repressive and more transparent, the American image of the Soviet Union as a repressive ideological state bent on global domination could change – and with it the American perception of threat.'[237] In *Red Heat*, Hill adopts a responsive stance apropos the thawing of the Cold War, whose narrative function here, as opposed to compelling any dramatic thrust or constituting any kind of military 'threat,' is straightforwardly to express the essential, potential goodness of masculine comradeship across boundaries (which are, notwithstanding concessions to domestic foibles, drawn from a resolutely American perspective). Coarse ethnic and national stereotypes, hardly less facile and reductive than those of D.W. Griffith, herein reluctantly but productively join forces to crush a bigger threat (or, my enemy's enemy is, so long as I understand his historical crux, my friend).

Focusing primarily on the disparate – but ultimately perhaps reconcilable – habits and personalities of its two policeman protagonists, Arnold's Captain Ivan 'Iron Jaw' Danko and James Belushi's Chicagoan cop Art Ridzik, *Red Heat* is a generic 'buddy movie' that seeks warily to shift serious enmity away from the war on ideology and onto the newly declared 'war on drugs,' as the pair pursue a Russian cocaine smuggler on the run in America. Backing down from the sometimes veiled but nonetheless underlying strategic fundamentalism of Schwarzenegger's earlier vehicles, the film displaces most, but not all (the drug lord visits his villainy upon the USA from a country depicted as inherently prone to organised criminality), of its hatred onto the reactionary's nightmare of substance abuse, an 'evil' now preoccupying those in power and fixating the White House:

> [T]he focus placed on the drug issue by President and Mrs. Reagan contributed to a national obsession. To an extent, the drug war replaced the Cold War as a national security issue. The administration and journalists friendly to the White House spoke of 'narcoterrorists,' often linked to left-wing regimes in Nicaragua and Cuba, who replaced the Soviet Red Army as 'enemy number one.'[238]

Moreover, the Reagan and incoming Bush administrations 'continued to define drug use as a criminal problem, with policy focussed on intercepting supplies, arresting dealers, and jailing users.'[239] Despite Danko's incessant sternness, which is throughout overplayed to ridicule the Soviet Union as a fossil whose actual power has dissipated to be replaced by ineffectual pomp, the insidiousness of the international cocaine trade is what draws the brunt of *Red Heat*'s illiberal ire. Hill's, though, is a fantasist's version of the anti-addiction crusade, in which the law concentrates on catching a large-scale, well-equipped operative rather than targeting poor Hispanics and blacks. Launched with Reagan's angry promise that the police would clamp down 'with more ferocity than ever before,' the war on drugs, according to the 1996 *Report of the National Criminal Justice Commission*, in reality focused 'almost exclusively on low-level dealers in minority neighbourhoods.'[240] Danko and Ridzik, consequently, must 'terminate' their Georgian prey (Viktor Rosta – Ed O'Ross) 'with extreme prejudice' in what amounts to a public execution via celluloid, so that justice can be served and American political, economic and moral dominion can be exerted over the twinned terrains of outgoing Communism and incoming narcotics.

Hill entertains no doubts that the newly sweetened East–West relationship is in essence still psychologically dichotomous, or that the United States and the Soviet Union remain strikingly contrapuntal localities. From the start, Arnold is unmistakably in Terminator mode, the name 'Iron Jaw' standing for intransigence and automaton-like adherence to the task (literally) in hand. Having walked, naked apart from a G-string, into a unisex, medieval-looking spa in search of Rosta, Danko's mettle is tested by fire: a scorching-hot pebble is placed in his palm by a mafioso – he grips it, unflinchingly, his pain negated by his devotion to policing, which even extends to fighting naked (hyper-homo-erotic via hyper-hetero overstress, of course) adversaries in the snow.

Red Heat is never progressive in terms of cultural representation; always simplified for the spectator's easy recognition, the signifiers of 'Russianness' are in shorthand wherever possible. Over shots of troops parading machine-like across a very grey Red Square (Hill, remarkably, was allowed to shoot in this actual location), and set to a parodically portentous march by James Horner, the titles are rendered in a quasi-Russian typeface, with Ns and Rs appearing backwards. This is as clear a reflection as any of Hill's cursory judgement of the Soviets, and indeed general contemporary American attitudes to the fading socialist spectre – attitudes that were by and large softening but ambivalent, reductive and mostly ignorant (partly because of the Soviets' entrenched policies of secrecy and pre-*glasnost* willingness to show only a militaristic or intractable public face, and partly because of people such as Senator Robert Dole, who warned that Gorbachev, whose reforms were in Dole's view implemented to pave the way for aggressive long-term ambitions, 'is more dangerous and threatening to our country and our ideals than all the brashness and bluster of a Krushchev; all the stolid determination of a Brezhnev.').[241]

The USSR, in *Red Heat*, is hence set up as a moribund entity, but one that must be approached with caution lest one lose sight of its nature as an enemy of American concepts of freedom. To make the point abundantly and immediately clear, ominously jump-cut shots of Lenin and Marx (or at least their statues) are interspersed, during the opening credits, with those of onion domes and uniformed drones, all barely in relief against the cinematographically contrived dreariness. Schwarzenegger, under Hill's tutelage and genuinely derisive of collectivist principles himself, does his utmost to complement this by-the-numbers depiction: his Danko coming over as a strange mixture of infantilised charmer, heavy-handed brute, contemptuous simpleton and – above all – political and social anachronism in thrall to a dying regime. 'Don't tell the Americans anything,' he is warned by his superior before embarking on his trip Stateside. 'Don't talk about our problems.' Although Arnold insisted that part of the reason the crew was allowed to film in Moscow was that 'this is the first time where a Soviet has been portrayed in a very heroic and positive way,'[242] his character is predominantly a dupe. Danko is unknowingly shackled by an 'inferior' worldview simplistically positioned by the film to reassert stereotypes, whereas the short-lived, real-life 'buddy movie of Mikhail and Ron'[243] – a partnership worrying to George Bush (to whose presidential campaign Arnold was in 1988 contributing) – constituted in effect a more optimistic and progressive enterprise than many could allow.

Upon arriving in Chicago to extradite Rosta (who has fled abroad after killing Danko's colleague in a typical revenge-quest set-up), Arnold provides comedy, somewhat in the vein of *Hercules in New York* and indeed of Peter Faiman's *Crocodile Dundee* (1986), only with the dubious innovation of additional topical currency. 'Iron Jaw' is an old-fashioned fish out of water and a foreign curio ignorant of the customs of the 'poisonous West,' which are instantly condensed by the presence of a Levi's billboard – the first thing we see of the United States, in a simple juxtaposition proving Hill is at least more or less fair when it comes to sketching easily construed philosophical schemes: the Russians get Lenin as a synecdoche, Americans get denim. Whilst the doughy Belushi munches fast food, endlessly wisecracks and ogles girls,

Schwarzenegger goes about his task with caricatured, monosyllabic efficiency: all buddy movies draw a distinction, and here it is between 'a one-dimensional cardboard cut-out of a Russian police officer with little identity of his own,'[244] and Ridzik's equally shallow foil, who initially considers Danko 'a jerk.' When the Soviet turns on the television in his room and is faced with a pornographic film, he bemoans to himself, 'Capitalism,' and we are of course in on a 'joke,' which nevertheless bears a serious message: Danko needs to lighten up in order that he might forge a relationship with Ridzik, acknowledge the fault-lines in his thinking and question the outmoded dogmatism of his homeland. For in the year of *Red Heat*'s production, Moscow would be holding its first beauty contest, four years after the BBC denounced the Miss World pageant as 'anachronistic and almost offensive.'[245] The Soviets, in a bid for economic viability, were emulating the West's passion for the 'beauty mystique'; yet here Schwarzenegger's notional aesthetic appeal (as the winner of numerous beauty pageants himself) is sublimated entirely to his function as a uniformed type, or a stolidly over-clothed, state-stifled body doing a job at odds with 'freedom' and choice: the women do not even appear to want him to molest them.

'Is that a Russian cop uniform?' asks a young, female police officer, as Danko walks into the precinct. 'Looks like a glorified postman, or something out of World War II!' 'Be respectful to our guest,' admonishes her superior, Commander Donnelly (Peter Boyle), addressing the spectator as directly as anyone. Danko may well be 'absurd,' but it is wise, so Connelly implies, to maintain diplomacy, even when prompting educes little response beyond the miserable. ('How do you Soviets deal with all the tension and stress?' 'Vodka,' replies Arnold, conveying an irony through the humour's dismissive tone: alcoholism's impact on Russian productivity, as Gorbachev had stressed, was immeasurably worse than the 'American poison,' cocaine.) Putting on a stiff, green suit, Danko goes 'undercover' to find Viktor, who has escaped custody following arrest for a driving violation. 'You look like Gumby,' mocks Ridzik, and it is true that Arnold, resplendent with what might be a Grace Jones-inspired flat-top, could not conceivably blend in. However, as we have seen, Schwarzenegger can never be part of the mass, part of the homogeneous whole: the hero abroad, regardless of his guise, is always a hero or champion of some kind to the culture that spawned him from its imagination.

At one point Danko is forced to explain to Larry Fishburne's officer that 'brigandage' no longer goes on in the Soviet Union, and that 'burning villages, raping women' was a thing of 'the past . . . During war. Not now.' Schwarzenegger's expression is different during this dialogue; he lets drop the sternness and instead adopts a countenance that suggests he is humbled and ashamed, perhaps by association guilty, of the acts he describes – atrocities that should not have happened within his dearly held socialist utopia, but that did, alongside many other disgraceful acts, under Stalin. In other words, there is an internal conflict implied, something that does not trouble Ridzik ('a good cop, but a total expert in fucking up') with regard to his physicality, licentiousness or vices; Danko ('the perfect weapon') is seen to be having a crisis of faith in Soviet socialism, whilst the commander consequently loses patience in bonhomie: 'I don't want you rolling through this town like the Red Army!'

On the way to visit a jailed informer, with Ridzik along to keep him in line, Danko comes out with a zinger that makes plain his reduction to aggressive clown. Ridzik warns: 'In this country, we try to protect the rights of individuals. It's called the Miranda Act, and it says that you can't even *touch* his ass.' 'I do not want to touch his ass,' says Arnold. 'I want to make him talk.' Where Ridzik failed in an attempt to make him talk by planting heroin, Danko does so by violently extracting

10. *Ridzik and 'Gumby' in* Red Heat

the information. 'Soviet method is more economical,' explains Danko, plainly averse to the touching of male buttocks, but not of digits. The Soviets did not, and do not, of course, have a monopoly on brutality. Chicago itself, since well before the landmark events of the 1968 Democratic convention, has had a reputation for uncompromising policing. In Los Angeles, the Rodney King incident would eventually force a public re-evaluation of tactics, but the findings of the 1996 report on *The Real War on Crime* suggested that, nationally, nothing had changed, and that excessive violence was 'a significant problem' at the heart of American law enforcement methods.[246] Accusing Danko, therefore, of unnecessary force due to an amoral Soviet system, and presenting the Chicagoan as an ethically dubious yet pacific pragmatist honour-bound to obey the Miranda Act, is in itself highly suspect in terms of moral and ethical probity.

After being criticised for breaking the captive's fingers, Arnold retorts: 'In your country it is okay to lie and put drug in pocket? We both go too far.' Drug dealers, it would seem, are beneath contempt and undeserving of humanity, according to *Red Heat*'s conservative-appeasing stance apropos judgements of good against bad. Arnold, employing the 'Soviet method,' gets what he wants, despite his part-ner's begrudging insistence that 'even scumbags have rights in this country.' The buddies are building a camaraderie based on mutual acceptance of each other's unprofessional conduct. It is, in the rather inconsistently constructed world of Hill's film, implicitly and funda-mentally acceptable in the war on drugs to be both a devious exploiter of human weakness and to 'roll around town like the Red Army'; all is apparently fair in this deployment of East–West forces in opposition to the new evil empire of narcotics trading, exemplified by the black-power-preaching prison inmate and cackling crime boss (a quasi-juju priest made mysterious with opaque, sightless eyes) who plans 'to sell drugs to every white man in the world. And his sister!' in spurious revenge for the injustices of slavery. His militant ethnicity, coupled with a lack of fear, is the only thing seen to frighten Danko, the harsh-ness of the Soviet system's inculcations not proving equal to such a beguiling, unfamiliar force.

Danko certainly does not fear, and has no qualms about assaulting, several members of the public – especially one thug who wants his parking space back and is unfortunate enough to find himself provoking a zinger: 'Do you know Miranda,' Arnold asks? 'Never heard of the bitch,' says the baseball-bat-wielding complainant, upon which Danko knocks him unconscious with a punch, earning the admiration of an increasingly Nixonian Ridzik, who seems to be gaining some vicarious enjoyment and common ground with the Russian via a newfound honesty and mutual appreciation of zero-tolerance crime-fighting:

Ridzik: Tell me something, Captain. If you've got such a fucking paradise over there, how come you're up the same creek as we are with heroin and cocaine?

Danko: The Chinese find a way. Right after the Revolution, they line up all drug dealers, all drug addicts, take them to public square, and shoot them in back of head.

Ridzik: Nah, that'd never work here. Fucking politicians would never go for it.

Danko: Shoot them first.

Presumably this is meant both to illustrate the pair's beautifully developing masculine bond and to elicit a laugh at the expense of those 'fucking politicians' and liberal intellectuals who would deride the enormously ineffective war on drugs. It is, it must be said, one of the crudest and most ideologically repugnant moments of dialogue in Schwarzenegger's entire Hollywood career – a hotly contested honour. What the star regards as a 'very heroic and positive' portrayal must, with consideration, be seen – at least by political moderates – as nothing of the sort. Beneath the diverting fig leaf of international bridge-building lies an endorsement of deep-seated American brutality, which finds a release at this extremely violent film's climax, when all pretence to going by the book is dropped by Ridzik. 'I give up,' he drawls, 'this whole thing's very Russian,' before Danko unloads every round in his pistol into Rosta. United in a hatred of 'scumbags,' the American and Russian policemen have bonded for the greater 'good': punishment and revenge.

The real war on drugs was an abject disaster. As Steven R. Donziger notes, the campaign:

did not succeed in its goal of stemming drug use. As the war heated up in the late 1980s, the street price of cocaine should have increased as police interdicted supplies and dealing became riskier. Instead, the street price of cocaine *fell*. Increased arrests and harsher sentences should have forced dealers off the streets. Instead, drug dealing in most communities remained steady or increased. Nor was there any evidence that the war on drugs succeeded in lowering drug use – drug use was in decline well before the war was declared.[247]

No matter to Hill – the import of his story stands as proud as his Soviet protagonist:

> We have a Russian commenting on America and its perceptions of Soviet society, so there's an attempt at a comedic element running throughout. The film questions certain American values in juxtaposition with a very theatrical Russian sensibility. The characters come together from a common objective; while not liking each other, they grow to respect one another on the way to becoming friends. Arnold hesitated for fifteen minutes, but he's a smart fellow, so he came around.[248]

A smart fellow indeed, and one, as always, who sensed his purpose. 'His choice of script,' comments Wendy Leigh, 'one that painted the Russians in human terms – was, in the light of *glasnost*, an inspired choice. Arnold, the brilliant intuitor, had predicted the mood of the nation.'[249] Sylvester Stallone, simultaneously working on *Rambo III*'s imprudent glorification of the Mujahideen, could only have felt outdone as Arnold and his crew shot in Red Square on the day that Gorbachev announced that the Soviets were withdrawing from Afghanistan. Within two years, the Berlin Wall would come down, and Pushkin Square would have a MacDonald's (and all the double-edged 'freedoms' that such things beloved of Art Ridzik et al. bestow. 'Funny how the 'true end of Communism' and 'birth of a new age of democratic consumerism' still involved standing in line for food,' muses Morgan Spurlock).[250] Arnold, naturally, was full of praise for the changes he saw taking place in Moscow during the shoot. 'The people were much more relaxed about their freedom,' he said. 'There are now privately owned restaurants in Moscow. I have seen breakdancing, heavy metal rock bands.'[251] A continent-sized souk was opening up as the Great, Grey Bear – deselected in the battle for global economic survival – lay dead under Golden Arches whilst Boy (or Girl?) George sang its requiem, 'the sicknesses of [its] system'[252] revealed by the *pars pro toto* meltdown of Chernobyl.

In *Red Heat*, Schwarzenegger (free enterprise embodied) stooped to play the fool to highlight his own superiority and satirical might as a representative of the United States' ultimate, comparative authority. It matters not that Americans are, in Hill's narrative, often unfit, vapid consumers of pornography and junk food: this is their constitutional right and prerogative. What is crucial is that Arnold, a bugler of democratic capitalist victory whose destiny brought him, like Danko, across the great divide, imparts the gift of American enlightenment upon the world. He may look, to the eyes of Ridzik – the disingenuous, earthy voice of envy and awe – 'like Gumby,' but it is the superman, the *Übermensch* 'Arnie' to whom audiences have paid admiration and respect at the shrine of the box office. He has on occasion deliberately swaddled his uniquely potent body and voice in the robes of political and sartorial ridiculousness, but he can never assimilate, become part of the whole, or, as he would see it, become part of the drift of a humanity seeking identity as a true *Volk*. 'Isolated from mere mortals,' Arnold rises out, or sideways, or above, always distinguished by virtue of his nature as the carrier of mythic, *useful* power.

Schwarzenegger, by the late 1980s, had fought long and hard to bring heroic ideals and archetypes into his age and vigorously personify subjective political ideals, whether explicitly or obliquely: this was, and in many senses remains, Arnold's Great Quest for Freedom. He recognised, however, that to stay relevant (and potent) he had to examine and retune his own essential meaning in the light of a post-Cold War shift towards geopolitical diffusion. Many dragons – figurative and literal – had been slain, and countless adversaries brought to hard justice, but a new growth phase was dawning for the 40-year-old, happily married (to John F. Kennedy's niece, journalist Maria Shriver) Austrian Oak. 'I want people to know the real me,' he implored. 'Because the reality is that I don't take a gun in my hand to solve the situation . . . I'm not a stern character who doesn't smile . . . I'm a peaceful guy who has a great time.'[253] Was it preferable, asked Machiavelli, for a prince to be loved or feared? Perhaps Arnold, to his broadening constituency, could be both. He was learning, with a cultural acuity beyond all his competitors, precisely what he meant to a 'kinder, gentler' America:

What enables [heroes] eventually to escape from their thrall to the dark power is that they develop a wholly new understanding. They 'see the light' in a way which transforms their attitude . . . They have escaped from their original state of limited consciousness and learned to 'see whole.' They have discovered who they are. They have grown up.[254]

Man of Irony
Or, How Arnie Learned to Grow and Love

We as a people have . . . a purpose today. It is to make kinder the face of the nation and gentler the face of the world.[1]

We don't have ideologies, we have mortgages.[2]

Despite the debacle of the 1986 Iran–Contra scandal (which Reagan survived by essentially claiming ignorance), huge trade deficits and vast national debts, Ronald Reagan bowed out with an approval rating suggesting great public love and forgiveness. He was happy to take credit for ending the Cold War, albeit seemingly unaware that the Soviet Union's reforms were implemented not because of the flaccid, technologically unfeasible SDI programme, but because of Gorbachev's bold recognition of flaws inherent to the Soviet machine. '[I]n the end,' writes John Lewis Gaddis, 'he gave up an ideology, an empire, and his own country, in preference to using force . . . it made little sense in traditional geopolitical terms, but it did make him the most deserving recipient of the Nobel Peace Prize.'[3] Reagan's overtures to the General Secretary and readiness to endorse his changes, though, without doubt contributed to a better inter-power relationship and 'hope for a new era in human history, an era of peace'[4] – notwithstanding the basic failure to obtain decisive results in terms of nuclear arms reduction and a general sense amongst hopeful politicos of theatrics and missed opportunity. When asked what had happened to the 'evil empire' about which he had cautioned in 1983, Reagan replied that he was 'talking about another time, another era.'[5] His enthusiasm, however, was not popularly matched by either progressives or conservatives: '[M]y view is that the jury is still out,' complained Vice-President Bush, in an unprecedented display of perfidy.[6] At home, the poor continued to languish in the economic shadow of restructured corporations and the mounting wealth of the few; vagrants roamed the inner cities while *Les Misérables* played on Broadway; environmental concerns went unheeded; and the populace remained in dispute over immigration, race, civil rights, abortion and sexual mores.

In an election that saw the lowest voter turnout since 1924, George H.W. Bush took the White House, beating Democrat Michael Dukakis to the title of 41st President. Five days prior to the election, Arnold – affectionately dubbed 'Conan the Republican' by his endorsee – gave a speech pitting the 'tough' Republicans against the 'weak' Democrats, the rhetoric of which highlighted his own convictions regarding the given pre-eminence of the 'superman':

> I saw [Ronald Reagan and George Bush] take over an economy that looked like PeeWee Herman and I saw them turn this economy around to make it look like Superman . . . I saw them inherit from the Democrats a pipsqueak defence and a foreign policy with training wheels on it, and I saw them give back to our country the Republican muscle it deserves.[7]

('Dear Arnold,' wrote Bush to Schwarzenegger, shortly prior to victory, 'What a great boost you gave my campaign . . . Thanks, thanks, thanks.')[8] Occupying a more centrist, avuncularly tinged position that his predecessor, Bush combined the 'attitudes of a hard-line but pragmatic Cold Warrior'[9] with the domestic intuition of a moderate conservative evincing 'more concern for meeting people's needs than for achieving ideological purity';[10] the 'son' was eager simultaneously to walk his own path and give the impression of continuity between administrations, yet this would prove a personally awkward task. As the Annapolis Group (a bipartisan council of policy specialists) stressed: 'You possess a unique inheritance from Ronald Reagan . . . If you accept and embrace this inheritance, you may enhance American security and your own political fortunes at the same time.'[11] Bush, however, wanted little to do with this legacy and everything to do with harking back to the Nixon-era climate of 'consensus.' Within a few weeks, Bush had sidelined or sacked hundreds of Reagan appointees, especially those, like George Schultz and Frank Carlucci, whom he deemed overly soft on issues of policy toward the USSR.

Bush's dilemma was akin to a high-wire act; he felt mandated to appear as though he were continuing the popular 'Reagan Revolution' – concurrently 'smoothing out the rough edges of Reagan's domestic policies'[12] – whilst at the same time asserting himself after years of playing second fiddle to a more charismatic statesman. Haynes Johnson notes that, from his first days in office, Bush:

> sent a subtle but strong signal that he was in fact attempting to dis-tance himself from his predecessor. He made known to congressional leaders that he would not continue to press the ideological battle to support the contras . . . [Bush aide] John Tower let it be known that another cherished Reagan goal – 'Star Wars' . . . was both too costly and impractical.[13]

According to Susan Jeffords, in a shrewd essay on the Reagan–Bush tran-sition and its relation to Hollywood masculinities, 'The presidency shifted from the single-imaged and hard-bodied style of the Reagan years to what might be seen as a sort of schizophrenia, as Bush tried to balance his Rea-gan inheritance with his own interests.'[14] Stressing ideas of reunification, togetherness, heritage, family values (and, by extension, a strong message about a new world order under American *noblesse oblige*), Ivan Reitman's *Twins* (1988) is a characteristically deft work of political expression focus-ing on the importance of the deeds of the present, rather than the past, in cementing American values around a 'guardianship presidency.'[15]

Bringing up Arnie: A Temple of the Hearth

Supporting a family is a central means for a man to prove to himself that he is a *mensch* . . . young males are essentially barbarians for whom marriage – meaning not just the wedding vows, but the act of taking responsibility for a wife and children – is an indispensable civilising force.[16]

[T]he love and common sense of purpose that unites families is one of the most powerful glues on earth.[17]

Twins, Arnold's first foray into outright comedy since his debut, in many respects marks the start of its star's maturation into an extraordinarily self-aware product of his own, ballooning myth, fed back at him from a public whose tastes, desires and fears he seemed to grasp as well as any career politician. Pairing Arnold with *Taxi* veteran Danny DeVito ('round and squat as a cartoon bomb')[18] as his eponymous, improbable sibling, the film sees the two separated-at-birth brothers reunited after thirty-five years with predictably jarring results. Schwarzenegger's character, the naïvely charming Julius Benedict, is the result of a federally funded genetic experiment to create the 'perfect' child; DeVito's minor criminal Vincent, as it turns out, conversely comprises the unexpected leftovers from this venture – he is a human side-effect, a living 'abortion' possessed of neither Arnold's statuesque, Aryan looks nor his moral righteousness. Engaging in an anti-intellectual, anti-scientific discourse about nature versus nurture, and propounding the societal benefits to be had from a close-knit, surrogate but loving familial unit under paternal sway, *Twins* attempts to fuse again the split ova of Julius and Vincent, and perhaps by the same token, as Susan Jeffords notes, Reagan (like Arnold/Julius, the 'golden twin' or 'father') and Bush (the 'son').[19]

The film, and Arnold's characterisation especially, proves convincing as simple entertainment; and it works mostly because Arnold is unafraid to toy with mass preconceptions. Established expectations regarding 'Arnie,' now a king of the action genre, were clearly on Schwarzenegger's mind as he voiced a plan to extol the values of the fireside: 'In my last five or six movies, my love relationship was basically with guns, with explosives, with grenades and missiles. *Twins* was for me a learning experience all the way through.'[20] Where Stallone was floundering amid gruffly played, law-and-order censures of liberalism (or too-numerously repeated, barely re-written outings for Rocky and Rambo), Arnold understood that his image could be lent new importance and cultural specificity by appealing sensitively to the needs of the American populace and its democratically voiced will – yearnings channelled through George Bush's thoughts on his acceptance speech, as sent to speechwriter Peggy Noonan: 'I know what drives me – comforts me: family, faith, friends . . . Words I like: family, loyalty, kids, freedom, grandkids, caring, love, heart, decency . . . What hurts? An abused child; a scared child; an unloved child.'[21] Many may have wanted Arnold – most often a gentle-eyed, semi-boyish imp even when on the warpath – to allow his softer, nurturing side some substantial screen time, but few (with quite probably the exception of Arnold, who signed on to the project with impatient zeal) could have expected it to generate a palpable spark and Arnold's first massive financial hit.

Ghostbusters (1984) director Reitman, despite much evidence then to the contrary, saw a natural lovability in Arnold, by contrivance the consummate people person: 'He has this lovely naïve quality in real life. He's also very intelligent, very dedicated and very sweet. You don't often see that sweetness, and I thought it would be great to design a character that way.'[22] (Adrian Wright, by contrast, speaks of a 'lurking suspicion that the niceness of Arnold's persona in this movie is so manipulated as to verge on the absurd.' Wendy Leigh likewise describes Arnold's personal humour as 'streaked with sadism.')[23] So confident was Schwarzenegger that he had struck gold and once more resonated exactly with consumers' feelings, he took the role for no salary, instead asking for 17.5 per cent of the gross takings, which amounted to more than $110 million.[24] Though a one-joke film, it was essentially a warm-hearted production – artificial his persona may have been, but Schwarzenegger had again made the sharpest of decisions, moving ever onward and upward in the course of his adventures in the West.

We first find Julius Benedict living on a remote South Seas island (for which read Mount Olympus, or any other distant pantheon of the imagination) as the assistant to a mysterious, Germanic scientist who also provides expository narration about Arnold's character's origins in a 'top-secret [governmental] experiment designed to produce a physically, mentally and spiritually advanced human being.' The sperm of six fathers, each 'chosen for their genetic excellence' (and all of them Caucasian), was blended and used to impregnate a beautiful young woman, who apparently died whilst giving birth – not solely to Julius, but also to a second child, Vincent.[25] Upon learning of his brother's existence and whereabouts, Renaissance man (and virgin, 'pure in body and spirit') Julius decides, much like Arnold's young Hercules, to disobey the genial, Josef Mengele-like scientist-in-exile, leave his cloistered paradise and head to the metropolis. Vincent, it is soon made clear, is a womanising cheat, impecunious liar and petty crook, predictably the physical – and, ergo, moral – contrary to Schwarzenegger's embodiment of fascistically imagined human purity, or at least the implied likelihood of such an ideal's end result.

Despite the film's eventual message regarding the primacy of upbringing over biology in determining behaviour, associations between base genetics and conduct are nonetheless made: DeVito, a diminutive Italian American (not black, Jewish or disabled, so therefore not exploited), is throughout set up as fundamentally low-grade, a wastrel in need of constant care – care that should ideally be provided not by the state, but by the all-important bosom of kin. Government alone, the President said, was not the key to universal meliorism: citizens ought to look instead to 'a thousand points of light,' as he called them, 'all the community organisations that are spread like stars throughout the nation, doing good.'[26] 'At home I'll push for a "kinder, gentler" nation,' reiterated Bush, 'but for those who measure a commitment to that solely in terms of federal money there may be disappointment (deficit deficit deficit).'[27] (Of Lyndon Johnson's Great Society programmes, Schwarzenegger's own surrogate father and philosophical mentor Ronald Reagan memorably declared: 'Liberals fought poverty, and poverty won.'[28]) As if answering another magical call, now to the aid of wayward 'sons' Bush and Vincent, Arnold, this time a gentle giant, finds himself again the superiorly built stranger-hero abroad. He is replaying the scenario that has dominated his life, his films, and his self-declared 'Master Plan' for global celebrity:[29] Schwarzenegger reaching down from the heavens to inspire, catalyse and resolutely guide the 'inferior' to genuflect salvation, all the while adopting the comportment of a beneficent paternalistic emperor on a civilising crusade for the moral New Right, whose ethos is summed up by A. Rogers and B. Clements's *The Moral Basis of Freedom* (1985):

> History confirms that the connection between declining morality and national decline is not just fanciful; the Roman Empire declined not just because of immorality and personal licence but because of the burdensome taxation and state superstructure which the former had made necessary . . . We should support the family as an institution.

The family is a real alternative to the state, in fact a force for individual freedom and the first-line safety net for the welfare of the individual . . . [I]t is through the caring authority of parents that individuals learn to be independent.[30]

In other words, 'To stem the economic decline of capitalist countries,' comment Pamela Abbott and Claire Wallace, 'it is essential to re-moralise them.'[31]

Arnold, fittingly for manifold, overarching reasons not intrinsic to this film alone, has obviously come to Los Angeles to conquer, and is not afraid of showing disrespect to fading idols. Gazing up at a poster of Sylvester Stallone, Julius compares his biceps favourably to the *Rambo* star's 'tortured into existence'[32] muscles, laughing in the face of Stallone's wounded expression. As Adrian Wright notes, 'it is not only Julius wondering at the absurdity of such macho grandeur in the sophisticated world beyond the backwaters he has grown up in, but Arnold pointing out that while Stallone might be content to be forever identified (and forever trapped) as a symbol of indomitable strength, Arnold was not.'[33] Thus opens *Twins'* persuasive campaign for its audience's hearts and minds. We are being asked to love Arnold anew for his self-referential nous. He understands – unlike Stallone, Jean-Claude Van Damme or Dolph Lundgren – the crux of his deceptively simple, unique appeal, and how he must knowingly be seen to adapt to survive, seeking out new avenues toward cultural and political potency as 'Arnie' the omniscient redeemer, acknowledging and forgiving us the very sins – of violent idolatry – that precipitated his own journey. 'Wherever the hero may wander,' wrote Joseph Campbell:

whatever he may do, he is ever in the presence of his own essence – for he has the perfected eye to see. There is no separateness. Thus, just as the way of social participation may lead in the end to a realisation of the All in the individual, so that of exile brings the hero to the Self in all.[34]

From the Benedict twins' initial meeting, in a prison in which Vincent has been incarcerated for a traffic offence, Julius begins to nurture his brother, showing him an unconditional, fraternal (though in essence paternal) love that the nuns by whom he was brought up could not.

Though Vincent is at first unresponsive, Julius's efforts and their gradual rewards in the way of Vincent's slow moulding into a Republican-friendly citizen, imply, as Susan Jeffords explains, 'that the family cannot be so controlled, that its members are tied together by a kind of unconscious bond that surpasses scientific intervention and social control. It argues, in other words, that the family is *natural*.'[35] 'I've been looking forward to this moment all my life,' enthuses Arnold to DeVito, flashing an obtuse-looking but deceptively passive smile from behind the jail's Perspex visitation screen. 'I'm your brother – I love you!' DeVito reacts with understandable disbelief, rebuffing Arnold's requests that the two might 'talk philosophy together, play chess together.' (It should be noted that in a film such as this, pursuits of the mind favoured by the demonised 'intellectual elite' are unlikely ever to figure heavily; Julius may be a chess-playing, polyglot genius, but his comedic appeal to 'Joe Six-Pack' lies in what is, until Julius has assimilated the 'positive' aspects of Vincent, seen to be lacking: the scepticism of all things cerebral on which most average, Republican [the 'party of anti-intellectualism, of rough frontier contempt for sophisticated ideas'][36] citizens pride themselves, and that they consider more important than scholarly prowess. Julius, therefore, a man who has acquired all his knowledge from books, will learn, from Vincent, to let his feelings – when appropriate – lead his head: this, or so it is suggested, is the reciprocal gift of old-fashioned family, US style; for who needs 'pantywaist book-learning' when one has friends?)[37] Arnold's

11. Twins:
Schwarzenegger and DeVito pair up

mettle as a force for redemption will hence be thoroughly assayed; as devoted father Bush conceded in a diary entry of January 1989, 'No one can have instant success, no one can make this nation kinder and gentler overnight, but we can try.'[38] *Twins*, then, constitutes a series of tests: of those encountering Julius/Arnold's restrained messiah, who must shed his academic past, and of the broader ideological strength of care-in-the-community conservatism, tinged with apprehension about possible future conflicts that might prove expensive in terms of lives and money.

Contradicting his earlier films' gung-ho pre-emptive aggression, Arnold, after skilfully disarming an undisciplined Mafia thug who has come to beat up Vincent, serves up a metonym for impossible US aspirations to the controlled, responsible wielding of strength as a global paterfamilias: 'The first rule in a crisis situation: you negotiate first, and attack last . . . You don't know what kind of enemy I am!' Impressed by Arnold's ability to defend with martial honour, DeVito starts to enjoy Arnold's company, realising that, as a bodyguard, he might be second to none: 'You tell your brother,' he shouts at the now soundly defeated mobster, 'he messes with me, he messes with my whole family!' 'Actually, I hate violence,' replies Julius. 'But you're so good at it!' replies Vincent, in as clear and insightful a comment on America's and Arnold's entwined recent narratives as could be scripted. The pair walk down the street, illuminating DeVito's attitudes, and, moreover, the moral conversion of Arnold-as-father:

> *Vincent*: I love it when you hit people, Julius! . . . Listen, I've got an idea, we should go into business together: you can be a boxer and I can be your manager!
>
> *Julius*: I don't think I could fight for money.
>
> *Vincent*: No problem. You do all the fighting, I'll keep all the money! . . .
>
> *Julius*: I'm really worried about you, Vincent . . . Now don't worry about anything, Vincent – as long as I'm with you, I won't let anyone harm you.

We might recall the strikingly similar exploits of Hercules and Pretzie; this time around, though, the *Untermensch* will be raised, via a great individual struggle, to a position of civic responsibility. Arnold will invest the time to teach his unruly charge, a duty for which a 'natural,' protective parent – and an imminent parent in real life – should be prepared.

One thing the paternalistic hero must negotiate, however, in order to become completely 'whole' (or completely *masculine*), is romantic, physical love. This, of course, is never a straightforwardly conveyable pro-filmic theme for Arnold, who confessed to viewing women as 'sex objects . . . another kind of exercise, another body function,'[39] an attitude in itself perhaps that is a psychological impediment to the on-camera erotic performance delivered following the line, 'I have the highest respect for women.' In *Twins*, Reitman wisely plays the entire troublesome matter for laughs, settling on a rite-of-passage sub-plot involving the beautiful sister (Marnie: Kelly Preston) of DeVito's on/off girlfriend Linda. Though Schwarzenegger scoffed at the idea of his playing a virginal naïf, archly describing how it 'took tremendous acting,'[40] such a role, as evidenced by *Conan's* awkward clinch, is far more suitable than might be cursorily surmised.

Curiously, Arnold is never more convincing as a lover – notwithstanding an element of spectatorial relief that we are not to be subjected to a serious attempt at emulating sexual passion involving a middle-aged bodybuilder and a muscle-fixated nymphet. The love scene, such as it is, during which Julius joyously loses his virginity, is in fact somewhat charming, all actual mechanics having been elided – this is, after all, a family film about family. (At one point, Arnold's tumescent bicep stands in for his penis, the built body now literally made phallic in a knowingly anti-erotic critique of Arnold's hitherto earnestly fetishised quintessence.) It does not appear to be merely a token gesture, but rather an essential step toward reconstituting Arnold by means of a wider demographic allure. The girlfriends are to a large degree sidelined in terms of the plot – *Twins'* concerns are with the authority of the 'father,' to be sure – yet 'Arnie' is lent another dimension of humanness by Reitman. If *Predator* saw him suffer revelatory crises of physical duress, *Twins* achieves something similar, forcing upon the star a hugely advantageous admission that although he will never be a conventional romantic lead, his magnetism can draw power from alternative, reflexive sources: 'parody' and 'burlesque,' modes of representation that would recur as Schwarzenegger vehicles, following the success of the *Twins* experiment. 'I think it's the key to success in everything,' wrote Arnold in his autobiography: 'be honest; know where you're weak; admit it.'[41] Reconciliation, at this stage, begins to become for Arnold a byword for personal growth, a necessary precondition for future accomplishments. Personal reconciliation with one's own past faults, the reconciliation of the lateral family tree (Arnold's overshadowed and ignored brother Meinhard had tragically died in a drunken car crash in 1971), and reconciliation between generations and genders start to seem important; it is as if Arnold, a mother's boy, were indeed starting afresh with a view to being a more kindly and wise 'King of the World.'[42]

Finding out that she is not dead, Julius, driven by an innate desire to reunite his kin, sets off on a quest to locate his mother (whilst Vincent, and by association Julius, become embroiled in a rather perfunctory story concerning the delivery of a specialised high-technology engine hidden in the boot of a car Vincent has been paid to deliver). On the way, Julius meets one of his fathers, who informs him of Dr Traven, the Los Alamos-based scientist who told his mother he had died at birth. 'Watch out for him,' warns the father, 'he's kind of a dickhead – if you know what I mean.' 'No, I don't, but I'm learning,' replies Julius, now by osmosis sympathetic to the beer-drinking, low-income, paradoxically working-class and conservative citizen of Red America by virtue of adopting the parlance of the tavern and wearing a T-shirt emblazoned with the words 'Born to be Bad,' whose significance suggests a simultaneous mockery and endorsement of genetic predisposition. Gaining entry to the laboratory, the Benedicts meet Dr Traven, a narrow-eyed counterpoint to the scientist who had raised Julius, as opposed to created him: Traven is a father, but not a 'daddy,' content only to deal in technical realities, not matters of the heart. 'You came out first, of course,' he says to Julius, viciously, 'We weren't expecting . . . Him [Vincent] . . . The embryo did split in two, but it didn't split equally. All the purity and strength went into Julius. All the crap that was left over went into what you [Vincent] see in the mirror every morning.' The dialogue continues, delineating clearly the film's intended ideological stall:

Vincent: You're telling me I'm the crap?
Julius: This is not true, Vincent . . . He's wrong.
Traven: Look at him.
Vincent: Are you saying that I'm . . . a side effect?

> *Traven*: You haven't got the brainpower to understand this and I haven't got the time. Show's over.
>
> *Julius*: [*grabbing Traven*] Hey! Dickhead! Tell us where our mother is.

Traven, the absent father and would-be abortionist, is hence constructed as evil, a 'dickhead,' and a coldly intellectual force of coastal rationality. He personifies via caricature the demonised, interfering 'arrogance' of the academic elite, and the resentment of the 'meddling' professional classes by the 'regular guy.' 'The genius of America, folks,' said Kansan conservative Phill Kline, 'is not found in the halls of power . . . The genius of America is found at our kitchen tables, and our living rooms, and our places of worship.'[43] Endorsing this view, though doing so not without an incoherent concession that Arnold is indeed truly 'superior' – for therein lies the film's real allure: DeVito, so shaped, could not have played anybody's conception of a Hollywood superman's *natural* brother – *Twins* alludes to class tensions, as well as the sanctity of brethren.

However, all men, Reitman's film ultimately (if accidentally) intimates, are not born constitutionally equal and at the mercy of their upbringing – some are born to lead, achieve and inspire, even to the point of affected humility. If science has got it entirely 'wrong,' and its eugenic endeavours are misguided, would Julius, who has devoted enormous amounts of leisure time to swathe his body in muscle, giving the further illusion of innately possessed might, gladly inhabit the body (or, in *Twins*, the mind) of DeVito? Regardless of whether both Julius *and* Vincent are the morally 'illegitimate' products of a test tube, it is Julius/Arnold who wields the immense power of his hereditary frame in a culture still obsessed with appearance, longevity and beauty conventions. That the epitome of the tall, brawny, square-jawed comic-book superhero appears as he does is far from accidental, for he is the 'fittest' according to our science, instinct *and* art: 'we do not,' remarks Edmund Morris, 'like our leaders to look unhealthy.'[44] For all the love and charm he certainly inspires, DeVito stands contrary to Western ideals of classical male beauty, their roots equally in culture and in the deeply ingrained human reproductive drives. It may be playing God for Dr Traven to engineer foetuses along fascistic lines, and it may be gauchely unkind to dismiss Vincent as 'crap'; but, the inevitable, unavoidable, uncomfortable subtext of Schwarzenegger's Herculean essence nonetheless exists.

Archetypes are created or imagined for a reason; the hero of tradition must be bodily suited to a guiding, mythological task of endurance, stalwartness, bravery, protection or passion. Though the idea of a 'superman' is geographically, racially and ideologically subjective (and the *Herrenvolk* fantasy repugnant), our mostly white culture repeatedly offers up powerful, usually Anglo-Saxon men as exemplars; it is, in part, the classical hero's job plausibly to reflect drives ingrained by millennia of societal inculcation. 'Any culture's or individual's myths of the hero,' emphasises Carol S. Pearson, 'tell us about what attributes are seen as the good, the beautiful, and the true, and thereby teach us culturally valued aspirations.'[45] Despite its benign themes of resolution and fusion, *Twins* sadly cannot reconcile its selective dismissal of genetic science[46] with the primal truths of tribal identity, any more effectively than DeVito could have played Conan. Non-scientific body-fascism in America did not die due to the overt madness of Hitler's Reich, nor was it invented by Nazism; the athletic male physique's potency in Western culture, mythology and warfare is irrefutably pervasive. For Hollywood to deny this, whilst helping to elevate Arnold to even greater stature by contrasting him with DeVito, is either deluded or disingenuous. The 'dream factory,' whose leading men are customarily symmetrical ectomorphs, forwards, through *Twins*, a tokenistic and entirely bogus case for Schwarzenegger's status as an egalitarian. To try to rehabilitate Arnold's image, concomitantly emplacing him as a hero within a narrative centring on New Right causes, looks suspiciously like pandering to the star's vanity and political ambition: a rejection of biological determinism would seem laudable coming from almost anyone other than a man who had both won Mr Olympia and allegedly professed a longing to have been 'one of those Teutonic breeders.'[47] Of course, Arnold said this in jest – he was just 'playing Tarzan' – but he nonetheless grasped the deeply disquieting, always-present historical resonances of his charisma, and their decisiveness in moulding popular opinion. 'The week of the [1988 presidential] elections,' writes Marsha Kinder:

Los Angeles was plastered with a pair of billboards advertising a new comedy called *Twins* . . . One showed the image of the muscular super-hero under the Italian name of DeVito, while the other showed the short, swarthy comic under the Germanic name of Schwarzenegger. Nothing was needed except those two mismatched signs because spectators were presumed to know how to distinguish the two paradigms and know how to privilege the Aryan superman over the ethnic peewee, as well as the image over the word. It was precisely the American public's competence in reading such visual signs and in privileging image over substance that the Republican campaign so successfully exploited – a competence that was powerfully demonstrated in the two nationally televised debates between Bush and Dukakis where their differences in size proved more significant than their differences in policies.[48]

Mutatis mutandis, the natural-born 'superman' will always assert his primacy.

The Benedict twins, moreover, want nothing more than to find their biological mother – a link to the womb, the teat, the cradle and the double helix. They care little about those who shaped their lives (the nuns and the scientist – but then Arnold is the de facto father), but seem to desire contact with the maternal creator. The quest has the brothers on a Freudian mission to reinstall the mother and obviate the father/s in favour of Schwarzenegger, whose manly credentials as Mr Universe, Hercules, Conan, Terminator and the Running Man make him the most able and resolute surrogate dad around. At this point, finding a tempering reassertion of familial gentleness and humour efficacious, Schwarzenegger was, thanks to his role as Julius, becoming complete and ready to bestow his boons fairly upon the world according to the essential tenets of the New Right. The twins do find their mother, Mary Anne, rendering her life as a woman 'complete'; and, during the film's finale, we see the twins, having married Marnie and Linda and set up in business together, with twin babies of their own – once again proving genetics cannot be easily dismissed, provided the genes are selected by good, *social, natural* determination. Generically, at *Twins'* close, the 'unreconciled dark figure,' Vincent, coached by Julius's proud parent:

> goes through the fundamental psychological shift which brings him to himself. As he is liberated from his own dark prison, this also breaks the darkness which has oppressed everyone else . . . Everyone

has been freed to become his or her 'proper self.' Amid universal celebration, the little world of the story has again been connected with life.[49]

Conclusions though, especially regarding Arnold, are never quite that simple, and the 'little world of the story' is seldom all it purports to be. *Twins* is a film of numerous, less-than-straightforward contradictions running counter to its central argument of the primacy of nurture (we are constantly asked to laugh at DeVito's inborn physicality), and a symptom of many reactionary anxieties specific to masculinist impulses of the late 1980s that not only seek to define the family as paramount, but also to ensure that authority within the home is wrested back from the hands of the matriarch:

> American families are moving dramatically away from the patriarchal model, with increasing numbers of single-parent households, mostly headed by women. Part of the ideological project of the right in the eighties – one that is reflected in pop culture as well as in the recent presidential election [of George Bush] – is the restoration of the family to its former status as a strong Ideological State Apparatus and the reinstatement of the father within this patriarchal stronghold. Hence, the focus on fathers and sons and the further marginalisation of the female.[50]

As is often the case, Arnold's function is to allay mass fears and promote a solution based on the precepts of neo-Reaganite philosophy. As Susan Jeffords writes:

> [W]hereas the Reagan years offered the image of a 'hard body' to contrast directly to the 'soft bodies' of the Carter years, the late 1980s and early 1990s saw a reevaluation of that hard body, not for a return to the Carter soft body but for a rearticulation of masculine strength and power through internal, personal and family-oriented values.[51]

Arnold, only ostensibly 'gone soft' and unthreatening, brings his hugeness to bear on this crisis of masculinity, learning from DeVito the importance of casual manliness so he may still fulfil his potential for super-heterosexual dominion over the women.

In addition, *Twins* exhibits extraordinary keenness to its social-scientific context, even constituting an unplanned response, of sorts, to precise events. In the 1980s, the University of Minnesota's controversial and expensive 'twin studies,' harking back to the vastly more perverse yet connected fascinations of Auschwitz's 'Angel of Death' Mengele, set out to study raised-apart twins to ascertain the degree to which behaviour is rooted in heredity. The project's leader, Thomas J. Bouchard, eventually concluded that 'the possibility of influencing intelligence and learning abilities is slim.'[52] An ethically dangerous and contentious undertaking, the thesis was used by many racist advocates as 'proof that genetic factors set the potential limits of human behaviour,'[53] a reductive stance shared by Dr Traven's analogue of notorious anthropologist Roger Pearson, author of *Race, Intelligence and Bias in Academe* (1991), which propounded 'the practical application of genetic science toward the improvement of the genetic health of future generations'[54] whilst labelling those scholars who disagreed dupes to a politically correct system. To its credit, *Twins* makes an idealistic, bravely conceived but only partly convincing attempt to rubbish claims of inherent destiny by turning one of the world's most obviously redolent symbols of the Third Reich's – and all white, eugenics-endorsing groups' – ideas of purity and strength against his own semiotic message. In effect, the film has Arnold Schwarzenegger, a film star legendarily known for and infatuated with his body, telling us that bodies are superficial and unimportant; that it is the character, especially as developed by exposure to masculine love, that truly matters. In short, Arnold is vainly (and rather tardily) trying to abnegate his own myth's worst features. Seconding Karen Armstrong's hope that these 'very destructive modern myths, which have ended in massacre and genocide' might be replaced by 'myths that will help us identify with all our fellow-beings, not simply with those who belong to our ethnic, national or ideological tribe,'[55] *Twins* admirably advocates, but does so weakly and naïvely, universal acceptance of diversity. The film relies on, and ironically perpetuates, the very models of difference it tries to sublimate by forwarding a union of genetic polarities for comedic effect.

Twins' basic message may be noble, yet the two halves of the warrior/father ovum, however – as Julius might have to concede – cannot easily be forever or entirely rent apart. There always remains the spirit of the selfish, aggressive fighter, naturally selected for his hunting prowess on the African savanna, in the protective father; behind the goofy smile suggesting harmless social retardation, and behind the attempts to remodel himself for a new political atmosphere, Arnold, forever in some respects the barbarian, could not shake the image he had created for himself, instead falling back on often brilliant, but often telling, reflexivity. His heritage was unavoidable in nearly every respect; even in *Twins'* happy ending can be heard an echo of tragedy:

> To the eugenic scientist, no subject was of greater value. Young or old, healthy or diseased, living or dead, they all wanted one form of human – twins . . . In other words, a world of never-ending multiple births was the best assurance that the planned super race would remain super.[56]

Partial Recall: Arnold on the Final Frontier

> When earthman finally walks on the sands of Mars, what will confront him in this mysterious new world? Will any of his conceptions of strange and exotic Martian life prove to be true? Will he find the remains of a long-dead civilization? Or will the more conservative opinions of present-day science be borne out with the discovery of a cold, barren planet . . .?[57]

> American empire is a colonisation of the future that becomes a total consumption of all space and time – rewriting history, changing the very stuff of life in our genetic structure, shifting weather patterns, colonising outer space, indeed, changing the very course of evolution itself! It is this height and breadth of arrogance that startles and, not surprisingly, terrifies most of the world.[58]

Arnold again nurtured the helpless by example, revisiting the New Bad Future on a violent, civilising excursion to the space-age outer limit of Mars. Drawing on Philip K. Dick's 1966 short story 'We Can Remember It For You Wholesale,' and consuming $60 million to realise Martian locations and extravagant special effects, Paul Verhoeven's *Total Recall* (1990) was at the time of its production the second most expensive film ever made (the most expensive then being *Rambo III*, a project that has, for obvious reasons, not yet challenged *Total Recall*'s popular status as a semi-classic). Taking place in the year 2084, *Total Recall* sees Schwarzenegger's (appropriately, as it turns out) improbably blue-collar protagonist, Douglas Quaid, embark on a schizophrenic virtual – and later, actual – voyage to Mars. Haunted by recurring dreams of a former life on the planet, Quaid seeks the services of Rekall, a futuristic travel agency that implants bespoke 'memories' of vacations within customers' brains. The construction worker selects a fantasy in which he is a spy sent under deep cover, running with a sexually alluring female guerrilla on a mission to discover the secret purpose of buried alien artefacts and in so doing save the planet from destruction. However, during the implantation procedure, Quaid has a seizure revealing the presence of already-existent, previously erased memories that are too similar in nature to the fantasy's to be overwritten; it would seem that Arnold's holiday has triggered the recollection of a somehow suppressed former life, in which he really was a secret agent on Mars.

Schwarzenegger explained that he wanted to make the film because, 'When you're alone and you stick your neck out for a particular cause, that's heroic. A lot of people want to do that in real life, which is why my movies are such a great escape.'[59] *Total Recall* is indeed a 'great escape,' and a well-orchestrated and intelligently labyrinthine thriller; yet the 'escape' of which Arnold speaks is not simply to the movies, or to a literal Mars-as-future-colony plot device, but to a much bigger dream world of contemporary conquest-fantasy based on innately imperialist themes. Of course, as Fred Glass comments, the film's political content typically (for a Schwarzenegger vehicle) 'keeps closely to the shadows of [its intended demographic's] unconscious, where the fears and hopes on which political manipulation thrives tend to stay in our depoliticised culture.'[60] Nevertheless, resonating with the often-expressed idea of 'outer space as our nation's new or final frontier, a challenge to all who possess the fortitude and sense of adventure to carry through the vision,'[61] the film sets up the red planet as a kind of Oriental Frontier, a Babylon of the mind populated by the descendants of Americans who have nonetheless 'gone native,' via mutation, and become characters in an exotically arrayed analogue of the old colonial Asiatic. These noble but as yet un-American people are, most importantly, unable to self-govern with decisiveness: this is at heart old-fashioned 'Injun country,' the Wild West with a pseudo-liberal twist (Mars's righteous populace are not going to get wiped out by Arnold's cowboy, at least) infused with narrative tropes concerning Euro-American, pan-global dominance as a God-given racial and ideological right – tropes that sit uneasily alongside the film's central, characteristically NBF-style message warning of the dangers of corporate greed. Schwarzenegger is essentially going to Mars to institute order over chaos, and to put in place compassionate, white-male-led governance to stop things falling apart under the 'inevitable' iron fist of dictatorship – which in *Total Recall* is personified by Ronny Cox's overwrought oxygen magnate Cohaagen.

The film opens by presenting a scene of apparent domestic harmony – notwithstanding that Arnold has been dreaming of an 'exotic' brunette – featuring Arnold and his 'wife' Lori (a feline Sharon Stone, who seems to intimidate Arnold as much as seduce him). We hear from a news report that Earth is troubled by a war between two totalitarian factions dominating the globe: this is obviously a state of (nearly) Orwellian inconvenience. The omnipresent symbols of corporate assertion (Sony, Fuji Film, Marlboro and Coca-Cola logos, in the film as announcements simultaneously of brand insidiousness – the 1990 brands themselves – and those brands' 'inevitable' long-term survival), appearing on billboards and television sets, are at once reassuring and ominous – the chattels of our own ethnocentric lifetimes present and unchanged in a future-vision shot through with a sense of confused and pessimistic cynicism about urban development and the 'sins' of international materialism. Product placement is everywhere, there being no obvious visual culture in 2084, only what exists for selling placebos, vicarious experiences or addiction to a populace inured by over-exposure to 'trashy' entertainment. A prerequisite for the NBF's paradoxical imaginings, such a doubly dystopian, telescopic backdrop, serves (as in *The Running Man*) to underline the need for a recasting of Hollywood ideology – a refreshing but superficial break from historical momentum to catch sight of fundamental aims that nonetheless always recapitulate the cyclical motifs of American history: escape, expansion, conversion, individualism, consumption, dominion, revolt, backlash and the eventual comfort of big-business conservatism with a smiling face.

In going to Rekall, Quaid seeks an analogous break from himself so that he might find out where things went astray and become the hero he knows (and we suspect) he has been all along, in the process revising his

12. Crises of identity in Total Recall

memories and casting himself as the natural master of a new fiefdom, able to understand the locals' behaviour and needs without recourse to assuming the native mindset. Ostensibly to block the signal from a locator chip implanted up his nose, but as much to convey the visual absurdity of Arnold – not a man possessed of many ethnic religious sensibilities – in a turban, Quaid wraps a towel around his head and picks up a briefcase sent by himself, or his alter-ego 'Hauser,' containing a baffling videotaped message: 'You are not you – you're me! There's enough shit [in your head] to fuck Cohaagen good! . . . Get your ass to Mars!' Quickly, the action relocates to Earth's neighbour, the film's locus of imperial renewal and testing ground for Schwarzenegger's agent of liberation. (Quaid's marriage, so it transpires, has been a sham contrived by the mysterious 'Agency,' whose operatives, including Michael Ironside's memorably thuggish Richter – who is Lori's jealous boyfriend – follow Arnold in pursuit.)

Narrowly avoiding being shot at immigration when his prosthetic disguise (as a middle-aged, overweight woman) malfunctions, our hero heads at first to a soulless hotel and then to the red light district, a carnival of the bizarre inhabited by triple-breasted prostitutes, mind-reading children, psychic soothsayers, one-eyed chiromancers and lusty dwarfs. It is here that Arnold meets the object of his nocturnal desires. She is the 'demure' but 'sleazy' Melina (Rachel Ticotin), an athletically built, Amazonian fantasy of Oriental concoction, who emerges from the intoxicating miasma of 'monsters, devils, heroes; terrors, pleasures, desires' residing, in the colonial mind, to the far-flung east, west and south of Europe.[62] 'Still bulging, I see,' she says, grabbing at first Arnold's bicep and then his crotch, in a forced and embarrassing attempt to endow the couple with an earthy sexuality. (Despite Fred Glass's opinion that Arnold 'may be understood as a swollen penis, throbbing his way through the receptive material of the narrative,' his phallic – but, as always, sexually juvenile – body as a whole, not his literal penis, are where his potency lies.)[63] Melina, though, goddess and 'world creatrix, ever mother, ever virgin,'[64] more obviously signifies a kind of purity amongst the supposedly corrupt, a perfectly formed physical specimen whose fragrant exoticism contrasts with her fellow anti-Cohaagen resistance fighters' deformities; she is hence the ideal romantic partner for Arnold's Romantic, Western adventurer, a 'sublime acme of sensuous adventure'[65] separated from the threateningly 'impure' mass by idealised dark physicality, the acceptable face of the Other adorned in the clothes of ethnocentric fantasy. As Edward Said writes, 'In most cases, the Orient seemed to have offended sexual propriety; everything about the Orient . . . exuded dangerous sex, threatened hygiene and domestic seemliness.'[66] Madonna and whore, fighter and mother, demure *and* sleazy, Melina is the embodiment of liberated femininity,

13. *Melina and Quaid* (Total Recall)

as recalled by Verhoeven et al., and put to the service of an adventurer-king's *mission civilisatrice*.

'To be a European in the Orient,' continues Said, '*always* involves being a consciousness set apart from, and unequal with, its surroundings. But the main thing to note is the intention of this consciousness: What is it in the Orient for?'[67] Schwarzenegger's journey, a voyage with several important connotative dimensions, finds explicit purpose in the fight for a collective good against a tyrant. While Cohaagen shuts down the air supply, intent on suffocating the dissenters in an equivalence to the Chinese government's 1989 slaughtering of students in Tiananmen Square, Melina shows Quaid where the 'first settlers are buried – they worked themselves to death, and Cohaagen ended up with all the money . . . Maybe you can change all that.' (The pioneers did not, obviously, have a charismatic Austrian to tutor them in the ways of resource management without recourse to unionisation.) He is then taken (by cab-driver Bennie, the film's only black character: a jive-talking con artist who later proves to be a mole) to meet Kuato, the resistance leader who has thus far remained unseen and who will read his mind to discover Hauser's secrets (Hauser was in fact a favoured henchman of Cohaagen; the plot henceforth gets tortuous). Residing in the belly of an otherwise normally developed human host, Kuato, whose emergence symbolises the horror of male-pregnancy anxieties (addressed later in Ivan Reitman's *Junior*, 1994) and evokes fears associated with tumours and parasitic organisms, is a tiny, grotesque gargoyle reminiscent of the beasts reported throughout *Mandeville's Travels*, a fanciful, medieval catalogue of foreign encounters including one with 'a race whose faces appeared on their torsos.'[68] Kuato's shocking otherness lies in his extreme mutation, a chance ability to read minds at the expense of bodily independence; 'ugly,' like the Predator, but literally dwelling within, the guru, like George Lucas's Yoda in *The Empire Strikes Back* (Irvin Kershner, 1980) – or indeed Ronald Reagan – is the wise old man figure, but this time gone horribly reliant on charity, sick without the support of a host, and lacking Arnold's super-humanly *independent* body ('in our culture,' notes Carol S. Pearson, 'practically a synonym for masculinity'),[69] which is as ever the key to freedom. 'A man is defined by his actions, not his memory,' intones Kuato, absolving Arnold/Quaid of any lingering guilt from his uncaring past, America from any remorse about previous conquests effected by the use of gunpowder and coercion, and Bush (who claimed to be 'out of the loop' during the Iran–Contra scandal) from his long legacy, as he pushed to assert the primacy of the values and deeds of the present over those of his predecessor. 'The public,' writes Susan Jeffords, in an essay on 'The Bush Style':

> was asked to judge Bush on his contemporary performances – his character – and not his past record ... George Bush cast his presidency in terms of his current expressions of sympathy for victims of disasters, his current outrage about international terrorism, or his current lament for individual laid-off shipyard workers, rather than in terms of his record on taxes, his service as ambassador to the UN, his brief tenure as CIA director, or his response to the Tiananmen Square massacre . . . At the beginning of his 1988 presidential campaign, George Bush declared, 'We don't need to remake society, we just need to remember who we are . . .' [S]o much of his philosophy of domestic policy was based not on an economic or social agenda but on popularising voluntarism and a revival of a class-based American spirit of obligation toward others and a commitment to helping those 'less fortunate.' In such terms, remembering who 'we' are required not a grand shifting of the social system or reform of malfunctioning institutions but a mere reminder that it is performance that counts, the kind of reminder that would produce heroes.[70]

'[S]alvation of the planet,' remarks Frank Grady in a lengthy essay on *Total Recall*, thus 'depends not on remembering an act of kindness but on forgetting acts of violence and espionage.'[71] This will be a compassionate takeover, a remodelling of the Martian country along 'kinder, gentler' lines: 'Morning again in America,' blue skies on Mars, and another amnesiacal chance to retell a story, now with the violence directed against a singular oppressor deemed by consensus acceptably 'bad' within the New Bad Future's curative diagnosis of capitalism: an old-style robber baron whose time has come.

Buried under Mars's pyramids, as Kuato's probing of Quaid reveals, is an ancient nuclear reactor that Cohaagen has been reluctant to turn on for fear it may emit endless, free, breathable air and put him out of business. Bennie, a mutant but a self-serving traitor to the minority cause (for which read a mercenary Black Power activist, sold out to cynicism) shoots Kuato, who has been found only because Schwarzenegger believed himself to be the 'good' Quaid, rather than the Agency-employed Hauser – this was the only way to get past the mutants' psychic abilities: 'Congratulations: you led us right to him!' 'Start the reactor,' Kuato implores to Quaid, with his dying breath: 'Free Mars!' At this point it is revealed that Hauser willingly had himself brainwashed and sent to Earth, in order to forget his own past and infiltrate the resistance free of readable mental traces of guilt. The slate was wiped clean, and now Quaid must fight against relinquishing his virtuously heroic new consciousness to its original host:

Cohaagen: Well, my boy! You're a hero.

Quaid: *[deadpan]* Fuck you.

Cohaagen: Don't be modest. Kuato is dead, the resistance has been completely wiped out and you were the key to the whole thing.

Quaid: *[to Melina]* He's lying.

Melina: You two-faced bastard.

Cohaagen: You can't blame him, angel, he's innocent . . .

Quaid: Well, Cohaagen, I have to hand it to you – that's the best mind-fuck yet.

During the procedure to reinstate Hauser in Arnold's body, however, Quaid, by sheer force of will, breaks free of his literal and figurative restraints. The present *must* prevail over the past, and 'bad' history must be erased to ensure progress and a refinement of the American Way relying on retooling, but not dramatically changing in essence, the underlying system. The 'kinder, gentler' 'Arnie' prevails: it is acceptable, and in fact necessary, to change one's mind, to acknowledge previous flaws so that the order of the NBF can be restored without troublesome revolutions, apocalypses, or the dreaded political sea-change of Marxism–Leninism taking hold.

Following a bloodthirsty penetration scene in which Arnold drills Bennie to death ('Screw you!' shouts Arnold, in an uncanny repeat of *Commando*'s zinger at the similarly monikered Bennett's expense), Quaid and Melina find the alien reactor's starter button. Triggering the machine, the pair are ejected by a rush of air out onto the Martian desert; Cohaagen suffocates, but Melina and Quaid hold on long enough to breathe, as clouds fill the sky with vapour, bringing a new dawn to Mars.

The Martians gaze out upon this vista, brought by Arnold's White Man with his revised imperialist consciousness; he can never be at one with the subjected race, but he has bestowed his boons – of life and a chance to start anew under the tutelage of his superman – upon the helpless and needy denizens of a world unable to see the light in his absence. Against a backdrop of swirling storm clouds, Quaid and Melina embrace in a parody of classical Hollywood endings: 'I just had a terrible thought: what if this is a dream?' says Arnold. 'Well then kiss me quick before you wake up!' This deliberately ludicrous finale, as we have come to expect, is not easily explicable. 'By implication,' Fred Glass ponders,

> the climactic sequence of *Total Recall* is fetishistic: it represents the wish to magically deal with a reality too threatening and complex to face directly . . . the ultimate meaning of his action remains somewhat murky. Can we be saved from the ravages of technological capitalism by the 'moral' use of a technology – perhaps the ultimate technology, atomic power – developed by that capitalism? Is Quaid a social agent, a stand-in for his people reclaiming their place in history and society, or just an individual action-adventure hero?[72]

The magical ending, then, is a surrogate for real political action, a trick accomplished by Quaid to pre-empt any difficult questions or coups running contrary to American convenience. The reactor, a neat way of sidestepping any discussion of America's addiction to oil and more akin in its effects to nature than the dangerous science of Three Mile Island and Chernobyl, was waiting all along to be set in motion by Arnold. As a metaphor it contains the awesome potential of the unexplored American mountains, or the challenging environs of the romanticised, dusky Orient; this potential is then released to rain abundance on those who show faith in Schwarzenegger's version of space exploration, an endeavour that has always appealed primarily to white males wanting to plant flags – real and metaphorical – of territorial claim on far-off lands.

Frank Grady notes:

> The film's politics deserve further attention. On the surface, of course, they are leftist, anticorporate and revolutionary . . . Beyond the literal level, though . . . the film offers a more conservative message

– heroism turns out, as usual, to be the province of the archetypally masculine, white, professionally rugged individual.[73]

Total Recall's dream is in the end not one solely of vanquishing evil, but also one of the imposition of benevolent rule by a 'caring' force of dominion. Its essential meaning, however, is located deep in the Western ideological will to conquer those coarser terrains (both of the land and the heart) that seem to ask for such guidance. To quote Briton James Balfour, lecturing in 1910 on 'the problems with which we have to deal in Egypt':

> Western nations as soon as they emerge into history show the beginnings of those capacities for self-government . . . You may look through the whole history of the Orientals in what is called, broadly speaking, the East, and you never find traces of self-government. All their great centuries – and they have been very great – have been passed under despotisms . . . We are in Egypt not merely for the sake of the Egyptians, though we are there for their sake; we are there also for the sake of Europe at large.[74]

Balfour and his like desired to cultivate a bond of friendship between the empire and the subject peoples – whom they painted as hopelessly uncomprehending – so as to make smooth the passage of administrative dominion. 'Lurking everywhere behind the pacification of the subject race,' writes Edward W. Said, 'is imperial might, more effective for its refined understanding and infrequent use than for its soldiers, brutal tax gatherers, and incontinent force. In a word, the empire must be wise; it must temper its cupidity with selflessness, and its impatience with discipline.'[75] Quaid's/Arnold's Manifest Destiny, then, is quite clear: he must go to Mars as an investigator, finding the sources of corruption where 'natives' have failed through innate incompetence; as an ethnologist, bringing home evidence of the intoxicating sexual, decorative and societal practices of the Martian East, a veritable Mappa Mundi of fantastic imaginings; and as an ambassador for caring, ecologically sound capitalism, imposing on the extra-terrestrial – and by connotation Third-World – 'savages' an example by which they might be encouraged to follow Arnold's god-like hierophant towards receptive civic existence. 'If you have a dream and it becomes reality, don't stay satisfied with it too long,' said Arnold in 1980, during another moment of lucidly accurate prophesying. 'When you have that dream achieved, make up a new dream. The Eastern philosophy is passive, which I believe in maybe three per cent of the times [*sic*], and the ninety-seven per cent is Western, conquering and going on.'[76]

Part T.E. Lawrence, part advertiser of the ultimate effectiveness of a NASA programme devastated by the Challenger disaster of 1986, and part Romantic visionary on a quest to 'revive a dead world, to quicken in it a sense of its own potential, one which only a European can discern underneath a lifeless and degenerate surface,'[77] Schwarzenegger, in *Total Recall*, follows Kipling's White Men along the road of self-appointed duty and obligation, 'When they go to clean a land.'[78] Frederick Jackson Turner was wrong to call the frontier closed in 1883; while President Bush defended his proposal to send a manned expedition to Mars (already long suspected to be a miserably barren and freezing destination) by announcing that 'throughout our history, America has been a nation of discoverers,'[79] Arnold, a politician of the popular imagination, was providing a vision of that mission's prospective result, and how efficacious management might bring about favourable ends. 'Imagination,' notes Howard E. McCurdy, 'recasts issues in terms that non-experts can understand . . . Imagination allows people to visualise a particular activity taking place, a key ingredient in convincing policy makers to undertake it.'[80] As Lyndon B. Johnson asserted:

> Control of space means control of the world, far more certainly, far more totally than any control that has ever or could ever be achieved by weapons, or troops of occupation . . . Whoever gains that ultimate position gains control, total control, over the earth, for purposes of tyranny or for the service of freedom.[81]

In every sense, Arnold made sure he was contributing to the discursive push in favour of outward expansion, an ethos close to his fundamental philosophies. Dreams of Mars, like dreams of the Deep South in *Stay Hungry*, cannot 'grow without burning,' but grow they must, and into an upwardly thrusting mould of material yearning informed by emissaries of empire on a crusade of self-reflexively 'soft' power, the cultural means by which capitalist, free-market democracy spreads the persuasive gospel of its own Providence. *Total Recall* and the whole NBF cycle register the need for a far-sighted projection of anxieties, though they see no practicable, realist solution that might accommodate the wishes of those not aligned with the Washingtonian power elite's vision of unending capitalist growth. According to George Soros, 'We must learn to confront unpleasant realities if we want to remain leaders in the world . . . a feel-good society does not want to be given bad news.'[82] Seconding the words of Professor Donald Michael, NBF works realise that, 'Our margin of error is very small . . . we must live in the future now,' but present only a glamorous cultural distraction from the need to contemplate an absolute revolution of thought.[83] Original writer Philip K. Dick, whose 1978 essay demonstrates acute understanding of the ironies involved in telling stories about the nature of blinkered, media-influenced reality in the information age, would no doubt be ambivalent regarding *Total Recall*'s treatment:

> We live in a society in which spurious realities are manufactured by the media, by governments, by big corporations, by religious groups, political groups. I ask, in my writing, What is real? Because unceasingly we are bombarded with pseudorealities manufactured by very sophisticated people using very sophisticated electronic mechanisms. I do not distrust their motives. I distrust their power. It is an astonishing power: that of creating whole universes, universes of the mind. I ought to know. I do the same thing.[84]

Total Recall went on to gross nearly $120 million; as Schwarzenegger enthused, 'such a great escape.'

'The Hunger for the King':[85] Two Dads

> One might reasonably argue that [the restoration of the father] is the dominant project, ad infinitum and post nauseam, of the contemporary Hollywood cinema . . . The Father must here be understood in all senses, symbolic, literal, potential: patriarchal authority (the Law), which assigns all other elements to their correct, subordinate, allotted roles.[86]

The machine partakes of, and represents, a larger social power, which it functions to maintain and celebrate. The machine – whose form recalls the supreme phallus itself – is a glittering pearl amongst fascism's working monuments to the power of the abstract father.[87]

We want to own big muscles and be like Arnold when we grow up.[88]

'Knee-deep in family values in 1990,'[89] Schwarzenegger further explored the lucrative themes of fatherliness and patriarchal assertion in Ivan Reitman's *Kindergarten Cop* (1990), and, subsequently, the actor's biggest box office success, *Terminator 2* (James Cameron, 1991). Both works in many respects pick up where *Twins* left off (although *Total Recall* of course sees Arnold as father to an entire people), and both works further emphasise Arnold's evolving desires in the way of sympathy with the political sphere. Made chairman of his friend the President's Council on Physical Fitness and Sports in January 1990, Arnold, with wholesome intentions for the nation's youth, 'made the position a bully pulpit to get America off its flabby behind,'[90] declaring that, 'A philosopher once said, "Let the world be a better place, and let it start with me." Think about that. It is the attitude each of us should take to help us make our youngsters more physically fit.'[91] In the heat of May, Schwarzenegger staged the 'Great American Workout' on the White House's south lawn, enrolling the President, his aides, and numerous celebrities in an enthusiastic (if for some slightly uncomfortable) demonstration of the benefits of exercise. Lobbying for the creation of a national fitness day, Schwarzenegger would 'lapse into *gemütlich* reverie,' remembering long-ago summers at sports camps in his native Austria.[92] 'He is determined to set a good example,' said George Bush. 'And he is.'[93]

Moreover, Arnold (now father to a toddler, Katherine) was determined to inhabit film roles that revealed this concerned side apposed with a certain macho toughness – a combination many would see as the ideal pattern for modern fatherhood. Accommodating sensitivity, empathy and the warrior's strident competitiveness, Schwarzenegger aimed to instil in the country's youngsters an empowering 'inner King,' whilst paying lip service to the post-feminist traits of the 'new man.' Arnold's 1990s daddies are therefore resilient, ultra-hetero playmates and mentors, whose purpose is the reclaiming of masculinity from the tempering influence of the women's movement, and the effective obviating of maternal power beyond the acts of birthing and early-years rearing. They represent, dilates Thomas B. Byers:

> a set of deep and persistent fears on the part of a formerly dominant order that has begun to recognise that it is becoming residual . . . The new image is reinforced by his constant discussion of his marriage and children on talk shows and in popular magazines. However, lest his domestication suggest a 'caving in' to the demands of women, Arnold's retooling has entailed a frontal attack on working mothers and feminists, whom he blames for the physical unfitness of America's TV-addicted children. 'The villain,' [he seems to say] 'is the economic situation and women's equal rights.'[94]

As 'mythopoetic men's movement'-champion Robert Bly proclaimed, in a 1990 masculinist tract entitled *Iron John: A Book About Men*:

> The journey many American and Western men have taken into softness, or receptivity, or 'development of the feminine side,' has been an *immensely valuable journey, but more travel lies ahead* . . . We know that for hundreds of thousands of years men have admired each other, and been admired by women, in particular for their activity. Men and women alike once called on men to pierce the dangerous places, carry handfuls of courage to the waterfalls, dust the tails of the wild boars. All knew that if men did that well the women and children could sleep safely. Now the boars have turned to pigs in the stockyard, and the rushing rivers to the waterfall in the Museum of Modern Art courtyard. The activity men were once loved for is not required . . . Young men coming into adulthood during the Reagan and Bush administrations have a difficult problem – the difficulty of finding anyone who can carry their King. Edwin Meese certainly could not do it, nor John Poindexter, nor any of the other men involved with the lies surrounding the Contras. Reagan, as an actor, played the part, but could not be honest. The betrayal of the country during the savings and loan scandal by both Democratic and Republican senators makes the situation worse. If the younger men have no public man to whom they can give their King, how can they develop the King inside?[95]

It was Schwarzenegger's assumed duty to be the 'public man to whom they can give their King,' and the saviour of traditional paternalism from the 'dangers' of the encroaching feminine, now posited as otiose via Arnold's repeated attempts at assimilation of the matriarchal identity also. Arnold's 'dominant quest,' during the Bush Senior and early Bill Clinton eras, would thus be the restoration of the idea of the humane yet manly father to its 'rightful' place, and concurrent atonement, on his own terms, with his own literal and symbolic father figures: Gustav and Ronald – apt, often distant family men of mid-century now forgiven their flaws as an inter-generational task is inherited, from father to 'dad.' 'The mystagogue (father or father-substitute),' so Joseph Campbell states, 'is to entrust the symbols of office only to a son who has been effectively purged of all inappropriate infantile cathexes . . . [The "invested one"] is the twice-born: he has become himself the father. And he is competent, consequently, now to enact himself the role of the initiator, the guide.'[96] It was for Arnold, and his mythic essence, a period of conversion from dragon-slaying 'adolescent' to something approaching full and capable maturity. 'The ego's rise to conscious action,' writes Joseph L. Henderson:

> becomes plain in the true culture-hero. In the same fashion the childish or adolescent ego frees itself from the oppression of parental expectations and becomes individual . . . We see the full hero image emerge as a kind of ego strength (or, if we are speaking in collective terms, a tribal identity) that has no further need to overcome the monsters and the giants . . . The 'feminine element' no longer appears in dreams as a dragon, but as a woman; similarly, the 'shadow' side of the personality takes on a less menacing form . . . This change, however, does not take place automatically. It requires a period of transition, which is expressed in the various forms of initiation.[97]

Kindergarten Cop immediately sets up Arnold's character, the trench-coat-wearing and bearded John Kimble, as a hard-body, hard-ego law-man designed to crystallise and parody 'the eighties man, the lethal weapon *par excellence*.'[98] Kimble Mk 1 is a mockingly crude, unconvincingly played (Arnold has always been too 'intrinsically attractive and comic' for Harry Callaghan-type parts),[99] one-dimensional distillation of the single-mindedly aggressive attributes Schwarzenegger was at the time already softening and shedding. '[A] Dirty Harry figure from hell'[100] expressing Arnold's assessment of Stallone and his ilk's anachronistic lack of self-awareness, Kimble exists in order that he might be initiated, re-formed or remoulded into an 'Arnie' for the 1990s, simultaneously rigidly disciplined (like the super-efficient machine audiences knew and admired) and maternally aware enough to supersede the female altogether. The film will constitute, then, a rite of passage for Kimble from dourly inchoate hunter/warrior to warrior-father, and a rehearsal for the bravura 'surprise' comeback of the Terminator in fully functioning protector mode. Arnold, naturally, was in reality a step ahead of Reitman's and writer Murray Salem's narrative; his own rejoinder to feminism and 'defective mythologies that ignore masculine depth of feeling'[101] was almost complete. The lesson herein – how to embody a responsible and apposite father figure in the post-Reagan 1990s – is aimed at all those obdurate, hard-to-teach men (Schwarzenegger's chief rivals included) who wished to heed calls for a tough-but-caring manhood cognisant of its potential bearing on a child's development, and make the transition from inexorable fighter to born-again guardian. 'For ten years,' complained Arnold, 'I have been telling writers, producers, directors, and studio executives that I would love to do a film where a kid or children are a very important part.'[102] The time was now at hand. 'The harmful side effects of warrioring,' notes Carol S. Pearson in *The Hero Within*:

> come in its more primitive forms . . . When it is freed from these more dualistic and absolutist forms, warrioring (like sacrificing) becomes a healthy, useful, positive human process . . . The stronger and more confident Warriors become, the less they must use violence, the more gentle they can be.[103]

Shorn of his Dirty Harry attire, guns and prehistorically redolent beard ('The mythological systems associate hair with the instinctive and the sexual and the primitive'),[104] Kimble, when his professional partner Phoebe falls victim to a stomach complaint causing perpetual vomiting, is assigned undercover to an elementary school in Astoria, Oregon; he must seek out the child and wife of routinely villainous drug-dealer[105] – and all-round inadequate father – Crisp (Richard Tyson), to coerce him into revealing his criminal contacts. Arnold, his confidence predictably misplaced, finds himself in charge of a classroom full of unruly infants whose job it will be to force 'Arnie,' and by the same token Hollywood 'musculinity,' through the growing process and into the light of a truly realised ego. 'They're six-year-olds,' says Kimble, 'how much trouble can they be?' Introducing himself to the school's principle, the tiny, literally belittled but matriarchically stern Miss Schlowski (Linda Hunt), Kimble, looking thoroughly aggrieved, announces that there has been 'a change of plan,' and that he, and not the expected woman, will now be the new teacher. Miss Schlowski commands respect from the children as she explains Kimble's presence as coverage for their usual teacher's absence, but they are lifelessly compliant – their spirit is lacking in zeal and the internal 'King.' When Arnold first enters the classroom, a subjective shot, from Kimble's point of view, he looms over the children; he bemuses them with his bulk as an awesomely big 'daddy' who must prove his size is a boon and not a danger or object of ridicule. When Kimble leaves to get assistance in undoing a girl's buttons so she can use the toilet, the children run amok, vandalising the classroom. The initiation has been officially pronounced a failure – 'Two more days of this, and he'll quit,' smiles Miss Schlowski, the voice of Spiro Agnew's 'nattering nabobs of negativism,' a hypothetical 'overeducated ruling class that is contemptuous of the beliefs and practices of the masses.'[106] But, Arnold, baptised by fire, returns the next day ready to face his trials anew.

Some female parents, having dropped off their children in the morning, express worries that the new teacher is 'obviously gay' for choosing his profession; when they see Arnold's physique, however, they are enraptured and made girlish by his hyper-masculine enormity, which thrills them from afar. J. Hoberman notes that *Stay Hungry* also 'includes a scene in which a woman enquires whether [Arnold's] character is gay.' Hoberman, though, misses the fact that in *Stay Hungry*, the woman is convinced his bodybuilder's physique is a sign of homosexuality; in *Kindergarten Cop*, the admirer is swayed against an initial supposition of Arnold's gayness by the same stimulus: the received significance of large muscles has seemingly reversed, at least as far as *Kindergarten Cop's* Oregon is concerned – a phenomenon in all probability only plausible due to the pervasiveness of Arnold's previous hyper-masculine film characters' stringent attempts to emplace the muscular frame as absolutely straight.[107] 'Welcome to Astoria: single-parent capital of America,' says a smitten mother, similarly desirous of Schwarzenegger's 'natural' roosting qualities. She has come to Kimble because she is worried about her son playing with dolls, sure in her conviction that a teacher so over-whelmingly strapping must have the answer she requires: she is right, Kimble revealing that the boy uses the dolls to look up girls' skirts. This is something of a relief: it is 'normal' and 'natural' behaviour, irrespec-tive of the boy's father (his sexual forebear and exemplar) having left his mother for a man. All Kimble seems to want during these moments of reflection on sexual conditions, though, is to meditate in various ways on the private meaning of fatherhood and family, his own 13-year-old son being estranged and raised – the implication is, for both the son and the father, emasculatingly – by a 'nice man.'

Undertaking to discover the identity of the child for whom he is looking, Kimble asks the children to come to the front and tell the class what their fathers do; a disparate catalogue emerges of fathers mostly driven by monetary gain, in sedentary jobs, boorishly regressive, or handicapped by circumstances: 'My dad repairs cars that are driven by women who are pinheads'; 'My dad is a psychologist'; 'My dad doesn't do anything since the crash'; 'My dad watches TV all day long.' Kimble's father, so the policeman later lies, was a 'teacher' in Austria – 'We have a tradition in Austria where we follow in the footsteps of our parents.' (Again, Arnold's art was commenting on his life. Speculation about Arnold's father's job was at the time rife, with the *News of the World* in Britain alleging that Gustav was a war criminal. Schwarzenegger, out of curiosity as to Gustav's [and hence his own] true identity and to head off potential embarrassments precipitated by his heritage, instigated an investigation by the renowned Simon Wiesenthal Center. No evidence of criminal acts was uncovered, despite Gustav having been a 'fervent Nazi.')[108] Clearly, the pupils of Astoria need a powerful male role model who will get them moving, and in whose footsteps they themselves can literally follow. After going to dinner with a young teacher, Joyce (an Eva Braun-styled Penelope Ann Miller, whom it transpires is the woman he seeks), Kimble's 'change of plan' begins in earnest. 'Listen, Kimble,' advises Phoebe, essentially a masculinised, overly work-fixated 'buddy' figure, whose boyfriend is absurdly feminised, 'you gotta handle this like any other police situation. You walk into it showing fear, and you're dead.' 'No fear,' replies Arnold, aware that he must now totally embrace the role of dominant warrior-father, the hunter-hero-settler whom the children seem to crave.

Whilst castigating an overweight child for overeating, the policeman formulates a fresh idea of what will instil in his charges the power of self-discipline and aspiration, motivate the 6-year-olds and give both him and them a focus: Kimble will enact a highly disciplinarian version of the fitness drives undertaken for President Bush, forcing the children to respect themselves *and* their tutor, as they flourish through regimented physical testing. 'You kids are soft. You lack discipline. Well I've got news for you . . . You're not going to have your mummies run along behind you an' wipe your little tushes, oh no. It's time now to turn this mush into muscles,' barks Arnold. This drill instructor-style approach, maybe surprisingly, instantly has an effect, the pupils now revering their new teacher as a longed-for source of fatherly order. 'It works . . . It works! This is great!' exclaims Kimble, his epiphany too much to contain. Putting the class through a junior version of what looks like army basic training, conveyed in a montage reminiscent of *Rocky*,[109] appears to be an ideal prescription. All the children craved was a chance to find delight in bodily development and health – a nation-building programme devoid of too much 'pantywaist book-learning,' and of which Reagan (and the New Right in general), the family Bush and Nietzsche alike would be proud: 'the right place is body, demeanour, regimen, physiology; the *rest* follows therefrom'; or, as Adolf Hitler put it in *Mein Kampf*, 'The folkish state must not adjust its entire educational work primarily to the inoculation of mere knowledge, but to the breeding of absolutely healthy

14. John Kimble: protector, drill instructor and kindergarten cop

bodies. The training of mental abilities is only secondary.'[110] ('Any nation,' laments Bill Bryson, 'where twenty million people can't read the back of a cornflakes box, or where almost half of all adults believe that human beings were created sometime in the past ten thousand years, clearly has its educational workload cut out for it.')[111] These vigorous and determinedly disciplinarian 'fathers' – their influences and mantras always, however indirectly, informing Schwarzenegger's career – had taught Arnold well, the heroic son in turn passing on a moderated version of the tenets of the elders. Arnold, as always with a twinkle in his eye and a calling in his heart, was beginning to think about the form his legacy might eventually take in literally moulding the United States' future. Channelling through Kimble philosophies he held dear (above all 'the philosophy of good living through physical endeavour'),[112] Schwarzenegger suggests, in *Kindergarten Cop*, that there is no shame in willing submission to authority as part of a functioning, 'healthy' American institution under reasserted *paternal* control. The female teachers, unable to instil such a spirit, look on with envy as if suddenly redundant; here is the superman, the super-*dad*, seizing jurisdiction back to the masculine realm and away from the mysterious feminine, now denuded of its softening, emotive potency and revealed, via Crisp's parental 'fairy godmother,' to be potentially bewitching and possibly evil if allowed sufficient rein. All need for female control over the most crucial (to Arnold) aspects of education and even nourishment (Kimble now apportions the symbolic milk allowance) rendered illusory, women can now function solely as generative, soothing vessels, driven back to their 'proper' sphere: birthing and its strange dreadfulness, homemaking (of the strictly passive kind), and attendance to the male's romantic needs.

Unavoidably, then, *Kindergarten Cop* strives to take seriously Kimble's relationship with Joyce – for the father must be restored as a totally male being, atoned also with the pre-feminist patriarchs' pride in conquering and making receptive the potential bearers, but not in every way makers, of the next generation. After all, as Pamela Abbott and Claire Wallace attest, citing Reverend Jerry Falwell:

> The ideal family [for the Moral New Right] is one in which the man sees his role as the disciplinarian as well as the economic provider and the woman sees her role as sacrificing herself to the needs of

household and children: 'The family is the God-ordained institution of the marriage of one man and one woman together for a lifetime with their biological or adopted children.'[113]

Though she is allowed to keep her job, as part of the compromise offered by Arnold's semi-liberalised 1990s revision of the mid-century father, Joyce is incomplete without subsuming her professional identity to Kimble's superior abilities. Because she is a single, professional mother (a potential danger to the fabric of society) and he divorced (denied of his female-conquering facet), they must unite to approximate Falwell's 'God-ordained' ideal, realising in the process an ostensible reconciliation of feminist and masculinist drives that in fact entirely favours the patriarch's desire to minimise women's psychological effect. It is for Arnold's remarkable occupation of both maternal and paternal roles that he is so desired. His uniqueness, obviously apparent to the women who lust after his supremacy, lies in the straddling of a supposed duality: here is a *male* kindergarten teacher, who is definitely *not* gay, and who can bring stability, warmth and the all-important toughness inherited from his former life as a policeman.

Admiring of Arnold's ability with his surrogate brood, and taken by the anti-intellectualism evident in the quasi-militaristic chant he has the class repeat as it marches ('Reading, writing, arithmetic, too much homework makes me sick!'),[114] Joyce falls for the giant, older suitor. Wiping his milk moustache from his face, she coyly invites him for dinner – for which she dresses in the unadorned contours of a 1930s Reich poster girl – at her old-fashioned, austere house, which has not been bought by hard work, but acquired through the charity of friends ('Her teacher's salary is less than I make, which is pathetic,' decries Phoebe, later in the film, hinting at a feminist critique of women's wages, but additionally eliciting an inference that women should simply not bother with extra-domestic work). 'Can you start a fire?' she asks when he arrives, immediately wanting a demonstration of manly prowess. During Joyce's preparation of the meal, her son, Dominick, takes Kimble to his hideaway in the garden, showing him his 'laser' to protect him from the 'bad people'; engaging in fake gunplay, the pair bond over games of defending the family 'fort' from marauders (Dominick's worries about other men's aggressive interests then prompt Arnold's realisation that this is the boy for whom he has been searching, and that he now has a doubly important duty to protect and to serve). Discussing with Joyce the nature of the 'nice man' (for which read a 'new man' of the 'pantywaist' variety) who now looks after his son, Kimble ascertains that her ex-husband (who transpires to be Crisp) does not pay alimony, and is hence not a provider in the mould of Arnold's rugged alpha male: 'I was so glad to see him go, I didn't worry about that part,' she sighs, clearly in need of a *real* man in her life.

Arnold, in the culmination of an extraneously unsubtle sub-plot, then proves his real-man credentials once and for all, by beating up the physically abusive father of one of the school's introverted children. While children and parents look on with goading awe, Kimble, as had Dutch in *Predator*, stops short of dealing a knockout blow that might imply anachronistic brutality along the lines of John Wayne – the mid-century man untamed by adherence to liberals' rules – swaggering through a 1950s Western: 'You're not worth it . . . I'm pressing charges.' 'I have no idea what kind of police officer you are,' Miss Schlowski says in response. 'But you're a *very* good teacher . . . What did it feel like to hit that son of a bitch?' 'It felt . . . great!' smiles Kimble, his law-and-order qualifications for any role *in loco parentis* secured. Schlowski, after the children's Kimble-directed play about the Founding Fathers, the Gettysburg Address and the concept of constitutional liberty, delivers a eulogy in acceptance of the all-subsuming, inexorable super-dad into the ineffectual world of the female: 'I'd like to introduce our kindergarten teacher. He came to us as a substitute teacher, and he's proven to be a wonderful asset. Let's welcome him into our community and hope that he considers staying on a permanent basis. Ladies and gentlemen – Mr John Kimble!' The children, surreally wearing giant, Lincoln-esque stovepipe hats, gather round Arnold's god-like presence, embracing the King who brings the fatherly gift of the King inside. Joyce is overcome with veneration; given the miraculous Mr Kimble, who would need a woman for anything other than passive procreation?

Now softened, submissive and symbolically infantilised in an oversized pink jumper, Joyce, having learned the truth about his identity, accepts Arnold's protection from Crisp's Oedipally troubled bogeyman. Kimble enters her home as a bodyguard – 'I don't want to lose you, I don't want to lose Dominick' – and they finally, and briefly, kiss, to the sound of swelling strings. His mastery is nearly complete; all he must now do is dispatch Crisp and survive the final showdown with matriarchal darkness as embodied by Crisp's mother, who is knocked unconscious, *deus ex machina*, by Phoebe, a woman-turned-man (a 'partner,' never a lover) in order to function fully in the sphere of custodial employment. In the end, Kimble elects to give up his former occupation as a policeman and become a full-time kindergarten teacher, saving the children from becoming effete or fat. United with Joyce as her protector and lover, all is well once the twin worlds of the female and male are likewise reconciled via Arnold's hard-body, all-encompassing carapace, tough, big and manly enough to embed the nation's founding principles within its heft. 'The message?' concludes Jeffords: 'The emotionally and physically whole man of the eighties would rather be a father than a warrior,'[115] although, as we have seen, only the path of the warrior can bring true completeness or atonement to Arnold's persona.

Christopher Booker writes of a 'perennial fault line which helps explain that fundamental opposition in politics between "right" and "left"':

> ... The right-wing view rests chiefly on the masculine values, centred on the exercise of power and the maintenance of order; what may be called the values of 'Father.' This is innately conservative because it believes in upholding the established structures and institutions of society. It supports those values which it sees as holding society together: the symbols of the nation state, tradition, patriotism, conventional morality, the family, discipline, the need for strength to defend the existing order against its external and internal enemies. The left wing rests essentially on the feminine values of feeling and understanding, what may be called the values of 'Mother,' in which it perceives the ruling order and the right-wing view in general to be so heartlessly deficient ... It believes in change and the vision of a future society which is fairer and more caring; in which everyone can have an equal chance; which is not bound by narrow exclusive nationalism but sees all humanity as one.[116]

Realising the bifurcating nature of this dichotomy and its import in fuelling an internecine sense of opposition between genders, Schwarzenegger once more addressed a perceived need for reconciliation – through the father's reasserted importance and newfound usefulness – in the enormously expensive, heavily effects-laden and vastly successful *Terminator 2*.

Using the trope of the apocalypse as a means to suggest the benefits to be gained from the everlasting influence of the strong but devoted dad on world order, James Cameron's follow-up seeks to bring a new stasis to future society, one in which mothers have been taught hard but necessary lessons in how to be better fathers. The mother is allowed to exist, to survive, but not to thrive or to express herself as anything other than the biological mother of the future and a surrogate, mechanised father: the 'historically female duty of bearing boy children'[117] already undertaken, Sarah Connor must run on into the unknown, perpetually supplemental to Arnold's macho but desexualised robot, an emissary of never-ending patriarchy. 'Never have I found the woman by whom I wanted children,' Nietzsche has Zarathustra sing, 'unless it be this woman, whom I love: for I love thee, O Eternity! For I love thee, O Eternity!'[118] When the inescapable 'Judgement Day' (the film's overtly religious subtitle) comes – and come it must, notwithstanding Sarah and John Connor's efforts – maleness, and all that the archetypes of hard-body maleness represent, will for many believers, such as televangelist John Hagee, be the default state of humanity:

> I'll know Jesus has reappeared when my glorified body sails past the Milky Way into the presence of God. I'll know I'm with the real Jesus when I stand in his glorious presence with my brand-new, disease-proof, never-dying, fatigue-free body that looks better, feels better, and is better than Arnold Schwarzenegger's.[119]

Following Judgement Day, 'real' men like Arnold's T-101 will be the exemplars of manhood; the future may be bleak, but its conflicts, mapped on to the schemas of the eternally renewed frontier, nonetheless give purpose to the lost, secular youth of the pre-millennial age. 'We should not forget,' explains Geoff King:

> that the 'New World' of America was itself seen by some early enthusiasts as marking the potential arrival of the millennial kingdom on Earth . . . rooted in notions of a fresh start, a sloughing off of the old and corrupt in favour of a new and supposedly more authentic beginning.[120]

After a recapping flash-forward to 2029, and the familiar scenario of resistance fighters battling skeletal robots in a darkened, fire-ravaged landscape, *Terminator 2* begins with Arnold's naked materialisation, as per the first film. Surveying his surroundings, he sees a convenient biker bar, enters, and takes the clothes and motorcycle of a suitably sized drinker. Schwarzenegger is by this point so comfortable with his own heterosexuality that he takes delight in co-opting the signifiers of the gay scene, perhaps a necessary prerequisite for Schwarzenegger becoming an ostensibly all-inclusive individual – by the 1990s, his spontaneous transmogrification into 'the world's first self-sufficient human being' looked to be well under way.[121] 'Fathers now worry,' said a 1987 tourist guidebook, 'if a son's hair is too short, if his dress is too macho, or his muscles too well-developed, since these are the trademarks of the new breed of San Francisco gay man.'[122] The gay community, perhaps sensing a hint of derogatory misappropriation, has never fêted Arnold; Schwarzenegger, though, did not mind adopting its codes of dress to elevate himself from the throng. Already engaging in camp self-parody, the Terminator requires only a pair of shades to top off his Tom of Finland look: a comedically ultra-butch apostle of Armageddon ('bad to the bone,' as the music ironically incants), this time sent back to guard John Connor (Edward Furlong) from the deadly intentions of his more slightly built rival, a superiorly designed, 'liquid metal' terminator.

Mimicking the appearance of a policeman – the T-1000 can adopt the form of anything it touches – Robert Patrick's mercurial shape-shifter has a distinct advantage: it can literally, if it so wishes, blend in to the mundanity of urban life, an amorphous and thus for Arnold detestable quality signifying amalgamation with the undifferentiated inner-city 'mass,' an 'arbitrary multiplicity of individuals [that] can never be the bearer of values.'[123] The handsome T-1000, most of the time, looks like a staunch (if, to the spectator, strikingly glacial) law officer and can thus insinuate itself with ease; 'he is our neighbour, our protector,'[124] a functionary, a *nonentity*. Arnold's T-101, a heavy-faced bodybuilder in tight leathers and sunglasses (these seem to have been conscious fashion decisions, programmed by John Connor upon sending his companion back in time), is solidly and defiantly conspicuous, a new man born not of sinful flesh but of the 'drill-machine, created without the help of a woman, parentless.'[125] As Klaus Theweleit states, 'The most urgent task of the man of steel is to pursue, to dam in, and to subdue any force that threatens to transform him back into the horribly disorganised jumble of flesh, hair, skin, bones, intestines, and feelings that calls itself human.'[126] The T-101 is not a devious, thin-lipped trickster, but a brazen, somatically *immutable* force of scientific nature in opposition to the 'weaknesses' of a woman's biology and Patrick's sinewy androgyne. He is a self-contained, apparently self-generating father, made possible only by our drives for war; a triumph of Puritan, logical will over underhand, 'feminine' psychology; a superlative locus for the acme of Arnold's post-*Pumping Iron* screen personae and the ideal rhetorical template from which to construct a masculinist scheme demonstrative of the power of father–son bonding rituals. If such a 'man of steel,' in many ways apt as a forward-striving, implacable parent, were taught how to sideline the mother, then the 'kinder, gentler' Schwarzenegger's cinematic rite of passage (and accidental citizenship of cyborg-theory proponent Donna Haraway's 'post-gender world,' even if with male hegemony in mind)[127] might be complete.

Sarah Connor, the bearer of the future leader John, has been incarcerated in an asylum, wherein she has been building her physique in readiness for the coming war, her femininity now secondary to her mission. Frustrated by Dr Silberman's insistence that she is delusionally psychotic, Sarah's resolve is strengthened by adversity. 'Like the T-101,' write Janice Hocker Rushing and Thomas S. Frentz:

> this 'new' Sarah is muscularly hardened, slimmed to fighting shape, and mean as Hell. No longer the virginal aspect of the Madonna/whore split who relies on men to teach her survival skills, Sarah emerges in the sequel as a full-fledged Amazon warrior, a Joan of Arc whose mission is to save the world.[128]

Sarah, 'who was a stereotypically weak woman in need of saving at the beginning of the first *Terminator* has, in effect, become a cold, deadly Terminator herself,'[129] to all intents and purposes, having functioned as a birth mother, a symbolic soldier-male adjunct to Arnold's King. Not entirely devoid of maternal feelings, though, Sarah dreams of the future apocalypse, and of its biblically destructive effects. Evoking Zechariah (14:12), an atomic-age realisation of his prophecy unfolds: 'Their flesh will be consumed from their bones, their eyes burned out of their sockets, and their tongues consumed out of their mouths while they stand on their feet.' Watching a younger version of herself playing with her infant son, Sarah's vision sees her incinerated where she stands, turned to a pillar of salt by a red-hot nuclear shockwave rushing across Los Angeles, once again Hollywood's chosen site of ultimate annihilation. She expresses, to Dr Silberman, a longing to be with her progeny, to save his life, but not to be his mother, for the knowledge she holds has changed her from soft-natured carer to angry defender. John must, however, be given the chance to become a multi-faceted man; he must be given the life examples he needs to lead the human race in the war against the machines: stoicism, calm authority, composure and compassion, all improbably contained in the T-101. The scene is set, then, for a battle of wills and bodies, fought for the survival of humankind, the masculine identity of the boy-saviour, and the pre-eminence of Arnold's all-conquering paternal ethos against the liquefying, glamorous, subsuming enemy. 'As before, the resistance was able to send a lone warrior, a protector for John,' narrates Sarah. 'It was just a question of which one of them would reach him first.'

John, when we first meet him, is living with 'white trash,' suburban foster parents, who by their lack of disciplinarian skills and inability to provide strong mentoring essentially leave him free to run riot and commit petty crime with his friends. The suggestion is that he is squandering his life without proper parental authority. Wasting no time, the polite T-1000 locates the foster family's house and obtains a photograph of his quarry, whom he describes as 'a good-looking boy' – an observation that would sound faintly deviant coming from Arnold's outlaw muscle-man, and that comes across as only marginally less so from Patrick. John, whose excursion to town saves him from the T-1000's initial attempt to discover his whereabouts, has learned to defraud banks, steal credit cards and manipulate machines to his own ends. Unlike the strangely disconnected, 'out of the loop' Reese (his real father), he is making technological systems – the eventual bringers of doomsday – work for him by learning their language; he is a product of the microchip revolution as much as are the warriors of Skynet. It was his mother who taught him to assimilate technology in order to fight fire with fire, to take what he can while he is still able, in preparation to do battle. Not believing her story ('She's a total loser'), he has turned this knowledge to pointless frittering. 'Let's go spend some money,' he says to his friend, as they head to the shopping mall, the vacuous destination of all young cinematic rebels of the 1990s: a temple to the frivolous lack of direction or ambition of 'Generation X', born of a despondence with political and educational leaders unable to offer a stewardship significantly appealing to the young.

The apotheosis of a 'slacker,' young Connor listens to nihilistic rock music (Guns 'n' Roses) and affectedly wears a T-shirt emblazoned with the name of a militant, black rap group – Public Enemy. A shirker acting out an orphan fantasy of disenfranchised, idle cool, John requires an old-fashioned example from an old-fashioned future, where the Injuns might be metal, but still represent a usefully self-defining enemy for the white-led resistance. Arnold's job will be to instil in John the 'solid,' hard-body virtues of rugged, coolly striving manhood, whilst teaching his obsessively hot-headed mother a long lesson on the true nature of modern American parenting. 'I consider it possible to convert men into republican machines,' asserted Benjamin Rush. 'This must be done, if we expect them to perform their parts properly, in the great machine of the government of the state.'[130] By the same logic, America does not need slackers, but technocrats, system-literate functionaries and authors of the national narrative. Though the apocalypse, in Cameron's world, may well be inevitable (and a constructive purge from which true grit can re-emerge), the descent of childhood into meaninglessness is not. Arnold's good Terminator catches up with John at the mall, replaying the window-smashing saloon fight from the first *Terminator* film prior to spiriting the boy away from danger on a stolen Harley-Davidson motorcycle, a surrogate, all-American horse made for two as opposed to the unwieldy lorry chosen by the liquid-metal villain. Deviously inventive the T-1000 may be, but its choice of vehicle betrays a limited understanding of outlaw cool; Schwarzenegger's robot is by far the more savvy in the ways of American individualist endeavour, realising the importance of mobility to the concept of freedom, and tacitly appreciating the romance of the duel. Arnold wields only a shotgun against the ultra-resilient T-1000, shown iconically resurrected from an inferno and oozing back into perfect shape; the good Terminator will wear each wound he incurs during the film's progress as an honorific badge of courage, and of sacrifice to his 'son.'

The T-101 and a remarkably unfazed John soon get things straight between each other, John establishing that the robot must obey all his commands, including the order not to kill any human, and the Terminator understanding that he has to 'lighten up' to form a social cohesion with the teenager. Though this goes against the basic wiring of his 'brain,' it seems that the T-101 can learn to adopt a stolidly intoned version of John's vernacular, not in a fashion implying an anxious desire to regain his own youth, as is the timeless case with many real fathers trying to connect with the younger generation, but in a detachedly knowing sense that rises above inter-generational power struggles of linguistic assertion and discursive encryption. Arnold's '*überdad*'[131] is sufficiently in touch with his own inner child, underneath the prosthetically adult muscles, to realise that a child does not really want its father attempting to assimilate its parlance. The retorts 'Chill out, dickwad,' and especially 'Hasta la vista, baby,' have entered the pop-cultural lexicon not because they are uttered by a middle-aged actor who thinks he is fashionably attuned to his juniors' slang, but because they are delivered by Arnold's super-aloof Terminator, culturally empowered by the very inabilities to effect humanness that render it a 'dork,' as John puts it. What a boy really needs, then, from a father like Arnold, is the vestige of a machine-like past (or future), evinced in the father's actions, voice and manners – in other words, a trace of paternal strengths alien to the demographic lost to Generation X. It does not matter that Arnold's robot never really gets it – never stops being a 'dork' – for an unstoppable dork is what we want him to be: impervious to fashions, impervious to feminism, impervious to emotions, and almost impervious to bullets. The Terminator cannot cry, but nor should he. His power lies in the deepest depths of old-style American manhood and a yearning for what this offers; his expressivity sits caged in the cold chrome around his skull, but he nonetheless cares, without feeling the vulnerability of pain or the need for deceit.

Springing Sarah from the mental institution, halfway through her own attempt at escape's imminent failure, the two become three. They retreat to a disused petrol station to repair the T-1000, who carefully stitches up Sarah's wounds, and to engage in some expository conversation about Arnold's character.

John: Do you know what you're doing?
T-101: I have detailed files on human anatomy.
Sarah: I bet. Makes you a more efficient killer, right?
T-101: Correct.

John: [*holding up Arnold's bullet-hole-riddled jacket to the light*] Does it hurt when you get shot?

T-101: I sense injuries. The data could be called 'pain.'

Sarah: Will these [bullet wounds] heal up?

T-101: Yes.

Sarah: Good. If you can't pass for human you're not much good to us.

John: How long do you live? I mean last, or whatever?

T-101: 120 years with my existing power cell.

John: Can you learn stuff that you haven't been programmed with? So you can be, you know, more human . . .?

T-101: The more contact I have with humans, the more I learn.

This long-lasting, precise new man, then, is willing to learn but not to become feminised or soft. He knows about pain – like *Predator*'s Dutch he entirely understands it – but he is not weakened or compromised by such human frailty. He can pass for human, but he is a *homo superior*; he requires neither sleep nor food nor water, staying up all night to guard his charges, as the supremely loyal custodian of woman and child. In an age of economic recession and endangered blue-collar or medium-skilled employment (with the exception of the military, which was at the time easily combating Saddam Hussein's occupation of Kuwait), Arnold's T-101 sees the *family* as his occupation. Trouser-presser Morris Rosenfeld lamented in his nineteenth-century poem 'My Boy':

> 'Ere dawn my labor drives me forth;
> Tis night when I am free;
> A stranger to my child;
> And stranger my child to me.[132]

There is no such quandary for Arnold; if there simply are no jobs to keep men from their children, then one should count oneself lucky and make a career out of fathering, finding the resourcefulness to travel and to exploit the hypothetical opportunity of the West, 'a thousand points of light' taking the place of welfare. The love he inspires from John is not a love the boy has known, the T-101 being in some respects to Reese's timorous and vulnerable 1980s pin-up what John Kimble is to the other teachers of *Kindergarten Cop*: a professional dad not susceptible to error or self-doubt. He does not have to be dragged to his feet, but unerringly remains the ideal soldier-hero, Walt Whitman's 'strong man erect.'[133]

Leaving Los Angeles, the group drives south, heading to the sterile, folkloric domain of the frontier outlaw and his attempts to live a life free of the metropolis's corrosive influence. When humankind has learned its lesson, Cameron suggests, it will be in the desert, on the frontier ripe for claiming, that it will 'slough off the old,' and find an 'authentic beginning' in the ashes of the world. '[F]ree land,' said Frederick Jackson Turner, 'made the democratic type of society in America . . . the frontier is productive of individualism.'[134] 'We're not going to make it, are we?' John asks the Terminator, a mentor and eschatological sage whose Old Testament wisdom speaks of the certainty of the end-times. 'It's in your nature to destroy yourselves,' he replies, realising the need for a new start. Sarah merely ignores her son, fixating on the horizon, while Arnold, increasingly, appears to be the focus of the Messiah's attention, the teenager attempting to instruct his giant guardian and friend in how to do high-fives. 'What had been,' avers Susan Jeffords, 'its most frightening feature in the first film – Reese tells Sarah, "It will never stop!" – is now in Sarah's words its most admirable feature: it will never stop caring for John . . . When [Sarah] is shown being a mother, it is of the most brutal and unreflective kind.'[135] And Sarah, as is made plain in the film's most memorable and discussed monologue, knows her own mind about Arnold's abilities:

> Watching John with the machine, it was suddenly so clear. The Terminator would never stop. It would never leave him, and it would never hurt him, never shout at him or get drunk and hit him, or say it was too busy to spend time with him . . . It would die to protect him. Of all the would-be fathers who came and went over the years, this thing, this machine, was the only one who measured up. And in an insane world, it was the sanest choice.

We thus have two hard-bodied fathers (Sarah and the T-101), but only Arnold 'measures up' both meta-phallically and as a calm, controlled influence. Los Angeles, 'one vast prison, one dead-end system, one ash heap, one already happened disaster waiting to repeat itself,'[136] was about to erupt in violence, triggered by fifty-six baton strikes by police officers on black man Rodney King; 'of all the would-be fathers,' of all the best-equipped solutions to a culture of increasingly scatter-shot rage and institutionalised aggression, Arnold, assimilating the positive tenets of a non-violent white youth – the Christ of a California waiting to be saved – is paramount. 'In 1991,' records Kevin Starr, 'a record 1,154 people were slain with firearms in Los Angeles County . . . gangbanging and drive-bys were moving toward yet another record year.'[137] Never, then, was there more need for a hero whose precisely focused aggression only targets the legitimate; never was there a more loaded message in Schwarzenegger's films than Arnold's acceptance that on occasion he must 'put the gun down,' lest things get out of control and ricochet back at us.

As Thomas Byers attests, 'the fascist potential in the strong leader fantasy seems obvious,'[138] *Terminator 2* representing the zenith of such concerns' obviousness in Arnold's films, his life and expressive perform-ances rippling time and again through history like Cameron's time-travel narratives. 'The good father of the Reagan–Bush years,' Byers continues, 'is one who is capable of the most extreme violence, but *who will not hurt us*.'[139] In an 'insane world,' a world of chaos, recession and doubt as to the homeland's place in the greater world, the Führer was likewise the 'sanest choice,' for he too would never hurt his own. Moreover, 'When we put together [John's] tears and the restraints on violence with the role of military leader/saviour, we get a pretty good idea of who John is going to grow up to be: not the Schwarzenator but Norman Schwarzkopf.'[140] Though J. Hoberman refers mainly to the film's advanced, computer-generated effects, he likewise makes the same connection: 'Politically, *Terminator 2* suggests the merging of Schwarzenegger and Schwarzkopf, techno-war and Technicolor,' he writes. 'This is truly the Desert Storm of action flicks.'[141] The war in the Persian Gulf (now known as Gulf War I) had been, to many US observers, 'a bloodless Nintendo game evoking passive spectator applause,'[142] as the tin-pot Stalin-styled Saddam was driven cowering back to his palace – but not, due to American govern-mental unwillingness to get involved in the complex internal sectarian politics of Iraq, killed. Bush could have learnt from John Connor's com-ment about his mother ('she always plans ahead') and saved his own son the eventual effort of a futile re-match that would descend into the closest analogue yet of America's Indochinese adventure. Instead, the President pulled out. 'By God,' exclaimed Bush after the Gulf War's overwhelming victory, ensured by the United States' 'precision bombing' campaign designed to avert media fears of another 'quagmire,' 'we've kicked the Vietnam Syndrome once and for all!'[143] There was no point, though, in Arnold fighting a fictionalised version of the Gulf War on screen: that phenomenon was already at play on television, thanks to the rolling news' constant coverage from cameras manned or unmanned, but mostly operated by the US Army. The conclusion of this particular battle, a war between militaries of massive inequality and 'the most covered and the least reported war in history,'[144] was in any case too foregone for Arnold's assistance to be necessary.

Arriving at the encampment of some stereotyped Mexican banditos, inhabiting 'a typical "inferior realm" in which the seeds of redemption are destined to germinate,'[145] the T-101, Sarah and John (who introduces the Terminator as 'Uncle Bob') assert their outlaw credentials, Sarah swigging tequila to prove her manhood. Arnold, of course, refuses the offer of a drink, being a robot, another attribute that makes him a better father: like millions of men before and after them, his own and Reagan's old-fashioned, hard-working dads had turned to alcohol to anaesthetise the pain of familial struggle, something the good Terminator takes in his stride. The T-101 and his entourage pick up some weapons hidden in the desert, the *Mater/Pater Dei*-cum-honorary-terminator echoing Arnold's demand of the bikers: 'I need clothes, food and one of your trucks ... *Now*, Enrique.' For a moment, Sarah, alone and tired, remembers motherhood, as she watches the Mexicans play with their children. Drifting off to sleep, however, a nightmare of the coming apocalypse stirs her back to Amazonian hardness. Fully armed with military-grade hardware, and resembling no one so much as Arnold in his pre-ego-birth days, she is resolute. Her mission is to kill: she absolutely will not stop until the man 'responsible' for Judgement Day, wealthy computer scientist and 'soft,' black father Miles Dyson, is dead. In another inversion of the first film's thrust, it is now Arnold, accompanied by John, who will attempt to pit himself against 'the machine' and stop the 'terminator' doing its job. Although, as the T-101 points out, Dyson's death might well avert the end of the world, the newly empathetic Terminator and his adopted son John temporarily put the life of one, misguided family man above the lives of millions.

At the Dyson family's house, Sarah attempts to assassinate the inventor, as the T-101 had previously tried to assassinate her, to prevent the future war. Dyson, ignoring his young son, is absorbed in his computer work, presumably investigating new ways to exploit the futuristic chipset (salvaged from the factory in which Arnold's first incarnation was terminated) he has secreted at his laboratory complex, and which will form the basis of Skynet's 1997 attack. The technologist is a 'girly-man' of intellect, puzzles and calculations, not rugged deeds. He cowers under attack, sensibly afraid for his life in contrast to Arnold's fearless, machine-like ability to protect the ranch; he is unable to shelter his brood from aggression; he does not comprehend the consequences of his actions; he is, in every way, the opposite of John Matrix. 'Nobody fucking move! Get down on the floor, bitch!' shouts Sarah to Mrs Dyson, gaining entry to the house by showering it with bullets; she has become a crazed killer, a slave to her impulsive anger and quick temper, traits the super-efficient Terminator has always been too impassive to possess. When it comes to the moment of execution, she cannot, despite (or maybe because of) her fervour, match the Terminator for dedication. The excursion, a risk deemed by the T-101 unacceptable, has been aborted by her humanity; distracted by a vestige of what she seems to consider 'illogical' emotion, she breaks down only to be comforted by John and his ever-loyal Frankenstein's Monster. Certainly, things have changed, and become not a little bizarre: Sarah is now shown up as a mother by a gay biker-styled robot assassin and her once-wayward son under his sway. As even the T-101 would now concede, she can not 'just go around killing people' – especially not Dyson, an undeveloped, cerebral black man who needs the Austrian Oak's prompting to redeem himself by martyrdom. That Dyson might technically be the T-101's 'father' is lost on everyone concerned; as an unwitting, blinkered and bourgeois black catalyst of the end-times, Dyson has in some way to be punished, in this case by being led to a contrite death amidst the ruins of his smouldering laboratory. Taking out an entire SWAT team with a single gun (Old Painless, which Arnold seems to have brought with him from *Predator*), all the while taking care not to kill any of the heavily armed men, Arnold again proves his manhood, simply taking all the fire they have to offer, even if it wears down his face to a half-skull. There are no casualties; there is no 'collateral damage'; and there will be no 'friendly fire.'

Climaxing with a lengthy showdown featuring Arnold versus the liquid-metal man, who tussle in a steelworks (a typical venue in aesthetic terms), *Terminator 2* champions Arnold's character's stolid determination in apposition to the fluid, 'mimetic polyalloy'-based Proteus. However hard it might try, and however it might re-form, mimic and coalesce, the T-1000 is unable to outperform its nemesis; in the end, what is really required is a shotgun blast from Arnold, which sends the T-1000 tumbling into a vat of molten metal and back to leaderless, undifferentiated sub-humanity, the faces of those it has assimilated screaming forth. The famous final scene, in which Arnold martyrs himself, is an extraordinary example of tear-jerking dramaturgy, orchestrated to maximise every spectatorial pang of emotional resonance. Lowered with excruciating slowness into the steel, so that his chips are destroyed (one remains intact, of course, in another severed hand), Arnold raises a thumb aloft as he sinks to his termination, whilst John and Sarah mourn the passing of an exemplary patriarch. It is the ultimate sacrifice by the man of steel, who has striven so hard to escape the drag of milling, nebulous, unbound civilisation, to subsume his consciousness into the liquidity from whence it came. Sarah's epilogue, spoken over a travelling shot moving forward down a darkened road, sums up the preceding lesson: 'The unknown future rolls towards us, and I face it for the first time with a sense of hope. If a computer can learn the value of human life, maybe we can too.'

Or, if 'Arnie' can learn the value of human life, his continued pre-eminence, at least for the time being, is assured. Both *Kindergarten Cop* and its successor evince a remarkable feat in convincingly metamor-phosing the Terminator into a man not only of steel, but also of encour-agement and inspirational paternalism: 'one of the more bizarre, hippo-in-a-tutu reinventions,' comments Tom Shone, 'since Garbo decided to laugh.'[146] 'While it was okay for the Arnold of the 1980s to kill 275 people,' said the star, in the self-distancing third-person language only the acutely business-like can conjure, 'it is not okay for the Arnold of the 1990s.'[147] Arnold wanted to be the perfect dad, the ideal hero-father figure for a nation whose patriarchal schemes, post-Reagan, were under threat. Middle age, the end of the Cold War, and the lack of a defining Other to fight meant that Schwarzenegger had to look at inhabiting new mythological realms – and provide apposite new examples – if he were to stay at the pinnacle of his game. Tempering the model his own, highly influential father (of whom the 10-year-old Arnold was so scared he had wet himself)[148] had provided, Schwarzenegger reconciled himself with the 'positive' aspects of Gustav and his ilk, whilst admitting a degree of the 'feminine'; by this process of osmosis, Arnold subtly implied a need for female input solely at the biological or recreational level.

A widely read pamphlet from the eighteenth century, entitled *Advice to a Daughter*, proclaimed: 'Your Sex wanteth our Reason for your conduct, and our Strength for you Protection: Ours wanteth your Gentleness to soften, and to entertain us.'[149] Doubtless Arnold would agree. Offering rejoinders to feminism, *Kindergarten Cop* and *Terminator 2* alike suggest a remodelling of the female role, as well as the male: the former allowing women to keep jobs so long as they comply with the *Advice to a Daughter* or act as anti-erotic sidekicks, the latter going a step further. *Terminator 2*, in tacitly conceding that feminists might be chagrined at *Kindergarten Cop*'s anachronistic dismissal of prettily beautiful, soft-contoured women's professional potential, allows its heroine some rein, on the condition she 'kicks ass as a man in drag'[150] whilst Arnold, big enough and man enough to take everything in hand, accepts mothering duties: the 'self-made man' par excellence was absorbing even the conventional role of the woman – an attempt, it would seem, at nullifying her by incorporation and reaching a compromise. ('I've always thought,' pondered Bill Moyers, 'that if you could get in touch with your feminine side, then you would know what the gods know.')[151] To quote a particularly reactionary passage from Robert Bly's *Iron John*: 'How can any complicated culture live without strong warrior energy? The outward warriors inside some women are today strong, sometimes stronger than those in men. Forces in contemporary society recently have encouraged women to be warriors, while discouraging warriorhood in boys and men.'[152] Although he speaks in figurative terms, Bly's worries are addressed literally by 'Arnie'; in the early 1990s, Schwarzenegger sought to diffuse and ultimately absorb his culture's 'warrior energy,' proffering a solution based on Hamilton's/ Sarah's journey of Arnold-tutored 'growth' from strong, independent, sexual woman, to stronger, but subsumed androgyny: 'A woman who grows and transforms on-screen is always a wonderful thing to play. Sarah went from a vulnerable, normal girl to someone who finds all of her deep reservoirs of strength and comes through it all.'[153] And the means of coming through it all? Gaining insight into motherhood from the Terminator's King. In 1852, Karl Marx observed that, 'Men make their own history [but] they do not make it just as they please; they do not make it under circumstances chosen by themselves, but under circumstances directly found, given and transmitted from the past.'[154] In *Terminator 2*, pondering the same issues, John Connor says, 'The future has not yet been written. There is no fate but what we make.' Out of our past, thus comes forth our destiny, brought on by endless, cyclical power struggles for domination over the Other and the shaping of the world to archetypal patterns – the end-times often only signifying a chance to claw back the status quo. As Susan Jeffords concludes, '[T]he future of masculinity has not yet been determined. But, at the same time, these films argue, if there is to be a future for mankind at all, it lies in the hearts of white men.'[155]

Clearly, the cinema-going public responded well to Schwarzenegger's comments on (and would-be remedies to) the precipitous state of the family, making *Terminator 2* Arnold's most lucrative film (it raised $205 million in gross receipts). Understandably tending to focus on the then-revolutionary morphing effects, critics reached no consensus. David Ansen of *Newsweek* noted Arnold's 'impressive, hilarious, almost touching performance,'[156] whilst J. Hoberman, at *Sight and Sound*, thought it 'proudly wasteful and bizarrely self-serving,'[157] a view that perhaps succinctly sums up the negative aspects of its star's narcissistic disposition. Schwarzenegger, it goes without saying, could afford a great deal of negative press: he was riding higher than ever before. Then, in the summer of 1993, a strange thing happened. Nearing the heat of the sun, Arnold faltered.

John McTiernan's *Last Action Hero* (1993) is an often clever, often confounding, and mostly misguided attempt to deconstruct and interrogate the 'Arnie' phenomenon from within. Using a *mise-en-abîme* device as its central conceit, the film sees Arnold, as an alternate-reality version of himself, emerge from the world of cinematic fantasy into modern-day Los Angeles, fulfilling the wildest dreams of his biggest fan: a flaxen young boy from a fatherless home. Replete with self-parodying mischief – something Arnold had conveyed for years with greater acuity and flair in his genre pieces – *Last Action Hero* enters a labyrinth of intellectually meretricious showboating and gets entirely lost. Arrogantly spoofing the nature of his own appeal (and arrogance), Schwarzenegger effectively tells his fans that they have been cheated; that he is a vacuous, violent and hollow product of a popular culture now so moribund it is forced to eat itself whole during a bafflingly telescopic burlesque. Arnold's zingers are sent up as wholly forced;

the ridiculousness of Arnold's apparent immunity to bodily injury is exposed as pure nonsense; and the villains, in a film not brave enough to comment on or deconstruct the xenophobia and racism so frequently at the core of Schwarzenegger's *oeuvre*, are sub-Bond caricatures or uglified grotesques.

Arnold's fans, understandably, did not take kindly to the insinuation that they had for years been duped out of their wages. Faring poorly at the box office (it recouped only $50 million worldwide, losing more than $20 million), *Last Action Hero*, its name optimistically suggesting the final word on post-modernity in mainstream cinema, proved a grave error of judgement. Put simply, it did not know what kind of statement it was trying to make, or indeed what kind of entertainment it most fundamentally was. In an age of 'ancient hatreds and new plagues' bedevilling a '"new world order" . . . rife with chaos and big, unresolved questions,'[158] *Last Action Hero* suffered from a schizophrenic confusion; whereas Arnold had previously offered certainty and direction, now there was a public crisis of confidence in his action-hero credentials.

Against the backdrop of Bill Clinton's popularly elected new Democratic administration – and the gradually lessening financial crisis it was mandated to solve ('It's the economy, stupid,' intoned Clinton's most famous mantra) – the film seems to glory in cynically spendthrift solutions to the formerly non-existent problem of how to effect Arnold's solipsistic enrichment. Moreover, and with suitable inconsistency, the film's irresolute text, which is one minute gratuitously explosive, the next derogatory of Hollywood excess, revels in sophomoric intellectuality and somewhat smug sleights of narrative hand at the expense of satisfying dramaturgy. To most, *Last Action Hero* represented neither value for money nor any significance beyond the mordant devaluing of long-standing generic codes; Hollywood was insulting the very consumers on whom it had always relied – Middle Americans whose tolerance for mockery was already being tested. The nation's biggest problems were those of prompting fiscal recovery and reducing deficit, but Clinton's attitudes to cultural expression – in the 1990s a number of controversial works prompted calls for federal censorship – were to some alarmingly open-minded. With no Cold War to distract them, citizens of patriotic persuasion (who comprised a large section of Arnold's audience) fought with renewed passion to reaffirm values and identities at home. Gunplay, implicit sexism, violence against the demonised Other and sundry related Americanisms were usually acceptable cinematic visions – blasphemy, superciliousness and nega- tivity less so. Helping to precipitate the 'culture wars' of the 1990s, ideologically pro- and anti-Clinton blocs fought hard to seize the dis- course of artistic expression for themselves. 'To deeply disappointed conservatives,' states James T. Patterson, 'Clinton was the epitome of all that was wrong with his baby boom generation – and with the elitist liberals, amoral Hollywood celebrities, and left-wing academics who supported him.'[159]

Arnold, who had posed nude for Robert Mapplethorpe *and* helped to elect George Bush, had no immediate answer but to dismiss the negative press amid suggestions that he was an anachronism unable to escape the mid-1980s' unfashionable immoderations. 'First of all,' he said, 'I don't believe that eras fall into neat decades. Second of all, I'm not a product of any era, I'm a product of myself.'[160] Caught between two stools in a perilous position of untenable prevarication, he could not please all of the people all of the time, no matter how he tried to incorporate everything before him into his capacious but nearly replete monad. 'Arnie,' at long last, was sensing his limitations. The province of the post-modern had been his for many years, yet the movie-going demographic did not want to see him explicitly emulating Godard, André Gide, Woody Allen or Jorge Luis Borges's works of recondite playfulness, whose techniques, in Arnold's hands, were rendered entirely devoid of affection or charm. *Halliwell's Film and Video Guide*, assessing *Last Action Hero* from the standpoint of a popular organ dedicated to serious film criticism, accurately derided it as a 'perfect example of cinematic self-hatred.'[161] Already, as J. Hoberman records, having masterfully reconciled 'America and Germany, and Russia, man and machine, freedom and authority, terminator and redeemer, Rambo and Cary Grant, gym class and kindergarten,' Arnold's 'potent symbol of international domination'[162] was experiencing something like inter-textual over-reach; in response, Joe Six-Pack had voiced severe disapproval. Alluding to McTiernan's portrayal of Arnold as Hamlet, Jonathan Romney sums up the manifold problems inherent to the venture:

[N]o one in Hollywood is immune to the slings and arrows of outrageous fortune, not even as apparently inviolable a sweet prince as him . . . *Last Action Hero* is already too thoroughgoing an exercise in self-reinvention, or at least self-deconstruction, to satisfy a market that prefers to take its stereotypes neat . . . The 'Arnold Schwarzenegger' we see at the *Jack Slater IV* screening – vain, garrulous, determined to plug his burger joint – seems a shadow of Jack Slater . . . when Slater and 'Schwarzenegger' meet, it's remarkable which seems more real.[163]

Last Action Hero, concludes Romney, is 'cinematic hara-kiri. It's hard to imagine that after it, any other Arnies will be possible.'[164] Schwarzenegger, though, would return triumphant with another parodic opus – featuring truly the last of his massively hewn action heroes – in which he finally gets to assume the duties of a post-Cold War, all-American Bond: James Cameron's bombastic *True Lies* (1994).

'Honey I'm Home!': 'Hasta La Vista, Fairness'[165]

The right wing's effectiveness rests . . . on certain points of contact with real problems of domestic life and foreign policy and widespread and deeply rooted American ideas and impulses.[166]

The movie theatre is the psychoanalytic couch of the average worker's daylight dream.[167]

The premise of *True Lies*, essentially a reworking of Frenchman Claude Zidi's 1991 *La Totale!*, is uncomplicated. Harry Tasker (Schwarzenegger) is a man who leads a double life. His demure spouse, Helen (Jamie Lee Curtis), thinks Harry is a nine-to-five computer salesman, when in fact he is a top-level governmental secret agent. Offering a barefacedly politically incorrect rejoinder to those championing sexual equality and relativism, whilst in addition exploring notions of what activities might or should comprise a matrimonially harmonious household, Cameron's mid-1990s updating of the James Bond cycle revels in countering what conservatives perceived to be the Clinton era's 'intellectually distorted emphasis on "multi-culturalism," women's rights, and minority groups.'[168] A big, loud and brash cinematic reclaiming of territory from liberal forces, *True Lies* expends the majority of its enormous budget on impressively staged (and usually computer-enhanced) action sequences. Epic in scale, though perhaps attempting, like *Last Action Hero*, to shoehorn too much into a crudely framed plot with the aim of achieving definitive 'Arnie' status, the film nonetheless sees Schwarzenegger return to what he knows best: the colourful politics of ideological disavowal, laced with subjective interpretation of contemporary experience.

'Bond's an aging, alcoholic Brit,' said Cameron, envisioning his ageing, hulking Austrian-American friend as the spy's natural successor, 'C'mon!! Let's pump some new blood into him!'[169] Cameron, of course, misses the point about both Fleming's dissipated hero and the film franchise's various adaptations, whose misogyny and violence, stoked by the Cold War's all-pervasive paranoia, went affectionately forgiven due to the compensatory suaveness of the leading men – projections of the everyman's desire to save the world *and* indulge in the bad habits of unreconstructed, 1960s manhood. Nonetheless, Cameron and Schwarzenegger strive to 'pump up' the formula, perhaps aware that Arnold's maturing physique and now oddly desiccated-looking physiognomy could only convincingly endure so many more energetic thrillers before succumbing to gravity. Still, Arnold was typically reluctant to slaughter the golden calf, retaining an almost religious faith in his corporeal resilience. 'Age is bound to catch up with us sooner or later,' he wrote in 1981. 'But later is better. No need to invite it in before its time.'[170] *True Lies*, an oxymoron coming after the personal humiliation of *Last Action Hero*'s implied termination of the genre's golden age, is an all-or-nothing, make-or-break gambit aimed at recovering Arnold's hitherto overwhelming dominance of Hollywood's action-blockbuster branch. It cares little for the facts of America's contradictions, evoked by the title. But then, Ronald Reagan once said, 'Facts are stupid things,' a statement, as Gary Indiana observes, 'which has become more than ever the reigning dictum of the faith-based Republican Party.'[171]

During the film's credit sequence, following a wetsuit-to-tuxedo conversion directly appropriating Bond, Tasker is established as a formidable yet loyal super-spy, whose typical day at work consists of feigning roguery and caddishness (Arnold is Bond rendered quasi-conscientious, without the air of mercenary threat) while infiltrating the circles of the ultra-wealthy. Speaking 'perfect Arabic,' as a subtitle informs us – lest we suspect that Arnold's talents or training leave anything to be desired – Tasker gains entry to a billionaire's party to steal secrets held on a computer at the mansion. Arnold saunters amongst the throng to the sound of Johan Strauss, insinuating himself as in such real-life situations via force of character; his 'almost mystical' aura clearly in full effect, the strangers universally submit to Tasker's arresting presence, giving him time to dance a tango with the exotically sexy Tia Carrere, the film's Southeast Asian villainess and dealer of nuclear arms to Islamic fundamentalists. When a security guard eventually asks for his invitation, Tasker's answer succinctly condenses Schwarzenegger's most frequent retort to pro-filmic enemies, journalistic critics, bodybuilding rivals and any industrial resistance met during his Hollywood career: 'Sure, here's my invitation,' says Tasker, detonating a firebomb that sends many bodies flailing through the air. Arnold needs no invitation to anybody's party, Cameron suggests: he is a bringer of unstoppable detonation whose brazenness is an asset.

Indeed, the absurdity of Schwarzenegger's/Tasker's domestic sub-terfuge in *True Lies* – that he is a sales representative for anyone other than himself – is central to the film's thrust. 'He's never gonna play a character where he sits around in an office all day and wrings his hands,' said Cameron. 'He is about direct action.'[172] The party is disrupted and Tasker makes a run for it, but we should not be surprised at this 'change of plan,' for Arnold always requires a physical release of some kind, 'direct action' without which he is unrealised. 'Ballsy,' comments his boisterous partner Gib (Tom Arnold, playing a sanitised revision of Belushi's Ridzik), who has been waiting in a surveillance van. 'Stupid, but ballsy.' When two Dobermann pinschers leap at him, Tasker knocks their heads together and admonishes them to 'Stay!' The unshakeable spirit of Hercules and his labours residing within him still, Arnold was embellishing his own legend. Tasker, the name itself implying devoted professionalism, is master of all beasts (later, he will verbally command a horse), men and women he surveys – the consummate, masculine, cowboy-spirited superpower made flesh who 'absolutely will not stop' until the job in hand is done, or the distractions of the homestead call him back.

Almost forgetting to reinstate his wedding ring before returning to his wife, such is his dedication to his calling, Tasker is driven to distraction by his duty to the nation as an anti-terrorist operative. While Harry has been away protecting national interests, Harry and Helen's marriage has lost its lustre, both partners' romantic interest in each other having been abandoned. The gift Harry gives his teenage daughter has been bought by his partner, with little thought to its specificity; she derides the trinket as 'pretty lame,' a comment applying equally, it would seem, to her father. Clearly something has to be done to reconcile the roles of father, husband and secret agent; Arnold, being the master of such processes whether as Terminator or teacher, is merely looking for a narrative catalyst that will not compromise his attention to espionage, and that will allow him to inhabit fully a catch-all parent-professional paradigm according to the precepts of the genre. Helen, it turns out, has embarked on a (thus far) non-physical affair with a puerile, sexually adolescent used-car salesman (Simon: Bill Paxton, earlier seen having his heart ripped out by Arnold in *The Terminator*) who is pretending to be a spy. Even worse, Simon, by no means able to bestow upon his would-be lover the lifestyle to which she is accustomed, lives in a trailer park and wears uncoordinated clothes – readily interpretable indications, to those with differing aspirations, of being exactly the kind of 'loser' Schwarzenegger could never be. Dissatisifed with her husband's apparently mundane life and persistent absences, she is looking for the very attributes and excitement that Arnold, with greater manliness, panache, and (we are subsequently told, by Paxton himself) a bigger penis, could of course provide, given the motivation and incentives to trust his beloved but exaggeratedly frumpy wife. (Curtis, the star of several prior films that exploit her open sexuality and lithe physique, is cast because of her status as an object of male fantasy. Her 'potential' for glamorous sexual reinvention, as observed by Simon, will not have gone un-noted by the average spectator; a repressed ugly duckling, Curtis plays up every nervous tick and over-endows Helen with the qualities of the stereotypical librarian.)

Upon learning of his wife's near-infidelity, Tasker confides in the beaten-down Gib, who offers condolence: 'Welcome to the club!' Called upon to convey this kind of anguish, though, Schwarzenegger appears to be in difficulty: he clutches his stomach, he gasps for air, and he is dumbstruck, but the performance is strained, revealing a shortcoming in Arnold's repertoire of emotions. Quite obviously, the actor is not a man who could ever even contemplate cuckoldry happening to him, so confident was he of his natural place as the ultimate alpha male. Playing Tarzan again, he told Michael Cartel of the *Valley Vantage* that, 'There was this thing with Tia and Jamie Lee . . . Who would get to kiss me

15. The interrogation of Helen Tasker (True Lies)

more? . . . So in reality there was this jealousy.'[173] Tasker could have Tia Carrere, it is implied, or the demure Helen, or perhaps both (demure *and* sexy, to remember *Total Recall*'s Quaid and his Madonna/whore complex); the spy is man enough, however, to save his marriage, but by entirely chauvinistic means. Helen is seized, with Gib's collusion, and questioned by the duo – who distort their voices into intimidatingly sonorous growls – from behind a two-way mirror. 'On trial for being a sexual person,'[174] Helen must undergo the first in a series of humiliating, gynophobic rituals for the men's pleasure. *True Lies*, avers José Arroyo, 'perpetrates astonishing emotional violence in the name of the traditional nuclear family. As Harry Tasker, Schwarzenegger can eavesdrop on his wife, stalk her through the city, kidnap her and even lock her up for questioning. All this is excusable because it proves Mrs Tasker is faithful and thus helps keep the family together.'[175] Arroyo is being generous – there is little sense that Harry cares about the integrity of the family, at least in the short term; rather, he is tortured by the thought of an 'inferior' such as Simon (a caricature of Joe Six-Pack, who did not seem to take offence) sleeping with his wife. Whilst this may be a refreshing honesty on the part of Cameron about his character's motivation, it remains that Tasker is the hero, the nominally virtuous and faithful man whom we have seen risking his life for American security. Now tested to his limits by anger and exacting excruciating revenge on an undeserving woman neglected beyond the point of irreconcilable differences, Harry, the protagonist, the *force for good* against the film's 'evildoers,' has become an obsessive manipulator with whom our sympathies and identificatory impulses are presumably supposed to be aligned. (Whereas Clinton, following the Monika Lewinski scandal, would be seen to be '"feminised" by his loss of control "to a series of fallen women,"' notes Gary Indiana, Schwarzenegger, during 2003 inconvenienced by accusations of sexual harassment, *equated masculinity with the nonconsensual humiliation of women*, thus gaining the approval of the locker-room set.')[176]

Harry coerces Helen, still unaware of the interrogators' identities, into choosing between her family's safety and accepting a job in the security services; obviously choosing the latter, Helen is given the chance to lead for real the exciting life of which she has dreamed. However, this opportunity depends on her making the transformation from legal secretary to overtly sexual seductress. Her 'audition' for the role of spy entails her going to a hotel under the guise of being a high-class prostitute, ostensibly to plant a bug, but in fact to perform a striptease for a wealthy guest – Harry, sitting in the dark so as to obscure his face. Approaching the room, she catches sight of herself in the mirror; realising that, although she has already 'dressed sexy,' as she has been told, she is still not quite sexy enough, Helen tears off the ruffles attached to her skin-tight mini-dress. She is willing, ready and able to occupy Harry's adolescent fantasy world in return for his dangerous romance and attention; she is Jamie Lee, The Body, the pin-up, a happily 'empowered' woman acting out the erotic as is her duty in order to maintain the Taskers' union. The antithesis of the feared (by conservatives) 'feminazi' Hillary Clinton, who likewise did not 'stay at home baking cookies,'[177] Helen now represents the 'ideal' working woman according to Schwarzenegger and Cameron's (the two seem remarkably like co-conspirators) juvenile daydreams. Upon finding out that it is Harry in the hotel suite, and that he is a government operative, she is initially enraged; soon, though, she learns to enjoy her life-endangering, action-woman lifestyle predicated on the 'capitalist myths of freedom of choice and equality of opportunity [and] the individual hero whose achievements somehow "make everything all right," even for the millions who never make it to individual heroism (but every man can be a hero – even, such is the grudging generosity of contemporary liberalism, every woman).'[178] The marriage can thus be saved, provided they share in Arnold's world of aggressive, *Boy's Own* escapism. All that remains, domestically speaking, is for the pathetically unworthy Simon to be subjected to such fear that he wets himself (as Arnold had done when confronted by his father – the abused has become the abuser), a hugely unnecessary ritual in narrative terms, but one that confirms Paxton's status as a hated, infantilised 'peewee' on a par with the film's Other villains: the fanatical 'Crimson Jihad' and its stereotyped leader, Art Malik's Aziz, or the 'Sand Spider.'

Typecast again, Malik must have bristled at the part. A mad-eyed, deranged, woman-slapping and constantly perspiring Arab nationalist, the Sand Spider (so named, we learn, 'because it sounds scary') proves incompetent, under-resourceful and humourless. (He does, though, partake in the film's most surreally entertaining dialogue. When asked, of a nuclear bomb, if he knows what it is, Arnold replies, 'I know what this is. It is an espresso machine. No, no, no – it's a snow-cone maker, that's what it is . . . Is it a water heater?') Beaten by Arnold in every direct confrontation, including one during which Arnold commandeers a horse to chase him – who rides a motorcycle, the conventional modes of transport reversed to show Tasker's 'native' aptitude on horseback – Aziz is an obsessive, hostage-taking ideologue on a mission to destroy the West, whose forces' presence in the Middle East he perhaps understandably resents: 'Crimson Jihad will rain fire on one major US city each week, until our demands are met,' he intones to a camcorder (which runs out of battery halfway through his speech, causing the minion filming to tremble in fear of his boss's temper).

Though Aziz is a hugely negative and unconstructive metonym designed to instil odium, *True Lies'* portrayal of Middle Eastern terrorism was and is in some respects accurate and topical. New Jersey Islamists had, in 1993, driven a Ford Econoline van filled with 1,500 pounds of urea-nitrate into the World Trade Center's basement intending to kill as many people as possible. (They killed six and injured over 1,000, prompting *Last Action Hero's* producers, in a show of obligatory compassion, to replace a stick of dynamite in the hand of a giant promotional inflatable of Arnold with a police badge.) Between 1993 and 1999, the federal counter-terrorism budget tripled, reaching more than $300 million per year, whilst a number of well-placed observers claimed that the United States was inadequately prepared for an attack on US soil. For the most part, Americans have never regarded themselves as imperial aggressors, and so have never considered themselves villains; striving for mass acceptance and easily construed dramatic opposition, the schematic details of Cameron's plot (as opposed to his characterisations) merely reflect public opinion in the midst of a small but genuine threat. A case might be made that the only significant distinction between actual Islamic militants and Cameron's terrorists is that the latter have managed to get hold of an effective weapon – via, naturally, a *femme fatale* whose 'whorish' ways disgust Aziz. All these diverting exploits, though, could reasonably be considered pernicious. When Osama bin Laden, in an interview aired by Al-Jazeera in 2001, spoke of America's 'unspeakable crusader grudge against Islam,'[179] he did so with a degree of justification. The West's long-standing cultural war (even irrespective of actual bloodshed in the name of oil, ideology or territory) fought against 'camel-riding, terroristic, hook-nosed, venal lechers whose undeserved wealth is an affront to real civilisation'[180] is not an insignificant contributor to anti-American feeling amongst Middle Eastern patriots. Hollywood, said author Jack Shaheen, 'finds it perfectly acceptable to vilify, to demonise whatever and whoever is Arab and Muslim.'[181] Muslims hate the West, and particularly the 'Great Satan' America, it would seem, partly because we insist on telling stories about how *we* hate *them* and why *they* will never change: 'For every benign us, we can nominate a malignant them . . . and for every distant they, a blessed and neighbouring we.'[182] The cycle hence endures, an unremitting exchange of animosity and ethnocentrism in which Schwarzenegger's oversize cipher for 'freedom' inevitably got involved. (When the film premiered, Arab reception was overwhelmingly hostile. 'Open your eyes and terminate the lies,'[183] read one placard, its holder aggrieved that yet another production had failed to say anything positive about Muslims or acknowledge any serious problems within Judaeo-Christian- or secular-based states.)

At *True Lies'* climax, Aziz, who has seized Tasker's teenage daughter – the implication is that he is after all white men's daughters as the ultimate bounty – is thrown around and genitally damaged, to add sterilising injury to insult and provide 'satisfying' retribution for daring to challenge Arnold's authority. 'You're fired,' says Arnold to Aziz, as he lets fly the villain on a missile launched from a Harrier jump jet, the *ne plus ultra* of grown-up boys' toys. 'Racist, sexist and shallow . . . an escape into a white boy's fantasy land,'[184] *True Lies* revels in comic-strip preposterousness of this kind, and in so doing attempts to emplace itself outside the discourse of political correctness, a discourse whose interrogation might prove as humiliating as that faced by Helen Tasker. *True Lies* suggests no remedy for, and even exacerbates, hypocrisies and deeply ingrained warrior tendencies inherent to the United States. It is a celebration of excessive consumption, modern-day tribalism and bloodlust, rendered, like its star, visually arresting yet peculiarly synthetic, searching for a definitive enemy at the gates onto whom to displace its internal rage, and by whom to make concrete its own identity. 'What are we waiting for, gathered in the market place?' wrote C.P. Cavafy, in a poem about ancient Alexandria whose import can be transposed onto the scheme of contemporary aggression in America: '[W]hat will become of us without barbarians? These people were a kind of solution.'[185] Or, as Phil Melling explains:

> War with Saddam . . . was no substitute for a replay of the Cold War, and the search for an errand behind which the nation could unite remained a terminally elusive quest in the next decade. In a society where the machinery of war had created vast, unexpended energies, the desire for confrontation and climax proved relentless. Hollywood, in particular, devoted itself to meeting the challenge of the demon lover by exploring the need for military vigilance . . . It lamented the loss of a Cold War culture while contextualising the Cold War theatre as a pathological site, one which attracted the manic energies of those who searched for cathartic action in border operations.[186]

Melding espousals of Reaganite family values, anti-Arab sentiment, rugged individualism, mythic heroics and female sexual acquiescence with Arnold's keen abilities to wage war on intellectuality and all notions counter to his philosophies, *True Lies* – the messages at its heart simultaneously as loud as bombs but as implicit as American faith in Freedom – is both the acme of Schwarzenegger's filmic endeavours and the plateau preceding a financially and critically disappointing period of cinematic frustration that would last nine years. As Arnold recognised, 'This run of success will end, it will, and of course one wonders what it will be like when that happens.'[187] Doing very well in terms of receipts ($146 million in domestic sales), *True Lies* was nonetheless outperformed by Robert Zemeckis's *Forrest Gump* (1994), a patronising affirmation of 'freedom of opportunity' whose central proverb ('Life is like a box of chocolates – you never know what you're going to get') is in diametric opposition to Arnold's ruthless perception of the American Dream: by all accounts he always knew exactly what he was going to get, and had a contingency plan for when he eventually ran out of soft centres.

In addition to Arnold's age, decreasing prudence and fading novelty, a number of political and cultural factors account for the considerable drop-off in Arnold's box office popularity over the mid–late 1990s. America was prosperous once more, its gross domestic product rising by 14 per cent between 1994 and 1998. It was almost invulnerable in those wars it chose to prosecute, often against enemies too ill-defined, parochial, or 'Old European' of purpose to inspire great public passions, and shameful of its celebratory attitude to greed in the 1980s. The Nixon-endorsing sanctuary Arnold had first encountered in 1968 was giving way to an environment less amenable to Schwarzenegger's brand of social Darwinism. Clinton's appointment had ushered in an age more tolerant of liberal ideals, integration, diversity, freedom of expression and racial and sexual equity. 'I feel your pain,' the President would say to the underprivileged and downtrodden he would make an effort to meet; Clinton was eager to please the gamut of his constituents, a quality at first seen as 'needy,' but that over time became an asset. 'Slowly but increasingly,' notes James T. Patterson, 'millions of Americans appeared to identify with him, regarding him – warts and all – as an unusually caring and sympathetic man,' seeing the President as 'the guy next door'[188] who nonetheless would not stand for censorship, prejudice, invective against non-nuclear families, or Arnold's attempts personally to get him to support state-sponsored fitness plans. Arnold's very muscles, inelegantly ossified in distinction to Clinton's relaxed posture, were a cliché: both metaphorically and literally redundant, the hard-body image was belittled in send-ups on comedy shows like *Saturday Night Live* and *The Simpsons*, a hugely popular, culturally immersed, perspicacious and irreverent marker of the shifted epoch. A new wave of versatile, delicately handsome leading men was emerging whose political leanings mirrored prevalent attitudes; equally adept in the realms of physical action, contemplative drama and sensitive romance, Keanu Reeves, Brad Pitt, Leonardo DiCaprio, Johnny Depp and Matt Damon embodied a persuasive conflation of traditional masculinity and emotional depth that made Schwarzenegger's recent forays seem like placebos. Perhaps in hindsight the defining film of the mid-1990s, Quentin Tarantino's post-modernist homage *Pulp Fiction* (1994) spearheaded and contributed to the commercial growth of independent cinema. Whereas *Last Action Hero* had seemed hatefully contemptuous, *Pulp Fiction* exuded soul. 'Unlike many of the traffic cop directors of studio entertainment,' notes Brian Neve, 'Tarantino, although he was aware that he was part of the selling process, clearly cared about the cinema as a battered twentieth-century metanarrative.'[189]

As Joseph Campbell states:

> The symbolic field is based on the experiences of people in a particular community, at that particular time and place. Myths are so intimately bound to the culture, time, and place that unless the symbols, the metaphors, are kept alive by constant recreation through the arts, the life just slips away from them.[190]

With no dragons left to slay, and an audience wary of the repetitious formulas he had helped to invent, Schwarzenegger faced a problem: for the first time in his until-now eerily prescient life, he was out of touch. Unconsciously evoking Norma Desmond ('I am big. It's the movies that got small'), Joel Silver put it succinctly: 'Nothing has changed with Arnold,' he said. 'But maybe the movies have changed.'[191]

IV Fall and Rise
The Will to Power

[O]nce a myth ceases to give people intimations of transcendence, it becomes abhorrent.[1]

The hero blessed by the father returns to represent the father among men . . . The hero of yesterday becomes the tyrant of tomorrow unless he crucifies *himself* today.[2]

Several efforts following *True Lies* tried, with mixed results and with little conviction, to probe new dramatic avenues whilst recapturing past glories. Working again with Ivan Reitman, Schwarzenegger, in 1994, took his notional power to embody and contain all mythical tropes a step further than his constituency must have expected: he would play a man who gets pregnant, thereby finally rendering feminine externalities superfluous as anything other than recreational distractions or the target of broad caricature. Even the virgin mother, queen of the mastery of creation, was not sacrosanct according to Arnold's compulsion to subsume all of legend on the way to bestowing his 'boons' ('The earth is my body. I am there. I am all over,' declared the 'word-redeeming' hero of the Jicarilla Apache, Killer-of-Enemies).[3] *Junior*, by reuniting Arnold with Danny DeVito in a scientific context (though this time *they* are the biologists), in effect replicates the *Twins* dynamic, positing the two stars' amiably dysfunctional characters in apposition once more. Dr Larry Arbogast (DeVito) is a fertility expert testing a new anti-miscarriage drug; needing a guinea pig, he turns to the only person he feels is ethically suitable for secret implantation: his colleague, the shy, serious and beleaguered Dr Alex Hesse, played with some charm by Arnold, who researched the role by carefully observing pregnant mothers' encumbered movements. The film, however, due to its revision of *Twins'* wholly negative attitude to scientific endeavour and its 'blasphemous' proposal that Schwarzenegger's body might be suitable for motherhood, angered and alienated a number of key audiences, especially in the religious South. Doing relatively poor box office business ($36 million), *Junior* was a challenging excursion into less familiar territory, but not the hit Arnold might have hoped for.

Briton Emma Thompson, who plays the bumbling, egg-donating scientist who falls in love with Hesse, saw another potential pitfall in allowing an element of vulnerability to encroach upon the superman's hitherto invulnerable, inviolable image. Lauding his bravery and willingness to diversify, Thompson was respectful of Schwarzenegger's conviction: 'I've always been fascinated by him. He is a self-made myth, someone who has invented himself and stayed in control of himself. Then he makes this film in which he loses control of his body. Arnold of all people.'[4] For Schwarzenegger, the film's key moment comes when he delivers the line, 'Does my body disgust you?' 'I have been working on my body,' he explained, with characteristic immodesty:

> and, by any accounts, from age 15 to 47, people have been telling me it is spectacular. You know, that's been my life. Then I have to have this big belly and feel that, maybe, I'm disgusting. That teaches me something about what a woman goes through. I mean, she must feel the same way.[5]

Shallow, unthinking and generalised, such comments reveal a deep-seated insecurity and sense of despondence with not only his anima, but also the frustrating stagnation of his filmic persona. An entry on Schwarzenegger's website (www.schwarzenegger.com), posted a decade later, allows a glimpse into Arnold's troubled relationship with his core fans' simple-minded expectations, and demonstrates the macho star's desire to abjure any prior insinuations of feminisation for fear they might compromise his alpha-male status:

I'm known for being this muscular guy and this heroic movie star, but to run around in dresses and wear earrings – it was fun to be able, in a legitimate way [for which read, 'in a heterosexual way'], to play that kind of feminine character, because in real life if I wear or do any of that, they would definately [sic] put me away.

However, Arnold would be the first to admit he doesn't know if seeing him in make-up really worked for his biggest fans:

One day I was sitting on a life cycle at World Gym . . . and this guy next to me was just staring at me and shaking his head. 'Nowwwww, you did it,' he said, and I was like, 'Did what?' He looked at me and said, 'You sold out. What happened? You marry a Democratic wife and now you have to make nice movies.'

Arnold recalls,

Basically I was verbally attacked, on the life cycle – I'd sold out, I'd become a Democrat, I'd become this feminine guy. All of that! So I said 'thank you for your comments' and called Ivan [Reitman]. I told him, 'Ivan, if the movie doesn't work in my gym, we have a problem.' And sure enough, the guys just wouldn't go for it – they thought it was a step too far.[6]

If the 'locker-room set' were more attentive, Arnold need not have worried. Countering any misgivings that *Junior* constitutes a truly progressive revelation of Schwarzenegger's maturity and willingness to 'make nice movies,' a number of scenes rife with clichés and ultimately reductive humour ridicule and stereotype women. At a party, Arnold, now glowing with hormonal effusion and unable to control his oestrogen-induced euphoria (and appetite for sausages), says that he 'had the most wonderful massage . . . One minute here, the next gone . . . We should be pausing to hear the joyful melody of life itself.' The guests comment on his 'radiance,' while DeVito's male midwife, irritated at the thought of news of his secret experiment getting out, is invited by Arnold to 'feel how soft my skin is!' Eventually, having refused DeVito's demand that he abort the child, his maternal traits – which include tastes for ice cream and the colour pink, nagging, clinginess, baking, a newfound sentimentality and empathy, and of course a swollen stomach – become too much to conceal: Schwarzenegger has no option but to drag up as an East German shot-putter, effect a falsetto and retreat to a health resort. 'They dispensed anabolic steroids as freely as you in America dispense Gatorade,' he says by way of explanation for his size, 'with no mention of the side-effects that are now so painfully apparent' (it should be appreciated that this is a brave and amusing broaching of a subject personally relevant to Arnold, and one of the film's more progressive and satisfactorily interrogative moments).

Highlighting both the absurdity of Arnold as a woman, and, more regressively, the basic absurdity of women themselves, *Junior* only partially allows Schwarzenegger to cast off the ideological yokes of his action-hero incarnation. 'A pro-life ode to the nuclear family,' writes Howard Feinstein, which 'smacks of the ubiquitous anti-abortion commercials ("Life: What a beautiful choice") running on television,'[7] Reitman's revisiting of the DeVito/Schwarzenegger coupling is perhaps a wasted opportunity. In the end, much as in *Twins*, Hesse and Arbogast, plus their all-important (if under-written and tokenistic) female partners, all celebrate the wonders of new life, regardless of its origin in the belly of a Teutonic weightlifter, and the joys of the two-parent unit. His hardwiring and chassis as dependable yet as obsolete as the T-101's, Arnold could evidently only take so much upgrading. Despite Feinstein's assertion that the film was 'clearly keyed to the mood of America . . . in the wake of the recent conservative Republican sweep of both Congress and the Senate,'[8] it did significant business only overseas, thanks to Arnold's still-powerful global product. 'For the most part,' notes Laurence Leamer, 'he was like any brand on the way down. Arnold had not made the complete devolution yet he risked endlessly repeating himself to oblivion.'[9]

Eraser (1996), directed by Charles Russell, is a return to the formulaic action genre, but played earnestly and lacking in imagination and verve. The story is of John Kruger, an agent (with the titular nickname) for the Witness Protection Program, who has been assigned to protect Vanessa Williams's disloyal employee of a corporation illegally selling military technology to the highest bidder. A fair amount of intrigue and a not-too-predictable twist ensure that *Eraser* seems superficially to meet all the generic criteria. However, the character of Kruger is simply too humanised, down-beat and slimmed to resound as the 'Arnie' audiences had come to expect from such productions. If Arnold's previous action efforts were not always of the highest calibre in terms of dramatic depth, they were usually leavened by a heartening sense of their own foolishness and Arnold's invulnerability (*Predator* being a brilliantly orchestrated exception to the rule). Arnold was again disavowing his past, and in the process alienating devotees.

The star, whose first major hit was after all *Twins*, had been successfully and increasingly dealing in self-parody and implicit satire for two decades; suddenly playing it almost entirely straight was one way of reinventing him, but it was not what most fans wanted of the Austrian and it did not re-ignite his career beyond the summer of 1996. *Eraser* has all the big, loud elements one expects from Schwarzenegger blockbusters, and it made a lot of money, but the critical reception was one of disdain for its repetitive, time-marking nature: 'Filmgoers may feel that they've been there, seen that. Fans will still flock,' predicted Alexander Walker;[10] Barbara Shulgasser of the *San Francisco Examiner* commented that 'Schwarzenegger is in great physical form and he handles the derring-do well, but for some reason he seems as bad – if not worse – an actor as ever.'[11] The presence of James Caan and James Coburn, who both appear uninterested, does not rescue the piece from its fate as an inferior, perfunctory and pointless entry in Arnold's once joyously destructive action *oeuvre*.

Brian Levant's *Jingle All the Way* (1996), featuring Arnold as Howard Langston, a father endlessly frustrated on a mission to procure an in-demand toy for his son Jamie, is a child-friendly Christmas comedy replete with what *Sight and Sound* accurately described as 'thudding comic timing' and 'wearisome slapstick overkill.'[12] In a tacit admission of Arnold's fading superstardom, the film sees Schwarzenegger mostly shrouded in a garish 'Turbo Man' outfit (Turbo Man has transparently been concocted to exploit the Power Rangers phenomenon), whilst the condescending, worldly conclusion has Arnold's hero-dad confer all-important social status upon the son of a black, jealous, mentally unstable blue-collar rival (Myron Larabee, played by Sinbad) in a fashion suggesting Arnold is naturally fitter for the job of parent than the parent himself. After a showdown between Howard and Myron, Langston's son generously donates the elusive (and now, to him, worthless) doll to the child, whose gratitude to the father–son team who have vanquished his inadequate father is beyond measure. Of course, Howard's formerly acquisitive son, having gone through a moral conversion effected by Schwarzenegger's trouncing of the villainous 'Dementor' (or Myron in disguise), does not now require the toy's totemistic power: it is his father who is the *real* hero, a far more valuable asset in playground power-struggles. This 'icky movie,' opined the *San Francisco Examiner*, 'in its attempt to mock the marketing fest Christmas has become, only congratulates us all for our materialism.'[13] The true meaning of Christmas, Levant hints, is gaining respect – through the repeated assertion of superiority and wealth – over those less fortunate, who include the Langston's neighbour, Ted – like Simon in *True Lies* crudely portrayed as a pitifully incompetent would-be suitor for Arnold's glamorous wife (Rita Wilson). *Jingle All the Way*, not for want of rapid-fire mania, seems tired, hackneyed and desperate – attributes not lost on the press. Derek Malcolm, of the London *Guardian*, called it 'a ghastly, paper-thin piece of Yuletide rubble . . . rather like that Christmas pudding you forgot to eat last year.'[14]

Arnold was by now seriously up against twin obstacles: his limitations as an actor and a decreasing capacity to discern between good and bad projects. Finding distraction in political workouts (endorsing conservative Republican Newt Gingrich ['Our leader!']; visiting Israel and Yitzhak Rabin, who gave him the keys to Tel-Aviv), Schwarzenegger was attracting speculation – which he always relished denying – that he would surely swap a film career for politics.[15] The occasional appearance in support of themed restaurant Planet Hollywood (co-owned with Bruce Willis and a strangely cooperative Sylvester Stallone) giving him added motivation to generate self-publicity, Schwarzenegger maintained a high profile, yet was consistently unable to secure a script worthy of his renown. Paul Verhoeven's promising-sounding but extravagantly budgeted *Crusades* had been abandoned, and so Arnold turned to pantomime. Playing the villain for the first time since *The Terminator*, Schwarzenegger took the role of Mr Freeze in Joel Schumacher's *Batman and Robin* (1997), a lurid, hollow sequel to Tim Burton's comic-book-inspired visions of gothic vigilantism. Delivering his poorly scripted puns ('Cool party!') with 'all the panache of a discount warehouse on legs,'[16] Schwarzenegger's usually endearing presence could not offset Schumacher's ugly, thoughtless execution. A festival of lavish camp, liberated by dint of monetary excess from the television series' famished production values and resultant cult allure, *Batman and Robin* is widely and fairly regarded as the nadir of Schwarzenegger's career.

Normally effective when fighting clearly delineated forces of evil, Arnold tried again to situate himself in a definite, consensually just conflict keyed in to the epochal mindset. With the millennium – and attendant religious, technological and environmental anxieties – approaching, an opportunity presented itself. Arnold, attuned to the importance of the task for both himself and his leaderless constituents without 'somebody to watch over them,' shouldered the burden of humanity's salvation and took on the only enemy left to fight: the Devil himself. Respected *Capricorn One* (1978) and *Outland* (1981) director Peter Hyams's *End of Days* (1999) pits Arnold's depressed former policeman Jericho Cane against the incarnation of Satan (Gabriel Byrne), come to America to impregnate the mother of the Antichrist. Generally reviled and overly reliant on computer-generated effects, the film nonetheless endeavours to bring a new depth to Schwarzenegger's acting repertoire; his hero is not an unstoppable superman, immune to hurt and emotion, but a bereft, unshaven alcoholic. Realising that guts and guns will not be sufficient weapons, he must instead find inner strength and faith to win the day; which, naturally, he does, in a climactic, church-set battle with Satan during which Cane martyrs himself to save the world. Though noble, Arnold's sacrifice (this time with no hope of glorious rebirth) is not enough to save him from ignominy.

One of *End of Days'* more serious problems lies in Arnold's character's flaws, which are by any standards acceptably human, but in this context thoroughly unbelievable. It is impossible to divorce preconceptions based on what we know of Schwarzenegger's life from his film parts, a slippage he has continually exploited with flair. Accusations that 'he always plays himself,' though more or less correct, have never hurt Arnold precisely because range and technical accomplishment (the 'craft' of acting) are not usually focuses of his intentions. When called upon to express psychological agony, as in *True Lies*, he seems incapable of fooling his ego into thinking he might be susceptible to the frailties of the shapeless, 'lazy,' working-class mass of an America he simultaneously relies upon and despises. Moreover, the import of 'Arnie' lies in an expansive, unconscious reverberation across our deepest fantasies of wish-fulfilment and adventure: sometimes we *need* a hero who cannot feel pain, who does not give up, who absolutely will

16. End of Days' Jericho Cane: Arnold as flawed saviour

not stop and who shamelessly personifies the myths upon which, ad infinitum, human understanding draws for inspirational guidance. The spectacle of Arnold drinking whiskey from the bottle (or being beaten in a fight by Miriam Margolyes) is somehow disquieting. Concocted for the *fin de siècle*, in another struggle to reclaim ground lost to fresher stars, Arnold's adaptation is perversely anti-Darwinian – his performance, and the character of Jericho Cane, goes against everything he believes, and every attribute that he has ever successfully sold. Here is Arnold, asking us to feel his pain, when we need only for him to cure ours by taking up his rightful sword without emotional reticence. Put simply, to fight the good fight, we need the old Arnold – with his zingers, muscles and minimal dialogue – back. All that was lacking, however, was a *good* fight, a situation not rectified by *The 6th Day* (2000), Roger Spottiswoode's tale of cloning that is little more than a dumbed-down revisiting of themes articulated with greater *élan* in *Total Recall*.

However, never one to give up before he was ready or sacrifice a cash cow to save his critical reputation, Arnold began work on a film featuring a tried and tested enemy: international terrorism. Scheduled for release in mid-September 2001, *Collateral Damage* (Andrew Davis, 2002), for a time at least, looked promising. A Bush was back in the White House (if not by a convincing majority), so the context was friendlier, and the jungle setting had served Arnold well before. Still, there was no denying that Schwarzenegger, as Laurence Leamer articulates, was 'squeezing every dollar he could out of the brand name, milking it to the end.'[17] Arnold was by this stage a cryogenic veteran of Hollywood's blockbuster age clinging to a hope of future revival. A constrainedly physical actor in well-preserved form but obviously succumbing to late middle age, Arnold's skin was now sun-baked and his thinning hair an unconvincing shade of russet. Stuck in a cycle of dismal retreads trading on long-faded splendours, something, somewhere, had to give.

In the end, it was not Arnold. On 11 September 2001, the United States experienced 'one of those moments,' as the *New York Times* ruminated, 'in which history splits, and we define the world as before and after.'[18] The Pentagon and World Trade Center bombings, executed by Islamic militants with vague-to-non-existent demands but a staunch hatred of the Western values espoused by Schwarzenegger, recast the world, to American eyes, in an us-and-them light. An anonymous, fraught woman, emerging from the dust cloud in Lower Manhattan, asked a simple but deliberate question of a television journalist: not 'Why?' but 'Why do they hate us?'[19] The situation was as shocking, epochal and inconceivable as the Japanese bombing of Pearl Harbor, which had roused a 'sleeping giant' out of isolationism; this time, though, it was not immediately clear who 'they' were. Blame, in a newly electrified climate of fear, was hurriedly apportioned, and targets for retribution singled out. Newspapers spoke of a 'fresh enemy . . . at civilisation's gate,' stoking an abhorrence of the Arab world on the Right, whose position was summed up by Victor Davies Hanson in the *City Journal*: 'They hate us,' Hanson declared, 'because their culture is backward and corrupt . . . they are envious of our power and prestige.'[20] Regardless of the militants' motives – which were a conflation of anti-'Zionism,' anti-Western ideological passions and a dislike of the West's global dominance – there was indeed a 'fresh enemy,' the menace of which was vastly inflated in the wake of its symbolically wounding strike. 'We're in for a difficult struggle,' perorated the President, slipping into the language of the Old West; 'it is a new kind of war; we're facing an enemy we've never faced before . . . You're either with us or against us . . . Wanted dead or alive, that's how I feel.'[21]

The Bush administration promptly decided to attack Afghanistan, despite the fact that many of the hijackers hailed from Saudi Arabia (a country whose ties to the US government made it immune to revenge). Easily removed from power but lingering for years in desert caves to launch sporadic insurgencies, the medievalist Taliban, supposed harbourers of master terrorist Osama bin Laden, conveniently denoted the 'evil' of Islam. Ill-advisedly using the word 'crusade' in a speech,[22] Bush made plain his stance – the months and years after '9/11' would be darkened by right-wing religion battling right-wing religion, neo-conservative 'crusades' against jihad and the Free World's campaign against its tormentors: the 'Axis of Evil.' Oil-rich Iraq, whose despotic ruler Saddam Hussein had drawn Bush's father's ire but not provoked him to the death, was the next country to suffer military anger from the United States. Though Saddam almost certainly had little or nothing to do with financing bin Laden's al Qaeda group, and did not, as it turn out, possess hidden weapons of mass destruction, the pretexts were sold with sufficient fervency to constitute a *casus belli*. America was engaged in a notional 'war on terror,' against mostly the wrong people, in mostly the wrong countries, and in a permanent state of medium-to-high domestic alert. 'As I see it,' muses George Soros, 'the terrorists touched a weak spot in the national psyche: the fear of death. The prospect of dying is the ultimate spoiler to feeling good. A feel-good society simply cannot accept death.'[23] Not for some years had feelings of vulnerability, confusion and uncertainty been so prevalent. Suddenly, for the first time since the Cuban Missile Crisis of 1962, the American narrative was going seriously awry.

Out of the Abyss: The Return of the King

[T]here is no ascent to the heights without a prior descent into darkness, no new life without some form of death.[24]

The king is dead: long live the king!

Perhaps America had indeed been on a decade-long 'holiday from history,'[25] blissfully immune to foreign threat and serious economic troubles since the end of the Cold War. A period whose zenith coincided with Arnold's Hollywood slump, the 'holiday' saw a change in the kinds of hero figures elevated by collective needs to high office and film stardom. Schwarzenegger's literal and metaphorical muscle atrophied proportionally as the perception of danger from outside shrank: without a calling, a mandate or a purpose born of mass desires, dreams and nightmares, 'Arnie' withered away to redundancy. He promised he would 'be back,' and he did not lie, but the context was not favourable until America once more needed his power to unify and communicate the big 'idea.' A poem posted outside Grand Central Station told the hijackers of 9/11 – and all enemies of America – why the nation would stay resilient, and strong: 'Well, you hit the World Trade Center, but you missed America . . . America isn't about a place, America isn't even about a bunch of buildings, America is about an IDEA.'[26]

Collateral Damage (another eerily predictive story from Arnold: of a Los Angeles fireman who loses his family to terrorism) was put back to 2002, by which time it had lost its potency in comparison to actual events. What was required of Arnold was a return to what had made him great – and useful – in the first place: his talent for endorsing the global interests of his adopted home by inhabiting roles that vibrated simultaneously on topical and mythical planes. 'We preach about values, democracy, human rights,' complained General Anthony Zinni, 'but we haven't convinced the American people to pony up . . . There's got to be the political will and support for these things.'[27] The *Terminator* star was preparing to 'pony up,' for one last battle, as the world-redeeming character that made his name; 'When troubles are dominant,' writes Eugen Weber, 'apocalypse is in the ascendant; should it be missing, people would begin to worry.'[28]

James Cameron, now preoccupied with diving on the wreck of *Titanic*, was not going to be involved in his friend's big comeback, which for several years looked as if it would never happen. The original *Terminator*'s production company, Carolco, had gone bankrupt in 1995, losing its chiefs Mario Kassar and Andrew Vajna the rights to the franchise. Spending the next few years re-acquiring the property from scattered investors and Cameron's former partner Gale Anne Hurd, who owned half, Kassar and Vajna finally created a new company, C-2 Pictures, specifically to bring *Terminator* back, with or without its designer. As Cameron tells it, he demurred from making a third instalment because, 'Working from someone else's script in a universe that I fucking originated held no appeal for me whatsoever.'[29] Enlisting in Cameron's place Jonathan Mostow, formerly in charge of *U-571* (2000) and *Breakdown* (1997), to direct, Arnold and his colleagues set about reviving his signature creation, while in the process laying to rest the ghosts of the previous decade's failures. 'There has been a hundred per cent "Want to see" with this movie and no negatives,' said Arnold, on the publicity trail.[30] For once, he was not exaggerating. Always readily (if sometimes abstractly) associated with apocalypses, holocausts and the remaking of history along American lines, 'Arnie' was slotting back into his natural place as the guardian of the future.

Terminator 3 (2003) opens with a familiarly apocalyptic image – a mushroom cloud enveloping a city – and a voiceover from John Connor (now played, due to Furlong's alleged drug problems, by Nick Stahl) reprising the last film's rumination: 'The future has not yet been written. There is no fate but what we make for ourselves.' But Connor is not so sure: 'I wish I could believe that,' he says, clearly a changed man who has been in the wilderness for some time, devoid of hope and, despite his experience of apparently stopping Judgement Day, quietly sure of the end-times' inevitability. A flash-forward shows Connor atop a hillock of broken machine parts, rallying his troops while a resistance general brandishes the Stars and Stripes, the flag ripped and burned by long exposure to firefights. This, or so the film proposes, is his Messianic destiny, as unstoppable as Arnold's eternally recurring masculinist whose glorious immunity to death and fear must inspire John to find his inner King.

Now in his early twenties and parentless (Sarah, we find out, died of leukaemia), Connor is living 'off the grid,' avoiding credit cards, phones and addresses in order to stop the machines tracking him down via electronic databases. 'I've erased all connections to the past. But as hard as I try, I can't erase my dreams . . . My nightmares.' And these nightmares, as we see, are of skeletal warriors marching over piles of human skulls. 'I feel the weight of the future bearing down on me – a future I don't want,' he says. He is going to have to be shown – by the father figure he knows surpasses all others, and who must continuously be sent back in time, by John, to shape his manhood – his responsibilities to lead with bravery and determination. For the nebulous enemy, John is aware, is gathering force under our feet and in our homes, waiting for the moment to strike upon a complacent world.

As before, a new model of terminator is sent to kill John. This time around, however, it is in the nubile shape of Kristanna Loken's flaxen fantasy for teenage boys (a key demographic, of course). Materialising in a boutique window, hence immediately soliciting scopophilic attention and hinting at a vacuous obsession with fashion and consumerist superficiality, the 'T-X' (or, as John puts it, the Terminatrix) is a sexist and exploitative remodelling of the T-1000. Inflating her breasts to distract a policeman who has stopped her for speeding ('I like your gun'), and targeting a well-dressed woman with an expensive sports car in order to steal her symbols of affluence, the T-X is hence set up as an aloof, shallow and sexually manipulative temptress in contrast to Arnold's old-fashioned renegade. 'She's the ultimate bitch,' said effects designer Stan Winston, a long-standing member of Arnold's boys' club. 'It was very easy to design her because I've been married for 30 years.'[31] The returned T-101 appears in the desert, the locus of manly endeavour and the wellspring of frontier renewal. He once more visits a bar, though this time a gay bar (in an acknowledgment of Arnold's always implicitly homo-erotic routines), and takes the stripper's leathers. Finding in the jacket a pair of star-shaped, disco-era sunglasses and trying them on, he rejects them, presumably for being a little too *outré* in design; upon stealing a car, he finds an appropriately butch pair, so as to look as reassuringly familiar as possible to both the spectator and John, who meanwhile is attempting to break into a vets' practice to procure drugs.

Without his mentor Arnold, John has become a weak-willed, drifting loser, working cash-in-hand at manual jobs whilst succumbing to self-pitying, pacifistic introspection. He doubts his fitness to lead the world yet worries about the aimlessness of his life without the warrior inside. The demons he needs to find his repressed soul haunt him, but above all he longs 'to renew ourselves in our own land,' via the apocalypse, and to realise his fate as the one, true embodiment of All-American fortitude, roused against the oppressor by a rude awakening from his 'holiday from history.' His future wife and general, Katherine Brewster (Claire Danes) is engaged to an unprepossessing, gentle 'girly man' about whose suitability she is having doubts. A sensitively inclined and pleasantly countenanced coastal professional, Scott is placed in symbolic opposition to Schwarzenegger's and the George W. Bush administration's thrusting rhetoric. Quite beyond hope of hawkish redemption and so destined to be absorbed and killed by Loken and her beguiling aura, Scott, with no self-defining demons to battle, will simply be assimilated. 'If you behave like a wimp,' Arnold once told the British magazine *Loaded*, 'then you're going to get stiffed, simple as that.'[32] There was no place for wimps in Arnold's post-2001 world, informed as it was by his attentiveness to the Republican cause. '[O]ur responsibility to history is already clear,' Bush intoned after 9/11: 'To answer these attacks and rid the world of evil.' As Bob Woodward comments, 'The President was casting his mission and that of the country in the grand vision of God's master plan.' We must, then, according to these precepts, be strong and look to vigorous anger to bolster our *selves* in the sight of God and Manifest Destiny, invoked to watch over Bush's destructive 'crusade' against insidious terror. 'It is said,' continued the proud 'war president,' 'that adversity introduces us to ourselves.'[33] For Bush, this was an accidentally brave admission; for John Connor, this is axiomatic.

In a passage likening America's armed forces to the Terminator, Niall Ferguson remarks that:

> In military confrontations, the United States has the capability to inflict amazing and appalling destruction, while sustaining only minimal damage to itself. There is no regime it could not terminate if it wanted to . . . What the Terminator is not programmed to do, however, is to rebuild. In his wake he leaves only destruction.[34]

As the war in Iraq dragged on into something approaching civil war, the President was having a hard time convincing the public that America must stay the course and rebuild the country, if only to exploit the trade advantage. 'The limits of American power,' concludes Ferguson, 'will be laid bare when the global Terminator finally admits, "I won't be back."'[35] Though it is ambivalent about the role of the military (after all, it is they, and chiefly Katherine's high-ranking father, who unwittingly bring about the nation's destruction), *Terminator 3* in essence implies that wars fought on the ground are traditional and therefore good, while wars fought remotely by machines are risky affairs. So long as we are vigilant, and keep 'humans in the loop' as individualist, dedicated warriors, then the cowards who have used our own technologies against us (including the illegitimately conceived, collectively conscious and hence un-American Skynet) will surely lose to the forces of inexorable free-market gigantism, as contained in the resurgent metaphor of Arnold's body. Finding John and rescuing him from the Terminatrix's wiles with no time to spare, the good Terminator makes himself known to his 'children.'

A looming, slow-motion avatar from the distant days of true men, the T-101 is a reminder not only of the first Gulf War and that campaign's regrettable truncation, but also of the need to finish a job, however long it may take and arduous it may seem. Twelve years have passed, but Schwarzenegger looks rejuvenated – *whole* – now fully atoned and reconciled with the dark paternal forces in his own life and three times born into ultimate fatherhood. It is obvious that Schwarzenegger, the bearer of the end and the beginning, has reconnected with his calling. 'It is time,' he says to John. 'You must live.'

After the film's most spectacular set-piece, a car chase involving Arnold getting hurled through various heavy obstacles to prove his resilience, the T-101, John and Kate remove themselves to the desert, where Arnold, in a joke calculated to stress the film's cognisance that it is a final bow for Arnold's action incarnation, says that he is 'an obsolete design.' Journeying to the supposed resting place of Sarah Connor, the T-101 reveals to his shocked charges a cache of weapons instead of a corpse, hidden there in accordance with Sarah's will. Halfway through the group's attempt to gather up the guns and flee, the police, who have been led there by the T-X posing as a now smirking Scott, besiege the mausoleum. Far from being obsolete in every respect, Arnold is here a template for masculinity striving to assert itself under crisis. John, reluctant to commit to the cause, has much to learn from Arnold's embattled stoic:

John: Leave me here, I'm not the one you want. You're wasting your time.

T-101: Incorrect. John Connor leads the resistance to victory.

John: How? Why? Why me?

T-101: You're John Connor.

John: Christ, Mum fed me that bullshit since the cradle. Look at me, I'm no leader, I never was . . .

T-101: *[lifting John by the throat]* You're right. You're not the one I want. I'm wasting my time.

John: Fuck you! You fucking machine!

T-101: *[letting John drop]* Better.

John: What, you were just dicking with me?

T-101: Anger is more useful than despair.

17. *'I'm back': Arnold returns for a last bow as the Terminator*
(*Terminator 3*)

'Basic psychology' being amongst his 'subroutines,' the T-101 provokes John into a moment of epiphanic truth. His passions must be roused if he is to be an effective man. It is impossible, the Terminator suggests, to fight wars with no conviction or a lack of emotional commitment; John must realise that, to become a warrior-hero himself, he has to find an all-consuming hatred of the enemy, even to the point of seeing the enemy in his surrogate father and coming to terms with it. This is a hard lesson, and perhaps one only an older Schwarzenegger could impart with authority. Of course, we are invited to laugh at the line, 'Anger is more useful than despair,' because Arnold's characters have always been so good at staunching emotion (as has Arnold himself) whilst taking up arms. It is, though, demonstrative of the T-101's function as a pedagogue, or a martial instructor instilling in a trainee the necessary impetus to risk his life and 'pony up' for the well-being of his own future troops. Going to war is agonising, and it involves sacrifice, but it is the duty of every American man to vanquish 'evil' from the earth, wherever it may hide, and whatever form it may take. When Arnold told GIs serving in Iraq, in 2004, that 'you are the real terminators,'[36] he was flattering them beyond sense; they can indeed be made to feel hate, but they will also feel pain. They know how to cry.

The unfeeling efficiency of the machines, a primal life force of one mind that is not afraid of expending soldiers, represents the antithesis of John's nature, which he must be coerced into appreciating and using. Akin to biology in its basest form, Skynet will take over the world because it does not see individuals, only the chance to spread its consciousness;

America must defend itself, or its 'IDEA,' against encroaching, silent dangers, and it is Arnold – gone against his 'programming' to start anew as a fighter for freedom – who in his most successful films unendingly exemplifies this struggle. Arnold's skeleton, his inner core, is of the machines – of the 'tirelessly forward-striving' Teutons whose ideals he cannot help signifying – but he is also an American, one of 'us,' bringing the repressed back to life to fight on the side of Freedom against 'them.' Again, the T-101 disables the assembled police without hurting them: he has become exemplary of the Bush (Senior and Junior) mindset, trained to kill only those Others not attuned to the West's outlook. As every flag-draped coffin shipped home was an embarrassment to the White House, every infliction of 'collateral damage' or 'friendly fire' is abhorrent to the upgraded Terminator.

Kate grieves over her fiancée, but is offered scant consolation from John, who, having seen the light, clearly understands Scott's uselessness to the fight: 'Look, I know this won't help, but sometimes things happen that you just can't change.' Scott was a casualty not of war but of his own redundancy in the changing scheme of things. A civilian unwilling to take up the sword, or get angry, he has been brushed aside to make way for John Connor's nascent plans. 'Are you sure, about me and her?' asks John of the T-101, now revealing more about Schwarzenegger's peccadillos than those of the robot: 'Your confusion is not rational. She's a healthy female of breeding age.' 'I think there's a little bit more to it than that!' he replies. 'My database does not encompass the dynamics of human pair-bonding,' says Arnold, in *Terminator 3* willing to concede not only his apparent obsolescence, but also his one-time promiscuity and career-long difficulty with cinematic romance. The two things the immortal father can never teach the son, it would seem, are how to love women for anything other than their bodies, or how to live beyond the shadow of mortality ('Humans inevitably die'). As the trio makes its way to the military research centre at which Kate's father works, to try and stop the T-X killing him before he can deactivate the autonomous weapons system that will instigate the war, Arnold tells John and Kate (whose orders he must obey) that it is he (or a similar model) who will eventually kill the resistance leader. 'John Connor was terminated on July 4, 2032. I was selected for the emotional attachment he felt towards my model number, due to his boyhood experiences. This aided in my infiltration. I killed you.' The tragedy is inescapable: only the father,

Arnold, can and will be reborn to serve again; though we will presumably never see the event of John's death, it highlights the T-101's meaningful endurance across time as an everlasting power to which mortals can only aspire. Whilst John and Kate share a light-hearted moment, the T-101 brings things back to the topic of human temporality: 'Your levity is good. It relieves tension, and the fear of death,' a statement that is a useful summation of another aspect of Arnold's career coming to an end in *Terminator 3*: the inflection of deadly violence with a paradoxical humour, as if everything fearful or hated can be diminished by Arnold's levity.

Indeed, we are reminded throughout of Schwarzenegger's career motifs, which are replayed and commented upon – although often merely with a detached reverence – repeatedly. Misogyny, something we have seen often in Arnold's *oeuvre*, is spectacularly conveyed during the film's prolonged confrontations between the T-X and the T-101. Stopping to check her reflection in a mirror, the T-X is ambushed by Arnold, who then slams her head repeatedly into a toilet; at one point, while the T-101 is injured, she uses her electronic capabilities (for which read feminine cunning) to re-programme Arnold to kill John Connor, an instruction he eventually, and impossibly, disobeys; and the *coup de grâce*, administered by Arnold (no mercy can be shown here), involves thrusting his ruptured power-cell into her mouth with the words, 'You're terminated.' ('Just die, you bitch!' shouts Kate, not immune to the temptation to demonise the T-X for being a woman.) Schwarzenegger, of course, enjoyed every second of humiliating his nemesis. 'I saw this toilet bowl. How many times do you get away with this – to take a woman, grab her upside down, and bury her face in a toilet bowl?'[37] How many times indeed, with a mind on political office.

The film's downbeat yet politically loaded conclusion underlines and forwards a perpetual need for John's American spirit and Arnold's resurrected mentor, here making his final, grandiose stand. Taken to a governmental fall-out bunker buried deep in the Sierra mountains, Kate and John find themselves unwittingly at the safest place around: a structure that appears to have been disused since the 1960s, and so one not online or plugged in to modern defence systems. They are, somewhat analogously to the Taliban, holed up in a cave to fight a war against aggressors, a last white hope for humanity in the long years of occupation that lie ahead. Nuclear explosions purge the earth of the weak and the lame, flattening dirty metropolises into one, big, character-building wilderness. Drawing down the curtain on Arnold's Hollywood career and a civilisation out of touch with the life-giving need to crush its enemies and see them driven before it, the end, and the beginning, are finally reached. Bidding farewell to John as he martyrs himself yet again, though perhaps now for the last time (at least in cinematic terms), the Terminator, the father, the eternal masculine, the warrior, the hero whose journey is almost complete – 'Arnie' – surrenders to the void. 'We'll meet again,' he says, by way of a goodbye, and it is hard not to believe him.

Epilogue
The Little Boy From Thal

You can call it mysticism if you want to, but I have always believed that there was some divine plan that placed this great continent between two oceans to be sought out by those who were possessed of an abiding love of freedom.[1]

It has been said that a leader is someone who discerned the inevitable and got in front of it.[2]

Terminator 3 was Arnold's biggest success in twelve years – his biggest success, in fact, since *Terminator 2*. Financially speaking, it was a fitting capstone to an often-remarkable film career that only in its tertiary decade began to tarnish. Critically, Mostow's belated revival of Arnold's cyborg attracted praise both for its well-staged action and its tongue-in-cheek portrayal of Arnold as an amiably monolithic old trooper whose notoriety had latterly outshone his talents. More importantly, the third *Terminator* represented a return to what Arnold does so well: packaging himself for contemporary popular consumption in the clothes of eternal myths, which cling to his off-screen persona and life seemingly as closely as they do to his uniquely continuous pro-filmic personality. From his lowly birth, call to adventure, fantastic voyages and quest for the father, to his ordeals, atonement with the father and final return to the real world with his gifts, Arnold is the consummate hero, now come 'home' to occupy the rightful headship of his kingdom.

As we have seen, Arnold's and America's narratives are inexorably intertwined; his superlative gift to American society – as the great bearer of culture he undoubtedly is – has been to help the United States come to terms with its own, flawed saga. It is thus reasonable to speculate, given the frequency with which Arnold is discussed in such terms, that Schwarzenegger understands the power and purpose of myth better than most of his contemporaries; not, in all likelihood, as a scholar of myth might, but in an intuitive way that has always guided his life, his film choices and his ambitions. He has always seen from afar his peculiar destiny, and that destiny's place in the world of human longing, an acuity that has allowed him to remain hugely famous and admired when others in a similar position have singularly disappeared. There is something of the mystical about Arnold's charm, as he has always sensed; without doubt, he sees his glorious life as an opportunity to help others less endowed (provided they share his perspective), but also as a chance to impose his pre-ordained rule upon the far-off land of dreams he made his own. 'I am your warrior,'[3] he told a crowd in Sacramento, betraying a far better grasp of what he truly means than those critics who would dismiss him as an 'unpronouceable dolt'[4] who got lucky. 'The fact remains,' aver Philip John Davies and Paul Wells, 'that the politics of the most powerful nation in the world cannot be divorced from the most far-reaching entertainment in the world.'[5] Straddling both worlds and working in the service of an idea, Arnold knew he and the movies were a natural fit.

Newly elected to the office of Governor of California, the Austrian Oak was sworn in on 17 November 2003, on the capitol's west steps. He had indeed, as many predicted, entered party politics – a logical next step after years of operating on the fringes of power and courting political celebrity. Perhaps only in California, a 'Land of Cockaigne'[6] set apart from the rest of North America by its status as a legendary outer limit of infinite opportunity, could Arnold have ascended the throne. He holds court over what he described as 'the absolute combination of everything I was looking for,'[7] a kingdom of fantasy and contradiction that can accommodate the balancing of big-tent policies with Arnold's own brand of oddly progressive strategies (but then, could Arnold, the ultimate individualist, ever be on the ticket of a major party for anything other than expediency's sake?). What matters, though, is that this once insecure child, brought up in the backwaters of Europe, shaped his own dreams in harmony with the aspirations of others. Believing self-advancing 'market fundamentalism' to be the best means of pursuing the common interest, he looked at the future, saw it was American, and, with a smile and an indefatigable personality capable of crushing all opposition, made that future swirl around him. Those who were not capable of attaining primacy on a par with Arnold, a living example of social Darwinism's cruel reality, learned the hard way that competition, not cooperation, was at the heart of Schwarzenegger's vision.

After all this, what next? There is speculation, based largely on the assumption that his ambition knows no bounds, that Arnold will follow Ronald Reagan in another respect and make a bid for the presidency.[8] This, however, seems unfeasible given the need for an amendment to the Constitution allowing foreign-born nationals this right – a difficult process to implement if essentially for the advancement of one man. As of mid-2008, Schwarzenegger's Hollywood career remains on hold while he continues to manage one of the world's largest economies; a comeback of sorts seems not unlikely, if he can choose roles that compliment his physical maturity whilst allowing him to function in his particular *oeuvre*. Mankind, we can be sure, will always need heroes of his ilk, creating for them adventures suited to the requirements of the times. In one shape or form, in this life or the next, 'Arnie,' when we really need him, will be back, the original collapsed into the receding, converging chronicles of folklore and legend as they are studied in distant millennia. It seems fitting, therefore, to bring this study to a close with a beginning of sorts, and the recollections of its subject:

> Call me Arnold . . . When I was ten years old, I had the dream of being the best in the world at something. When I was fifteen, I had a dream that I wanted to be the best body builder in the world and the most muscular man. It was not only a dream I dreamed at night. It was also a daydream.[9]

But, it seems overly generous to give a man so used to having the last word yet another finality. In consequence, I shall let T.E. Lawrence respond:

> All people dream: but not equally.
> Those who dream by night

in the dusty recesses of their minds
wake in the day to find that it was vanity.
But the dreamers of the day
are dangerous men,
for they may act their dream with open eyes
to make it possible.[10]

Notes

Introduction

1 Ronald Reagan, in his acceptance speech to the 1980 Republican National Convention, quoted in John Ehrman, 2005: *The Eighties: America in the Age of Reagan*, New Haven, Yale University Press, p. 84.

2 Arnold Schwarzenegger and Douglas Kent Hall, 1977/1994: *The Education of a Bodybuilder*, New York, Simon & Schuster, pp. 42, 34, 66–7.

3 See Michael Blitz and Louise Krasniewicz, 2004: *Why Arnold Matters: The Rise of a Cultural Icon*, New York, Basic Books.

4 Nigel Andrews, 2004: *True Myths: The Life and Times of Arnold Schwarzenegger, from* Pumping Iron *to Governor of California*, New York, Bloomsbury, p. 93.

5 'However much his career may be stalling,' notes Simon During, Schwarzenegger 'remains a unique phenomenon [and] the most popular movie star during the period in which the contemporary global popular emerged.' See During, 'Popular Culture on a Global Scale: A Challenge for Cultural Studies?,' in *Critical Inquiry* 23:4, summer 1997, p. 809.

6 Quoted in Richard Dyer, 1998: *Stars* (new edition), London, BFI, p. 6.

7 See especially John L. Flynn, 1993: *The Films of Arnold Schwarzenegger*, New York, Citadel; and Arian Wright, 1994: *Arnold Schwarzenegger: A Life on Film*, London, Hale.

8 Blitz and Krasniewicz, *Why Arnold Matters*, p. 36.

9 'The Culture Industry: Enlightenment as Mass Deception,' in Theodor W. Adorno and Max Horkheimer, 1944/1997: *Dialectic of Enlightenment* (trans. John Cumming), London, Verso, p. 148.

10 Alexander Walker, 1970: *Stardom: The Hollywood Phenomenon*, London, Michael Joseph, p. xi.

11 Walter Hill quoted in Wendy Leigh, 1990: *Arnold: An Unauthorized Biography*, Chicago, Condon & Weed, p. 256.

12 John Berger, 1972: *Ways of Seeing*, Harmondsworth, Penguin, p. 88.

13 See Joseph McBride, 2003: *Searching for John Ford: A Life*, New York, St Martin's Griffin, p. 11.

14 Leigh, *Arnold*, p. 89.

15 'This is a land in which foreigners who respect the laws are welcomed as contributors to American culture, not feared as threats. The United States has been strengthened by generations of immigrants who became

Americans through patience, hard work, and assimilation. Like generations of immigrants that have come before them, every new citizen has an obligation to learn this Nation's customs and values. At the same time, America will fulfill its obligation to give each citizen a chance to realize the American dream.' President George W. Bush's 'Strategy for Comprehensive Immigration Reform,' 2005, online at: http://www.whitehouse.gov/infocus/immigration, accessed on 16 January 2006.

16 'The Culture Industry: Enlightenment as Mass Deception,' in Adorno and Horkheimer, *Dialectic of Enlightenment*, p. 147.

17 Laurence Leamer, 2005: *Fantastic: The Life of Arnold Schwarzenegger*, London, St Martin's Press, p. 174.

18 Quoted in Studs Terkel, 1980/1985: *American Dreams: Lost and Found*, London, Paladin, p. 168.

19 Quoted in Leamer, *Fantastic*, p. 177.

20 Robin Wood, 'Ideology, Genre, Auteur,' in Barry Keith Grant (ed.), 1995: *Film Genre Reader II*, Austin, University of Texas Press, p. 66.

21 Stephen Prince, 1992: *Visions of Empire: Political Imagery in Contemporary American Film*, New York, Praeger, p. 7.

22 Janice Hocker Rushing and Thomas S. Frentz, 1995: *Projecting the Shadow: The Cyborg Hero in American Film*, Chicago, University of Chicago Press, p. 47.

23 Christopher Booker, 2004: *The Seven Basic Plots: Why We Tell Stories*, London, Continuum, p. 69.

24 Saul Friedlander, 1993: *Reflections of Nazism: An Essay on Kitsch and Death*, Bloomington and Indianapolis, Indiana University Press, p. 49.

25 *Ibid.*, p. 47.

26 Joseph Campbell, 1949/1973: *The Hero with a Thousand Faces*, Princeton, Princeton University Press, p. 4.

27 V.G. Kiernan, 1978: *America: The New Imperialism, from White Settlement to World Hegemony*, London, Zed, p. 206.

Chapter 1

1 *Beowulf: A Verse Translation* (trans. Michael Alexander, 1973), Harmondsworth, Penguin, p. 59. 'For what is "Beowulf,"' argues Ken Tucker, 'if not an Arnold Schwarzenegger prototype flick?' ('"Beowulf" is So Now it Could Open in a Cineplex,' in the *New York Times*, 13 July 1997, p. H5.)

2 The 'anti-fan,' quoted in Andrews, *True Myths*, p. 222.

3 Schwarzenegger quoted in *ibid.*, p. 20.

4 Schwarzenegger and Kent Hall, *The Education of a Bodybuilder*, p. 17.

5 Arnold Schwarzenegger, 1998: *The New Encyclopedia of Modern Bodybuilding: The Bible of Bodybuilding, Fully Updated and Revised*, New York, Fireside, p. 18.

6 Campbell, *The Hero with a Thousand Faces*, p. 55.

7   Andrews, *True Myths*, p. 21.
8   Leamer, *Fantastic*, p. 12.
9   Quoted in Paul Kennedy, 1989: *The Rise and Fall of the Great Powers*, New York, Vintage, p. 360.
10 Andrews, *True Myths*, p. 21.
11 The 'common theme' of the 1958 Milan Samples Fair, quoted in Victoria de Grazia, 2005: *Irresistible Empire: America's Advance through 20th-Century Europe*, Cambridge, MA, Belknap/Harvard, p. 453.
12 Dick Tyler quoted in Leigh, *Arnold*, p. 87.
13 See Mark Mazower, 1999: *Dark Continent: Europe's Twentieth Century*, London, Penguin, pp. 77–8.
14 Knight Dunlap, 'The Great Aryan Myth,' in *The Scientific Monthly* 59:4, October 1944, p. 296. Dunlap's language in this article is, perhaps understandably given the year of writing, rather fervent; nonetheless, it is a cogent indictment of the Nazis' propagandising appropriation of national folklore in the 1930s–1940s.
15 Mazower, *Dark Continent*, pp. xiii–xiv.
16 Antonia Fraser (ed.), 1980: *Heroes and Heroines*, London, Weidenfeld and Nicolson, p. 14.
17 Quoted in Bill Bryson, 1994/1998: *Made in America*, London, Black Swan, p. 178. In the first half of the twentieth century, over 60,000 Americans – usually minority members, the poor and the illiterate – were forcibly sterilised to eradicate supposedly deficient genes. See Stefan Kühl, 1994: *The Nazi Connection: Eugenics, American Racism, and German National Socialism*, New York, Oxford University Press.
18 See Sontag, 'Fascinating Fascism,' reprinted in Susan Sontag, 1980: *Under the Sign of Saturn*, New York, Farrar Straus & Giroux, pp. 73–105.
19 'There's an obvious overlap of Fascist and Socialist Realist styles with the corporate heroic style in the art of the [Rockefeller] center; it has often been noted that the face of Lee Lawrie's 'Atlas' in front of the International Building looks a lot like Mussolini, while muscle-bound heroic workers led to a picture of Lenin. Competing systems come to look alike.' See Adam Gopnik, 'Higher and Higher: What Tall Buildings Do,' online at: http://www.newyorker.com/critics/books/?031215crbo_books, accessed on 23 February 2006.
20 J. Hoberman, 'Nietzsche's Boy,' in José Arroyo (ed.), 2001: *Action/Spectacle Cinema: A Sight & Sound Reader*, London, BFI, p. 32. Emphasis added.
21 Thilo von Trotha, 'Der Heros des Deutschtums,' in *Die völkische Kunst*, 1934, p. 5.
22 Quoted in Kühl, *The Nazi Connection*, p. 17.
23 Quoted in Charles Gaines and George Butler, 1977/1986: *Pumping Iron: The Art and Sport of Bodybuilding*, London, Sphere, p. 128.
24 Advertisement for the New American Physique Chest Developer, featured in *The Incredible Hulk Annual 1976*, New York, Marvel Comics Group, p. 4.

25 See the official National Park Service website at http://www.nps.gov/whho/ PPSth/boysctmem, accessed on 21/02/06.

26 Quoted in Leigh, *Arnold*, p. 88.

27 Although, cautions Kevin White, 'There is no question that Burroughs's work is deeply embedded with the early twentieth-century discourse of Anglo-Saxon/white racial superiority.' Review of John F. Kasson's *Houdini, Tarzan and the Perfect Man,* in *Journal of Social History* 36:3, 2003, p. 796.

28 Keith Ansell-Pearson, 'Who is the *Übermensch*? Time, Truth, and Woman in Nietzsche,' in *Journal of the History of Ideas* 53:2, April–June 1992, p. 326.

29 Leigh, *Arnold*, p. 19.

30 Friedrich Nietzsche, 1887/1974: *The Gay Science: With a Prelude in Rhymes and an Appendix of Songs* (trans. W. Kaufmann), New York, Vintage, p. 36. See also p. 226: 'Sitting in moral judgement should offend our taste. Let us leave such chatter and such bad taste to those who have nothing else to do but to drag the past a few steps further through time and who never live in the present . . . We, however, want to become those who are – the ones who are new, unique, and incomparable, who give themselves laws, who create themselves.'

31 Schwarzenegger in Leigh, *Arnold*, p. 42.

32 Schwarzenegger and Kent Hall, *The Education of a Bodybuilder*, p. 19.

33 See Susan Jeffords, 1993: *Hard Bodies: Hollywood Masculinity in the Reagan Era*, Brunswick, NJ, Rutgers University Press, p. 24.

34 Peter Adam, 1992: *Art of the Third Reich*, New York, Harry N. Abrams, p. 178. Emphasis added.

35 Blitz and Krasniewicz, *Why Arnold Matters*, p. 167.

36 Jerry Siegel and Joe Shuster, 1934/1939: *The Superman Newspaper Adventures*, online at: http://superman.ws/tales2/adventurestrip/?page=1, accessed on 12 Febraury 2006.

37 Quoted in Chester Wilmot, 1997: *The Struggle for Europe*, Ware, Wordsworth Editions, p. 706.

38 Samuel P. Huntington, 2004: *Who Are We? America's Great Debate*, London, The Free Press, p. 117.

39 Hoberman, 'Nietzsche's Boy,' in Arroyo (ed.), *Action/Spectacle Cinema*, p. 29.

40 Fraser (ed.), *Heroes and Heroines*, pp. 14–15.

41 Campbell, *The Hero with a Thousand Faces*, p. 44.

42 Howard A. Zinn, 1980: *A People's History of the United States*, New York, HarperCollins, p. 416.

43 Schwarzenegger and Kent Hall, *The Education of a Bodybuilder*, p. 59.

44 See Leamer, *Fantastic*, p. 80.

45 Roland Barthes, 1957/2000: *Mythologies*, London, Vintage, p. 20.

46 Hans-Jürgen Syberberg, 1977: *Hitler, a Film from Germany* (trans. Joachim Neugroschel), New York, Farrar, Strauss & Giroux, p. 61.

47 Andrews, *True Myths*, p. 36.

48   Bernard Rudofsky, 1971: *The Unfashionable Human Body*, New York, Doubleday, p. 52.

49   Kenneth R. Dutton, 1995: *The Perfectible Body: The Western Ideal of Physical Development*, London, Cassell, p. 43.

50   John Boardman, 1996: *Greek Art* (fourth edition), London, Thames & Hudson, p. 158.

51   Andrews, *True Myths*, p. 38.

52   The character of Pretzie in *Hercules in New York* bears comparison to Dustin Hoffman's Ratso Rizzo in John Schelsinger's 1969 film.

53   Quoted in Flynn, *Arnold Schwarzenegger*, p. 39.

54   Mosse quoted in Uli Linke, 1999: *German Bodies: Race and Representation After Hitler*, London, Routledge, pp. 48–9.

55   See John Micklethwait and Adrian Wooldridge, 2005: *The Right Nation: Why America is Different*, London, Penguin, p. 330.

56   The montage style suggests a half-hearted tribute to Sergei Eisenstein.

57   Peary quoted in Wright, *Arnold Schwarzenegger*, p. 38.

58   Jon Solomon, 2001: *The Ancient World in the Cinema*, New Haven, Yale University Press, p. 314.

59   Friedrich Wilhelm Heinz quoted in Klaus Theweleit, 1989: *Male Fantasies, Volume 2: Psychoanalysing the White Terror*, Cambridge, Polity, p. 13.

60   See Neil Baldwin, 2001: *Henry Ford and the Jews: The Mass Production of Hate*, Cambridge, MA, Public Affairs, p. 80.

61   White, review of *Houdini, Tarzan and the Perfect Man*, in *Journal of Social History* 36:3, p. 796.

62   Quoted in Maurice Isserman and Michael Kazin, 2000: *America Divided: The Civil War of the 1960s*, New York, Oxford University Press, p. 261.

63   Michael Senior, 'The Age of Myth and Legend,' in Fraser (ed.), *Heroes and Heroines*, p. 20.

64   Daniel Jonah Goldhagen, 1997: *Hitler's Willing Executioners: Ordinary Germans and the Holocaust*, London, Abacus, p. 77.

65   See Erik Barnouw, 1993: *Documentary: A History of the Non-Fiction Film* (second revised edition), New York, Oxford University Press, p. 110. As State Excellency Dr Theodor Lewald exclaimed in a quasi-historical speech before the 1936 Games in Berlin, the Olympic torch represented, for the National Socialists, 'a real and spiritual bond between our German fatherland and the sacred places of Greece founded nearly 4,000 years ago by Nordic immigrants.' Quoted in Guy Walters, 2006: *Berlin Games: How Hitler Stole the Olympic Dream*, London, John Murray, p. 193.

66   Martin Flanagan, 'The Chronotope in Action,' in Yvonne Tasker (ed.), 2004: *Action and Adventure Cinema*, London, Routledge, p. 114.

67   Quoted in Steve Neale, 'Action-Adventure as Hollywood Genre,' in *ibid.*, p. 72.

68   Joseph L. Henderson, 'Ancient Myths and Modern Man,' in Carl Jung (ed.), 1964/1978: *Man and his Symbols*, London, Picador, p. 101.

69 Leroy G. Dorsey and Rachel M. Harlow, '"We Want Americans Pure and Simple": Theodore Roosevelt and the Myth of Americanism', in *Rhetoric and Public Affairs* 6:1, spring 2003, p. 65.

70 See Micklethwait and Wooldridge, *The Right Nation*, p. 235.

71 Burgin et al., 'Video Replay: Families, Films and Fantasy,' in Victor Burgin, James Donald and Cora Kaplan (eds), 1986: *Formations of Fantasy*, London, Methuen, p. 172.

72 Max Weber quoted in Dyer, *Stars*, p. 30.

73 *Ibid.*, p. 135.

74 Within the filmic narrative, this return fits with the Campbellian archetype; it might be said that Hercules's 'boon' to Olympus is the gift of fun, and specifically to his father, who subsequently copies Hercules's flight to Earth.

75 Michael Billington, for the *Illustrated London News*, wrote that *The Long Goodbye* was 'a spit in the eye to a great writer.' For both quotes see Flynn, *The Films of Arnold Schwarzenegger*, p. 29.

76 C. Vann Woodward, 1993: *The Burden of Southern History* (third edition), Baton Rouge, LA, Louisiana State University Press, p. 19.

77 Quoted in Leigh, *Arnold*, p. 133.

78 *Ibid.*, p. 136.

79 As Samuel P. Huntington writes, 'Identities are imagined selves: they are what we think we are and what we want to be.' See Huntington, *Who Are We?*, p. 23.

80 Joseph Goebbels quoted in Theweleit, *Male Fantasies*, p. 237.

81 Friedrich Nietzsche, 1896/2004: *Twilight of the Idols and the Antichrist* (trans. Thomas Common), Dover, Mineola, NY, p. 66.

82 Rafelson quoted in Schwarzenegger and Kent Hall, *The Education of a Bodybuilder*, p. 30.

83 Wright, *Arnold Schwarzenegger*, p. 46.

84 Rafelson quoting Schwarzenegger in the Director's Introduction to the 2004 MGM DVD re-release of *Stay Hungry*. The filmmaker also claims herein that Schwarzenegger told him, in 1975, that he would one day be governor of California.

85 See Robert Dallek, 2004: *John F. Kennedy: An Unfinished Life*, London, Penguin, pp. 594–5.

86 See Rafelson, Director's Commentary.

87 Bill Bryson, 1989/1999: *The Lost Continent: Travels in Small Town America*, London, Black Swan, p. 73. The *Smokey and the Bandit* series, also starring Sally Field, is one notable exception.

88 President Gerald R. Ford, 1974: 'Pardoning Richard Nixon,' online at: http://www.historyplace.com/speeches/ford.htm, accessed on 23 March 2006.

89 Quoted in Bob Woodward, 1999: *Shadow: Five Presidents and the Legacy of Watergate*, New York, Simon & Schuster, p. 43.

90 Jimmy Carter, 1977: *A Government as Good as Its People*, New York, Simon & Schuster, p. 128. Emphases added.

91 See C. Vann Woodward, 1955/2002: *The Strange Career of Jim Crow*, New York, Oxford University Press, p. 176.

92 James C. Cobb, 2005: *Away Down South: A History of Southern Identity*, New York, Oxford University Press, p. 305.

93 *Ibid.*, p. 303.

94 Thomas Carlyle, 1843/1998: *Past and Present*, Whitefish, MT, R.A. Kessinger, p. 37.

95 Quoted in Dyer, *Stars*, p. 22.

96 *Ibid.*

97 Rafelson, Director's Commentary.

98 Blitz and Krasniewicz, *Why Arnold Matters*, p. 116.

99 Quoted in Pauline Maier et al., 2003: *Inventing America: A History of the United States*, New York, W.W. Norton, p. 984.

100 *Ibid.*

101 Quoted in Tom Shone, 2004: *Blockbuster: How Hollywood Learned to Stop Worrying and Love the Summer*, New York, Free Press, p. 23.

102 Joseph Campbell with Bill Moyers, 1991: *The Power of Myth*, New York, Anchor, p. 163.

103 Ralph Stevenson and Guy Phelps, 1990: *The Cinema as Art* (revised edition), London, Penguin, p. 230. Emphasis added.

104 For a discussion of narrative 'incoherence' (or cross-purposes) within the New Hollywood, see Robin Wood, 1986: *Hollywood from Vietnam to Reagan*, New York, Columbia University Press, pp. 46–69.

105 Wood, *Hollywood from Vietnam to Reagan*, pp. 270–1.

106 Theweleit, *Male Fantasies*, p. 108.

107 Dick Tyler, 2004: *West Coast Bodybuilding Scene: The Golden Era*, Aptos, CA, On Target, p. 147.

108 Gaines and Butler, *Pumping Iron*, pp. 22, 96, 24. Emphasis is as in original text.

109 *Ibid.*, p. 8.

110 Maier et al., *Inventing America*, p. 1008.

111 Christopher Lasch, in *The Culture of Narcissism: American Life in an Age of Diminishing Expectations* (1979: New York, Warner, p. 201), contended that 1970s America was dominated by personality types he described as 'excessively self-conscious,' 'constantly searching for flaws and signs of decay,' and 'haunted by fantasies . . . of eternal youth.'

112 Marla Matzer Rose, 2001: *Muscle Beach: Where the Best Bodies in the World Started a Fitness Revolution*, New York, LA Weekly Books, p. 138.

113 Yvonne Tasker, 1993: *Spectacular Bodies: Gender, Genre and the Action Cinema*, London, Routledge, p. 78.

114 Samuel W. Fussell, 1991: *Muscle: Confessions of an Unlikely Bodybuilder*, New York, Avon, p. 24.

115 Erich Fromm, 1941: *Escape from Freedom*, New York, Holt, Rinehard and Winston, p. 203.

116 Barbara Creed quoted in Yvonne Tasker, 'Dumb Movies for Dumb People: Masculinity, the Body, and the Voice in Contemporary Action Cinema,' in Steven Cohan and Ina Rae Hark (eds), 1993: *Screening the Male: Exploring Masculinities in Hollywood Cinema*, London, Routledge, p. 232.

117 Christine Anne Holmlund, 'Visible Difference and Flex Appeal: the Body, Sex, Sexuality and Race in the *Pumping Iron* Films,' in *Cinema Journal* 28:4, summer 1989, p. 47.

118 Leamer, *Fantastic*, p. 106.

119 *Ibid.*, p. 107.

120 *Ibid.*

121 Holmlund, 'Visible Difference and Flex Appeal,' in *Cinema Journal* 28:4, p. 44.

122 Leigh, *Arnold*, p. 141.

123 Leamer, *Fantastic*, p. 106.

124 The mythical trickster is a transitory, juvenile character whose 'physical appetites dominate his behaviour. Lacking any sense of purpose beyond the gratification of his primary needs, he is cruel, cynical, unfeeling.' See Henderson, 'Ancient Myths and Modern Man,' in Jung (ed.), *Man and his Symbols*, pp. 103–4.

125 *Ibid.*, p. 109.

126 Alexander Eliot, 1990: *The Universal Myths: Heroes, Gods, Tricksters and Others*, New York, Truman Talley, p. 154.

127 Henderson, 'Ancient Myths and Modern Man,' in Jung (ed.), *Man and his Symbols*, p. 104.

128 Eliot, *The Universal Myths*, p. 81.

129 Leigh, *Arnold*, p. 143.

130 *Ibid.*, p. 144.

131 *Ibid.*, p. 145.

132 Gary Arnold, '*Pumping Iron*: A Witty Psych-Out by Mr Olympia,' in the *Washington Post*, 19 February 1977, p. B1.

133 In these years flanked by significant roles, Arnold featured in Hal Needham's *The Villain* (1979), as Handsome Stranger, and the made-for-television – and rapidly forgotten – *The Jayne Mansfield Story* (Alan Landsburg, 1981), as Mickey Hargitay. Both appearances evince competence and appeal, yet both do Schwarzenegger no favours in the way of enhancing his mythos, relegated as he is in favour of co-stars not here at their best.

134 Many others have outlined the birth, blossoming and supposed decline of the New Hollywood. See, for example, Geoff King, 2002: *New Hollywood Cinema: An Introduction*, London, I.B.Tauris.

Chapter II

1   Campbell, *The Hero with a Thousand Faces*, p. 321.
2   John Milius speaking in 'Iron and Beyond,' a short documentary included on the 2004 Warner DVD re-release of *Pumping Iron*.
3   Zinn, *A People's History of the United States*, p. 574.
4   Andrew Sinclair, 1999: *A Concise History of the United States*, Stroud, Sutton, p. 200.
5   Quoted in Maier et al., *Inventing America*, p. 1010.
6   Ehrman, *The Eighties*, p. 74.
7   Quoted in *ibid.*, p. 75.
8   Maier et al., *Inventing America*, p. 1008.
9   Ronald Reagan, 1989: *Speaking My Mind*, New York, Simon & Schuster, p. 60.
10 Tim Raphael, 'The King is a Thing: Bodies and Memory in the Age of Reagan,' in *TDR* 43:1, spring 1999, p. 56.
11 Brian Massumi and Kenneth Dean quoted in *ibid.*, p. 49.
12 Ronald Reagan, 1990: *An American Life*, New York, Simon & Schuster, p. 591.
13 Andrews, *True Myths*, p. 86.
14 Quoted in Michael Schaller, 2007: *Right Turn: American Life in the Reagan–Bush Era*, New York, Oxford University Press, p. 78.
15 See Diane Rubenstein, 'The Mirror of Reproduction: Baudrillard and Reagan's America,' in *Political Theory* 17:4, November 1989, p. 589.
16 Campbell, *The Hero with a Thousand Faces*, p. 109.
17 Thomas Frank, 2005: *What's the Matter with America?: The Resistible Rise of the American Right*, London, Vintage, p. 146.
18 See David C. Smith, 'A Critical Appreciation of John Milius's *Conan the Barbarian*,' in *Bocere* 1:3–2:1, August 1995–April 1996, available online at: www.barbariankeep.com/ctbds.html, accessed on 4 May 2006.
19 The actual aphorism reads something like: 'From the military school of life: What does not kill me, strengthens me.' Nietzsche, *Twilight of the Idols and The Antichrist* (trans. Thomas Common), p. 3.
20 Quoted in Leamer, *Fantastic*, p. 143.
21 *Ibid.*, p. 131.
22 Smith, 'A Critical Appreciation of John Milius's *Conan the Barbarian*,' online at: www.barbariankeep.com/ctbds.html.
23 Quoted in Leigh, *Arnold*, p. 193.
24 See Joel Porte (ed.), 1982: *Emerson in his Journals*, Cambridge, MA, Belknap Press, p. 81.
25 C.G. Jung, 'Approaching the Unconscious,' in Jung (ed.), *Man and his Symbols*, p. 73.
26 Campbell, *The Hero with a Thousand Faces*, p. 121.
27 Kirby Farrell, 'The Berserk Style in American Culture,' in *Cultural Critique* 46, autumn 2000, p. 186.

28 Noam Chomsky, 2004: *Hegemony or Survival: America's Quest for Global Dominance*, London, Penguin, p. 116.

29 http://en.wikipedia.org/wiki/Foreign_Interventions_of_the_Reagan_Administration, accessed on 5 June 2006.

30 John Milius interviewed online at: http://www.nypress.com/print.cfm?content_id=9373, accessed on 5 May 2006.

31 'Big Loud Action Pictures,' writes Larry Gross, 'make up an enormous percentage of those films that gross over $200 million in the United States, and go on to make five times that in foreign and ancillary markets.' ('Big and Loud,' in Arroyo (ed.), *Action/Spectacle Cinema*, p. 3.)

32 James F. Iaccino, 1998: *Jungian Reflections within the Cinema: A Psychological Analysis of Sci-Fi and Fantasy Archetypes*, Westport, CT, Praeger, p. 6.

33 Michael Rogin in Bruce Miroff, 'Ronald Reagan and American Political Culture,' in *Polity* 20:3, spring 1988, p. 547.

34 Whilst dining with black GOP senator Edward Brooke, Reagan apparently joked that in Africa, 'when they have a man for lunch, they really have a man for lunch.' Quoted in Schaller, *Right Turn*, p. 132.

35 Volkan and the Committee on International Relations quoted in Huntington, *Who Are We?*, pp. 26–7.

36 Reagan, *An American Life*, p. 346. Emphasis added.

37 Milius in the Director's Commentary accompanying the 2002 Twentieth Century Fox DVD re-release of *Conan the Barbarian*.

38 Huntington, *Who Are We?*, p. 31.

39 Wood, *Hollywood from Vietnam to Reagan*, p. 172.

40 Tasker, 'Dumb Movies for Dumb People,' in Cohan and Hark (eds), *Screening the Male*, p. 232.

41 Henry David Thoreau, 1848/1989: *On the Duty of Civil Disobedience*, Chicago, Charles H. Kerr, p. 16.

42 Nietzsche, *Twilight of the Idols and the Antichrist* (trans. Thomas Common), p. 20.

43 Quoted in Flynn, *The Films of Arnold Schwarzenegger*, p. 53.

44 Reagan, *An American Life*, p. 267.

45 See Leo Marx, 1964: *The Machine in the Garden: Technology and the Pastoral Ideal in America*, New York, Oxford University Press, p. 246.

46 Joseph Conrad, 1902/1950: *Heart of Darkness*, New York, New American Library, p. 69.

47 See Leslie A. Fielder, 'Mythicizing the Unspeakable,' in *Journal of American Folklore* 103:410, October–December 1990, p. 396.

48 John P. Diggins, 1973: *The American Left in the Twentieth Century*, New York, Harcourt Brace Jovanovich, p. 161.

49 Reagan, *An American Life*, pp. 239, 312.

50 Quoted in Leigh, *Arnold*, p. 195.

51 *Ibid.*, p. 194.

52 Leamer, *Fantastic*, p. 131.

53   Theweleit, *Male Fantasies*, p. 50.

54   Friedrich Nietzsche, 1997: *Thus Spake Zarathustra* (trans. Thomas Common), Ware, Wordsworth Editions, p. 8.

55   Diggins, *The American Left*, p. 190.

56   Campbell, *The Hero with a Thousand Faces*, p. 123. More simply, an archetypal hero's amorous encounter with a sexy woman, as Christopher Booker notes, frequently represents a frustrating distraction from a chief goal: '[O]ften the danger the hero runs is simply that he will be seduced and lulled into forgetting the great task he has undertaken, and will abandon his Quest under some beguiling spell.' (Booker, *The Seven Basic Plots*, p. 74. Booker cites the Sirens, Circe, and Calypso as examples of 'Temptations.') According to a literal reading of *Conan the Barbarian*, this 'great task' is of course revenge; in the case of Arnold's broader life and intertwined filmic career, the great task might be seen as his overarching quest to bolster American standing according to precepts rooted in his own, politically subjective opinions.

57   Diggins, *The American Left*, p. 190.

58   'It is almost axiomatic,' wrote the concerned correspondents of *Time*, 'that people attracted to the hippie culture are suffering from mental confusion.' Joe David Brown (ed.), 1967: *The Hippies*, New York, Time Incorporated, p. 27.

59   Quoted in Flynn, *Arnold Schwarzenegger*, p. 71.

60   Gary Arnold, '*Conan*: Barbarian Balderdash,' in the *Washington Post*, 14 May 1982, p. C8.

61   Rita Kempley, '*Conan*: Chopped Livers,' in the *Washington Post*, 14 May 1982, p. W15.

62   Flynn, *Arnold Schwarzenegger*, p. 68.

63   Quoted in Miroff, 'Ronald Reagan and American Political Culture,' in *Polity* 20:3, p. 547.

64   Taft and Wilson quoted in Chomsky, *Hegemony or Survival*, p. 64.

65   Theweleit, *Male Fantasies*, p. 266.

66   Kaplan and Schuck in Huntington, *Who Are We?*, p. 139.

67   *Ibid.*, p. 138.

68   Frank, *What's the Matter with America?*, p. 183.

69   Reagan, *An American Life*, p. 219.

70   Quoted in Miroff, 'Ronald Reagan and American Political Culture,' in *Polity* 20:3, p. 543. Reagan went some way to remedying this situation in *An American Life*, first published in 1989.

71   Klayton R. Koppes, 1994: *Ronald Reagan in Hollywood: Movies and Politics*, New York, Cambridge University Press, p. 237.

72   Rubenstein, 'The Mirror of Reproduction,' in *Political Theory* 17:4, p. 589.

73   Reagan, *An American Life*, p. 104.

74   Carol S. Pearson, 1989: *The Hero Within: Six Archetypes We Live By*, New York, HarperCollins, pp. 77, 81, 83.

75 Vincent P. Pecora, 'Nietzsche, Genealogy, Critical Theory,' in *New German Critique* 53, spring 1991, p. 129.

76 Gary Indiana, 2005: *Schwarzenegger Syndrome: Politics and Celebrity in the Age of Contempt*, New York, The New Press, p. 19.

77 Quoted in Jeffords, *Hard Bodies*, p. 5.

78 Niall Ferguson, 2004: *Colossus: The Price of America's Empire*, New York, Penguin, p. 290.

79 Indiana, *Schwarzenegger Syndrome*, p. 133.

80 Ronald Reagan quoted in Raphael, 'The King is a Thing,' in *TDR* 43:1, p. 52.

81 H.A. Highstone (1936), 'Frankenstein – Unlimited,' in Peter Haining (ed.), 2003: *The Frankenstein Omnibus*, London, Bounty, pp. 547, 554.

82 Mark Rowlands, 2005: *The Philosopher at the End of the Universe: Philosophy Explained through Science Fiction Films*, London, Ebury Press, p. viii.

83 Cameron was forced to acknowledge Ellison's influence by including a prominent credit.

84 Wright, *Arnold Schwarzenegger*, p. 75.

85 Quoted in Sean French, 1996: *The Terminator*, London, BFI, p. 39.

86 Quoted in Andrews, *True Myths*, p. 104.

87 *Ibid.*, pp. 102, 108.

88 French, *The Terminator*, p. 41.

89 Philip Lamy, 'Millennialism in the Mass Media: The Case of *Soldier of Fortune* Magazine,' in *Journal for the Scientific Study of Religion* 31:4, December 1992, p. 409.

90 Eugen Weber, 1999: *Apocalypses: Prophecies, Cults and Millennial Beliefs through the Ages*, London, Hutchinson, pp. 235, 237.

91 Lamy, 'Millennialism in the Mass Media,' in *Journal for the Scientific Study of Religion* 31:4, pp. 409, 411.

92 See Weber, *Apocalypses*, p. 209.

93 Robert A. Monson, 'Star Wars and Air Land Battle: Technology, Strategy and Politics in German-American Relations,' in *German Studies Review* 9:3, October 1986, p. 602.

94 Quoted in Robin Headlam Wells and Johnjoe McFadden (eds), 2006: *Human Nature: Fact and Fiction*, London, Continuum, p. 179.

95 David Thompson, 2006: *The Whole Equation: A History of Hollywood*, London, Abacus, p. 174.

96 Theweleit, *Male Fantasies*, p. 162.

97 Richard J. Evans, 2005: *The Third Reich in Power: How the Nazis Won Over the Hearts and Minds of a Nation*, London, Penguin, p. 168.

98 *Ibid.*, p. 708.

99 Quoted in Valerie Steele, 1996: *Fetish: Fashion, Sex and Power*, New York, Oxford University Press, p. 157.

100 Roz Kaveney has discerned that the punks' 'presence at the viewing platform of the Griffith Observatory in LA links them, and him [Arnold],

to James Dean in Nicholas Ray's *Rebel Without A Cause* (1955), a key scene of which takes place at the same location.' Kaveney, 2005: *From* Alien *to* The Matrix, London, I.B.Tauris, p. 122.

101 Thompson, *The Whole Equation,* p. 254.

102 Shone, *Blockbuster,* p. 143.

103 French, *The Terminator,* p. 42.

104 *Ibid.,* p. 43.

105 Quoted in Marx, *The Machine in the Garden,* p. 145.

106 Goldman, 'Images of Technology in Popular Films: Discussion and Filmography,' in *Science, Technology and Human Values* 14:3, summer 1989, p. 289.

107 Doran Larson delineates *The Terminator*'s moral contradictions with admirable clarity: '[We are] offered the moral satisfaction of demonizing that cycle of consumerism . . . in which we are caught. We are allowed to feel triumphant over the global Skynet even as we watch films bounced from satellites.' See Larson, 'Machine as Messiah: Cyborgs, Morphs and the American Body Politic,' in *Cinema Journal* 36:4, summer 1997, p. 67.

108 French, *The Terminator,* p. 51.

109 Geoff King, 2000: *Spectacular Narratives: Hollywood in the Age of the Blockbuster,* London, I.B.Tauris, p. 148.

110 Quoted in Carl N. Degler, 1984: *Out of Our Past: The Forces that Shaped Modern America,* New York, Harper & Row, p. 369.

111 Historian Kevin Starr writes of coastal California during the 1980s: '[S]cience and science fiction were closely allied . . . science, science fiction, and religion often intersected. Given the importance of science, given the dream of California itself, with its utopian/dystopian rhythms, it was perhaps not too far-fetched to see an affinity for science fiction at the very centre of California culture.' Starr, 2006: *Coast of Dreams: A History of Contemporary California,* London, Penguin, p. 33.

112 Stewart and Harding, 'Bad Endings: American Apocalypses,' in *Annual Review of Anthropology* 28, 1999, p. 293.

113 Joan Didion, 1968/2001: *Slouching Towards Bethlehem,* London, Flamingo, p. 150.

114 Quoted in Frances Fitzgerald, 2000: *Way Out There in the Blue: Reagan, Star Wars and the End of the Cold War,* New York, Touchstone, p. 24.

115 Frank Ninkovich, 1999: *The Wilsonian Century: US Foreign Policy Since 1900,* Chicago, University of Chicago Press, p. 261.

116 Kevin Starr, 1985: *Inventing the Dream: California Through the Progressive Era,* New York, Oxford University Press, p. 186.

117 King, *Spectacular Narratives,* p. 148.

118 Quoted in Robert Dallek, 1999: *Ronald Reagan: The Politics of Symbolism,* Cambridge, MA, Harvard University Press, pp. 148–9.

119 Rockhound (Steve Buscemi) in Michael Bay's *Armageddon* (1998).

120 See King, *Spectacular Narratives,* p. 145.

121   Robert Torry, 'Apocalypse Then: The Benefits of the Bomb in Fifties Science Fiction Films,' in *Cinema Journal* 31:1, autumn 1991, p. 8.

122   'And along with this,' continues Campbell, 'there runs another realisation; namely, that the social group into which the individual has been born, which nourishes and protects him, and which, for the greater part of his life, he must himself help to nourish and protect, was flourishing long before his own birth and will remain when he is gone.' Joseph Campbell, 'The Emergence of Mankind' (1966), in Campbell, 2000: *Myths to Live By*, London, Souvenir Press, p. 22.

123   Andy Medhurst in Arroyo (ed.), *Action/Spectacle Cinema*, p. 56.

124   Richard Dawkins, 1995: *River Out of Eden*, New York, Basic, pp. 12–13.

125   As Brenda E. Brasher states: 'To privileged first-worlders cyborg identity can bring with it an explosion of the self, an expansion of the human . . . To those less privileged becoming borged can entail one's humanity being annexed by machines.' Brasher, 'Thoughts on the Status of the Cyborg: On Technological Socialization and its Link to the Religious Function of Popular Culture,' in *Journal of the American Academy of Religion* 64:4, winter 1996, p. 817.

126   Rushing and Frentz, *Projecting the Shadow*, p. 180.

127   As a Google search will reveal, many Internet-based Schwarzenegger fan groups exist, and all are male-dominated (and usually male-administrated). The Arnold Fans website's staff, for instance, is entirely made up of men: http://www.thearnoldfans.com/staff.

128   Toby Johnson, 1992: *The Myth of the Great Secret: A Search for Spiritual Meaning – An Appreciation of Joseph Campbell*, Berkeley, Celestial Arts, p. 69.

129   Quoted in French, *The Terminator*, p. 39. In Jung's terms, 'the cinema . . . makes it possible to experience without danger all the excitement, passion and desirousness which must be repressed in a humanitarian ordering of life.' Quoted in V.F. Perkins, 1972: *Film as Film*, Harmondsworth, Penguin, p. 144.

130   Reagan, *An American Life*, p. 491.

131   Schwarzenegger quoted in Andrews, *True Myths*, p. 117.

132   Quoted in Prince, *Visions of Empire*, p. 117.

133   Schwarzenegger quoted in Wright, *Arnold Schwarzenegger*, p. 87.

134   Thomas Docherty, 'Review: *Rambo: First Blood Part II*,' in *Film Quarterly* 39:3, spring 1986, p. 51.

135   Gerard Jones, 2005: *Men of Tomorrow: The True Story of the Birth of the Superheroes*, London, Arrow, pp. 145, 170.

136   Jonas, 'Central America as a Theater of US Cold War Politics,' in *Latin American Perspectives* 9:3, summer 1982, p. 127. Italics are mine.

137   Reagan, *An American Life*, p. 471.

138   Dallek, *Ronald Reagan*, p. xv.

139   'If we could survive without a wife, citizens of Rome, all of us would do without that nuisance,' declared Roman general Quintus Caecilius Metellus

Macedonicus, in 131 BC. See Elizabeth Finkel, 'A Plague of Men,' in *Cosmos* 15, June/July 2007, p. 63.

140 Reagan, *Speaking My Mind*, pp. 152–3.

141 '*Commando*,' notes Yvonne Tasker, 'goes to great lengths to present Schwarzenegger/Matrix as well-adjusted.' Tasker also here emphasises the West's conceptual conflation of physical and moral health; the association of mental robustness with the built, 'spectacular' male soma is, of course, a trope that is more or less omnipresent throughout Arnold's film career. See Tasker, *Spectacular Bodies*, p. 81.

142 Quoted in Uta G. Poiger, 'Rock 'n' Roll, Female Sexuality, and the Cold War Battle over German Identities,' in *Journal of Modern History* 68:3, September 1996, p. 586.

143 Quoted in Andrews, *True Myths*, p. 122.

144 John Milius quoted in Blitz and Krasniewicz, *Why Arnold Matters*, p. 112.

145 Theweleit, *Male Fantasies*, p. 162.

146 '[M]ontages,' observes Eric Lichtenfeld, 'are so prevalent in the action, sports, and music-themed films of the decade . . . that in the 1980s, the montage itself is a ritual.' Lichtenfeld, 2004: *Action Speaks Louder: Violence, Spectacle, and the American Action Movie*, Westport, CT, Praeger, p. 82.

147 Jonathan Shay, 1994: *Achilles in Vietnam: Combat Training and the Undoing of Character*, New York, Touchstone, p. 141.

148 Quoted in *ibid.*, pp. 141–2.

149 Larson, 'Machine as Messiah,' in *Cinema Journal* 36:4, p. 65.

150 Quoted in *ibid.*, p. 57.

151 http://www.imdb.com/name/nm0920460/bio, accessed on 20 September 2006.

152 Lichtenfeld, *Action Speaks Louder*, p. 86.

153 Reagan, *An American Life*, p. 479.

154 For detailed statistics, see Colin Wilcox and Dee Allsop, 'Economic and Foreign Policy as Sources of Reagan Support,' in *Western Political Quarterly* 44:4, December 1991, pp. 941–58.

155 Creed in Tasker, *Spectacular Bodies*, p. 78.

156 Quoted in Evans, *The Third Reich in Power*, p. 127. Emphasis is as in source.

157 See Oliver Stone's *Salvador* (1986), for an alternative and altogether more sagacious view.

158 Dutton, *The Perfectible Body*, p. 219.

159 *Ibid.*, p. 220.

160 *Variety* called *Commando* 'palatable' and 'inoffensively silly'; *Halliwell's* dismisses it as 'nonsense with the saving grace of humour.' See *Halliwell's Film and Video Guide 1999*, London, HarperCollins, p. 167.

161 Flynn, *The Films of Arnold Schwarzenegger*, p. 95.

162 Deibel, 'Why Reagan is Strong,' in *Foreign Policy* 62, spring 1986, p. 109.

163 Tasker, *Spectacular Bodies*, p. 83.

164 Flynn, *The Films of Arnold Schwarzenegger*, p. 95.

165 Jay Maeder of the New York *Daily News*, quoted in *ibid.*, p. 104.

166 From the *Toronto Star*, in Leamer, *Fantastic*, p. 189. No byline is given.

167 Leigh, *Arnold*, pp. 237-238.

168 Quoted in Wright, *Arnold Schwarzenegger*, p. 91.

169 Michel Foucault, 'Interview,' in *Edinburgh '77 Magazine*, 1977, p. 24.

170 Edward W. Said, 1994: *Culture and Imperialism*, London, Vintage, p. 7.

171 Richard Dyer, 1997: *White*, London, Routledge, p. 156.

172 In which the two protagonists, Enkidu and Gilgamesh, venture to a labyrinthine forest to kill the ogre Huwawa – a forerunner of the Minotaurs.

173 Prince, *Visions of Empire*, p. 107.

174 Schwarzenegger quoted in Flynn, *The Films of Arnold Schwarzenegger*, p. 104.

175 'Dutch' was, of course, Ronald Reagan's childhood nickname.

176 Quoted in Flynn, *The Films of Arnold Schwarzenegger*, pp. 111–12.

177 Dyer, *White*, p. 156.

178 Quoted in Andrews, *True Myths*, p. 134.

179 Prince, *Visions of Empire*, p. 107.

180 Keith Beattie, 1998: *The Scar that Binds: American Culture and the Vietnam War*, New York, New York University Press, p. 41.

181 Hoberman, 'Nietzsche's Boy,' in Arroyo (ed.), *Action/Spectacle Cinema*, pp. 31–2.

182 *Ibid.*, p. 31. Joseph Campbell told Bill Moyers that preachers, misguidedly, try to 'talk people into belief; better they reveal the radiance of their own discovery.' Campbell with Moyers, *The Power of Myth*, p. xvi.

183 Dyer, *Stars*, p. 97.

184 Jerry Lembcke, 1998: *The Spitting Image: Myth, Memory, and the Legacy of Vietnam*, New York, New York University Press, pp. 136–7.

185 'The function of the Shadow in drama is to challenge the hero and give [him] a worthy opponent in the struggle. Shadows create conflict and bring out the best in a hero by putting [him] in a life threatening situation.' See Christopher Vogler, 1999: *The Writer's Journey: Mythic Structure for Storytellers and Screenwriters*, London, Pan, p. 72.

186 Reagan, *An American Life*, p. 289.

187 'The American,' according to Richard Slotkin, 'must cross the border into "Indian country" and experience a "regression" to a more primitive and natural condition of life so that the false values of the "metropolis" can be purged.' Quoted in King, *Spectacular Narratives*, p. 17.

188 David E. James, 'Rock and Roll in Representations of the Invasion of Vietnam,' in *Representations* 29, winter 1990, pp. 80, 83.

189 See William M. Hammond, 1996: *The U.S. Army in Vietnam: Public Affairs – The Military and the Media 1968–1973*, Washington DC, US Army Center of Military History, pp. 175–6.

190 As the nineteenth-century military theorist Carl von Clausewitz wrote: 'To someone who has never experienced danger, the idea is attractive.' Quoted in Shay, *Achilles in Vietnam*, p. 9.

191   Prince, *Visions of Empire*, p. 107.

192   Shay, *Achilles in Vietnam*, p. 34.

193   Michael Herr, 2004: *Dispatches*, London, Picador, pp. 62, 95.

194   Campbell, *The Hero with a Thousand Faces*, p. 116.

195   In 'racialist mythography,' observes Uli Linke, quoting René Girard, an 'analogic affinity of menstruation and blood spillage confirms the metaphoric linkage between "sexuality and those diverse forms of violence that inevitably lead to bloodshed." Masculinist ideology can thus reconfigure the flow of blood as a social threat, an attack on manhood and the national body politic . . . blood spilled by violence is read as a stigma, a red stain of contagion.' Linke, *German Bodies*, p. 123.

196   *Beowulf: A Verse Translation* (trans. Michael Alexander), p. 132.

197   Quoted in Susan Jeffords, 'Debriding Vietnam: The Resurrection of the White American Male,' in *Feminist Studies* 14:3, autumn 1988, p. 536.

198   *Ibid*, pp. 537–8.

199   Pearson, *The Hero Within*, p. 81.

200   Lichtenfeld, *Action Speaks Louder*, p. 91.

201   Shay, *Achilles in Vietnam*, p. 127.

202   J.C. Nott and G.R. Glidden (1868) quoted in Anthony Synnott, 1993: *The Body Social: Symbolism, Self and Society*, London, Routledge, p. 243.

203   Quoted in *ibid.*, p. 244.

204   The monster strikingly resembles Tlaloc, the Mexican rain-god with a face made of two serpents.

205   *Ibid.*, p. 95.

206   Prince, *Visions of Empire*, p. 108. Niall Ferguson saliently points out that it 'was the people of Vietnam and Cambodia who paid the horrifically high price of American failure; Americans themselves were able to walk away from the wreckage of "containment."' Ferguson, *Colossus*, p. 107.

207   Prince, *Visions of Empire*, p. 107.

208   Fielder, 'Mythicizing the Unspeakable,' in *Journal of American Folklore* 103:410, p. 399.

209   J. Carcopino in Donald G. Kyle, 1998: *Spectacles of Death in Ancient Rome*, London, Routledge, p. 6.

210   Michel Foucault, 1987: *Discipline and Punish: The Birth of the Prison*, London, Peregrine, p. 46.

211   *Cf. Aliens* (1986), *Escape from New York* (1981), *Outland* (1981), *Blade Runner* (1982), *Robocop* (1987) and *Total Recall* (1990). See Prince, *Visions of Empire*, p. 159.

212   Fred Glass, 'Totally Recalling Arnold: Sex and Violence in the New Bad Future,' in *Film Quarterly* 44:1, autumn 1990, p. 2.

213   David D. Hale, 'Picking up Reagan's Tab,' in *Foreign Policy* 74, spring 1989, pp. 145–6.

214   Quoted in Flynn, *The Films of Arnold Schwarzenegger*, p. 119.

215   Quoted in Schaller, *Right Turn*, p. 102.

216 Geoff King (in *Spectacular Narratives*, p. 132) notes the 'tendancy [in action cinema] to cast the heroes as maverick figures who perform beyond the borders of large institutions and bureaucracies.' This also usually extends to the hero – who is almost always a bastion of individualism – operating beyond total commitment to ideological revolutionary or underground groups also; collaboration is one thing, partisan alignment another.

217 Andrews, *True Myths*, p. 149.

218 Quoted in Flynn, *The Films of Arnold Schwarzenegger*, p. 120.

219 Christine Gledhill, 'Recent Developments in Feminist Criticism,' in Leo Braudy and Marshall Cohen (eds), 1999: *Film Theory and Criticism: Introductory Readings* (fifth edition), New York, Oxford University Press, p. 259.

220 Ferguson, *Colossus*, p. 302.

221 *Ibid.*, p. 293.

222 General Anthony Zinni quoted in *ibid.*

223 John F. Kennedy, (ed. John W. Gardner), 1962: *To Turn the Tide*, London, Hamish Hamilton, p. 10.

224 Quoted in Bertram Gross, 1980: *Friendly Fascism: The New Face of Power in America*, New York, M. Evans, p. 135.

225 William Fisher, 'Of Living Machines and Living-Machines: *Blade Runner* and the Terminal Genre,' in *New Literary History* 20:1, autumn 1988, p. 197.

226 Quoted in Schaller, *Right Turn*, p. 121.

227 *Ibid.*

228 For two prominent contemporaneous cultural criticisms of materialism, see Oliver Stone's film *Wall Street* (1987), and Tom Wolfe's novel *The Bonfire of the Vanities*, from the same year.

229 Schaller, *Right Turn*, p. 150.

230 De Grazia, *Irresistible Empire*, p. 3.

231 Franklin, 'Visions of the Future,' in Annette Kuhn (ed.), 1992: *Alien Zone: Cultural Theory and Contemporary Science Fiction Cinema*, London, Verso, p. 31.

232 Constance Penley, 'Time Travel, Primal Scene and the Critical Dystopia,' in *ibid.*, p. 116.

233 See James T. Patterson, 2005: *Restless Giant: The United States from Watergate to Bush v. Gore*, New York, Oxford University Press, p. 186.

234 Campbell with Moyers, *The Power of Myth*, p. 164.

235 De Grazia, *Irresistible Empire*, p. 459.

236 Schaller, *Right Turn*, p. 106.

237 Phil Williams, 'US–Soviet Relations: Beyond the Cold War?,' in *International Affairs* 65:2, spring 1989, pp. 273, 286.

238 Schaller, *Right Turn*, p. 154.

239 *Ibid.*, p. 155.

240 See Steven R. Donziger (ed.), 1996: *The Real War on Crime: The Report of the National Criminal Justice Commission*, New York, HarperPerennial, p. 115.

241 Charles William Maynes, 'America's Chance,' in *Foreign Policy 68*, autumn 1987, p. 89.
242 Quoted in Andrews, *True Myths*, p. 154.
243 Fitzgerald, *Way Out There in the Blue*, p. 438.
244 Flynn, *The Films of Arnold Schwarzenegger*, p. 142.
245 See Anthony Synnott, 'Truth and Goodness, Mirrors and Masks, Part I: A Sociology of Beauty and the Face,' in *British Journal of Sociology* 40:4, December 1989, p. 609.
246 See Donziger (ed.), *The Real War on Crime*, p. 168.
247 *Ibid.*, p. 116.
248 Quoted in Flynn, *The Films of Arnold Schwarzenegger*, p. 136.
249 Leigh, *Arnold*, p. 257.
250 Morgan Spurlock, 2005: *Don't Eat This Book*, London, Penguin, p. 64.
251 Quoted in Andrews, *True Myths*, p. 153.
252 Mikhail Gorbachev quoted in John Lewis Gaddis, 2005: *The Cold War*, London, Penguin, p. 231.
253 Quoted in Andrews, *True Myths*, p. 155.
254 Booker, *The Seven Basic Plots*, p. 223.

Chapter III

1 George Herbert Walker Bush, 'Inaugural Address,' in *Weekly Compilation of Presidential Documents*, January–March 1989, p. 100.
2 An anonymous Bush aide quoted in Schaller, *Right Turn*, pp. 63–4.
3 Gaddis, *The Cold War*, p. 257.
4 Reagan quoted in Fitzgerald, *Way Out There in the Blue*, p. 458.
5 *Ibid.*, p. 457.
6 *Ibid.*, p. 461.
7 Marsha Kinder, 'Back to the Future in the '80s with Fathers & Sons, Supermen and PeeWees, Gorillas & Toons,' in *Film Quarterly* 42:4, summer 1989, p. 2.
8 George Bush, 1999: *All the Best: My Life in Letters and Other Writings*, New York, Touchstone, p. 403. As Bush himself noted, dismissively, 'The choice between Bush and Dukakis will be very clear. He is the consummate traditional McGovern-type liberal.' (*Ibid.*, p. 389.)
9 Maier et al., *Inventing America*, p. 1044.
10 Schaller, *Right Turn*, p. 63.
11 Quoted in Fitzgerald, *Way Out There in the Blue*, p. 468.
12 Fred I. Greenstein, 'The Prudent Professionalism of George Herbert Walker Bush,' in *Journal of Interdisciplinary History* 31:3, winter 2001, p. 388.
13 Quoted in Jeffords, *Hard Bodies*, p. 91.
14 *Ibid.*
15 See Maier et al., *Inventing America*, p. 1048.

16 American social scientist Charles Murray (writing in 1989) quoted in Pamela Abbott and Claire Wallace, 1992: *The Family and the New Right*, London, Pluto Press, p. 85.

17 Ronald Reagan, *An American Life*, p. 27.

18 Andrews, *True Myths*, p. 160.

19 See Jeffords, *Hard Bodies*, p. 93.

20 Quoted in Flynn, *The Films of Arnold Schwarzenegger*, p. 150.

21 George Bush, *All the Best*, pp. 391–2.

22 Quoted in Andrews, *True Myths*, p. 161.

23 See Wright, *Arnold Schwarzenegger*, p. 109, and Leigh, *Arnold*, p. 258.

24 In 1989, Schwarzenegger, according to *Forbes'* estimation, earned $35 million, making him the sixth-highest-earning show business star. See Leigh, *Arnold*, p. 259.

25 This is, of course, bunkum 'science.' *Twins* dismisses the overall ethical probity and societal validity of genetic research, whilst fancifully suggesting that a blending of DNA in a sperm 'milkshake' might be feasible. Regardless of theoretical technicalities elided for brevity's sake, one wonders how many laymen might believe this to be a practical possibility, and if *Twins'* central conceit might adversely have influenced public perception of biological scientists. Part of *Twins'* undertaking, effected through the condensatory device of the 'milkshake,' also seems to be addressing worries described by the *National Journal* in 1987: 'Today, a child can have up to five people claiming to be its parents: a sperm donor, an egg donor, the woman providing a womb for gestation and the couple raising the child can all call a child theirs. And that's before any step-parents become involved.' Quoted in Sar A. Levitan, 1988: *What's Happening to the American Family? Tensions, Hopes, Realities*, Baltimore, Johns Hopkins University Press, p. 195.

26 Quoted in Patterson, *Restless Giant*, p. 238.

27 George Bush, in a letter to Willie Morris dated 7 January 1989, in *All the Best*, p. 408.

28 Quoted in Micklethwait and Wooldridge, *The Right Nation*, p. 10.

29 See George Butler, 1990: *Arnold Schwarzenegger: A Portrait*, New York, Simon & Schuster, p. 21.

30 Quoted in Abbott and Wallace, *The Family and the New Right*, pp. 7, 9.

31 *Ibid.*, p. 7.

32 Richard Dyer compares the two bodybuilders' auras: 'Schwarzenegger's body is simply massive, his characteristic facial expression genial, his persona one of Teutonic confidence . . . [Stallone's] eyes and mouth express vulnerability, iconic images have him bruised (*Rocky*) or scarred (*Rambo*).' Dyer, *White*, p. 155.

33 Wright, *Arnold Schwarzenegger*, p. 111.

34 Campbell, *The Hero with a Thousand Faces*, p. 386.

35 Jeffords, *Hard Bodies*, p. 93. Emphasis is Jeffords's.

36 Frank, *What's the Matter with America?*, p. 195.

37 *Ibid.*, p. 195. The fear of liberal intellectuality amongst Middle American Republicans is often astoundingly misguided and defensive, as in the following piece from *The American Enterprise* magazine: 'Most Red Americans can't deconstruct post-modern literature, give proper orders to a nanny, pick out a cabernet with aftertones of licorice, or quote prices from the Abercrombie and Fitch catalogue. But we can raise great children, wire our own houses, make beautiful and delicious creations with our own two hands, talk casually and comfortably about God, repair a small engine . . . shoot a gun and run a chainsaw without fear . . .' Missouri farmer Blake Hurst quoted in *ibid.*, p. 21.

38 Bush, *All the Best*, pp. 408–9.

39 Schwarzenegger and Kent Hall, *The Education of a Bodybuilder*, p. 27.

40 Quoted in Andrews, *True Myths*, p. 161.

41 Schwarzenegger and Kent Hall, *The Education of a Bodybuilder*, p. 35.

42 'He told us of a recurring dream. In it, he was king of all the earth and everyone looked up to him.' See Butler, *Arnold Schwarzenegger: A Portrait*, p. 21.

43 Quoted in Frank, *What's the Matter with America?*, p. 232.

44 Edmund Morris, 1999: *Dutch: A Memoir of Ronald Reagan*, London, HarperCollins, p. 412–13.

45 Pearson, *The Hero Within*, p. xxv.

46 'The world's knowledge and use of eugenics will progress far into the next millennium, increasing the possibility of jeopardising the future of mankind, but at the same time improving the human race to immeasurable heights.' Parendi Mehta, 'Human Eugenics: Whose Perception of Perfection?,' in *The History Teacher* 33:2, February 2000, p. 228.

47 Manfred Thellig quotes Arnold in Leigh, *Arnold*, p. 88.

48 Kinder, 'Back to the Future in the '80s,' in *Film Quarterly* 42:4, p. 2.

49 Booker, *The Seven Basic Plots*, pp. 152, 224.

50 Kinder, 'Back to the Future in the '80s,' in *Film Quarterly* 42:4, p. 4.

51 Jeffords, *Hard Bodies*, p. 13.

52 Kühl, *The Nazi Connection*, p. 9.

53 *Ibid.*

54 *Ibid.*, p. 4.

55 Karen Armstrong, 2005: *A Short History of Myth*, Edinburgh, Canongate, p. 142.

56 Edwin Black, 2003: *War Against the Weak: Eugenics and America's Campaign to Create a Master Race*, New York, Four Walls Eight Windows, p. 348.

57 Extract from the narration of a 1957 Disney television broadcast, 'Mars and Beyond,' quoted in Howard E. McCurdy, 1997: *Space and the American Imagination*, Seattle, Smithsonian Institution Press, p. 115.

58 Ziauddin Sardar and Merryl Wyn Davies, 2006: *Why do People Hate America?*, Cambridge, Icon, p. 198.

59 Quoted in Flynn, *The Films of Arnold Schwarzenegger*, p. 153.

60   Glass, 'Totally Recalling Arnold,' in *Film Quarterly* 44:1, p. 6.

61   Ray A. Williamson, 'Outer Space as Frontier: Lessons for Today,' in *Western Folklore* 46:4, October 1997, p. 256.

62   Edward W. Said, 2003: *Orientalism*, London, Penguin, p. 63.

63   Glass, 'Totally Recalling Arnold,' in *Film Quarterly* 44:1, p. 6.

64   Campbell, *The Hero with a Thousand Faces*, p. 114

65   *Ibid.*, p. 116.

66   Said, *Orientalism*, p. 167.

67   *Ibid.*, p. 157.

68   See McCurdy, *Space and the American Imagination*, p. 118.

69   Carol S. Pearson, *The Hero Within*, p. 57.

70   Jeffords, *Hard Bodies*, pp. 102–3. My argument here is indebted to Frank Grady, who likewise utilises Jeffords's prose in connection to *Total Recall* in his 'Arnoldian Humanism, or Amnesia and Autobiography in the Schwarzenegger Action Film,' in *Cinema Journal* 42:2, winter 2003, p. 50.

71   Grady, 'Arnoldian Humanism,' in *Cinema Journal* 42:2, p. 50.

72   Glass, 'Totally Recalling Arnold,' in *Film Quarterly* 44:1, p. 13.

73   Grady, 'Arnoldian Humanism,' in *Cinema Journal* 42:2, p. 44.

74   Quoted in Said, *Orientalism*, pp. 32–3.

75   *Ibid.*, pp. 36–7.

76   Terkel, *American Dreams*, p. 168.

77   *Ibid.*, p. 172.

78   Rudyard Kipling quoted in *ibid.*, p. 226.

79   Quoted in McCurdy, *Space and the American Imagination*, p. 144.

80   *Ibid.*, p. 4.

81   *Ibid.*, pp. 75–6.

82   George Soros, 2007: *The Age of Fallibility: The Consequences of the War on Terror*, London, Phoenix, p. 127.

83   Quoted in Michael Davie, 1972: *In the Future Now: A Report from California*, London, Hamish Hamilton, p. 250.

84   Quoted in Bryan Appleyard, 2006: *Aliens: Why They Are Here*, London, Scribner, p. 153.

85   I appropriate this subtitle from Robert Bly's 1991 book *Iron John: A Book About Men*, Shaftesbury, Dorset, Element, p. 92.

86   Wood, *Hollywood from Vietnam to Reagan*, p. 172.

87   Theweleit, *Male Fantasies*, p. 369.

88   A child co-star of *Kindergarten Cop*, quoted in Andrews, *True Myths*, p. 182.

89   *Ibid.*, p. 178.

90   Leamer, *Fantastic*, p. 209.

91   Andrews, *True Myths*, p. 169.

92   See Greg Critser, 2004: *Fat Land: How Americans Became the Fattest People in the World*, London, Penguin, p. 64.

93   Andrews, *True Myths*, p. 170.

94   Thomas B. Byers, 'Terminating the Postmodern: Masculinity and Pomophobia,' in *Modern Fiction Studies* 41:1, 1995, pp. 4, 15–17.

95   Bly, *Iron John*, pp. 4, 60, 111–12. Emphasis added.

96   Campbell, *The Hero with a Thousand Faces*, pp. 136–7.

97   Joseph L. Henderson, 'The Eternal Symbols,' in Jung (ed.), *Man and his Symbols*, p. 119.

98   Jeffords, *Hard Bodies*, p. 141.

99   French, *The Terminator*, p. 38.

100   Flynn, *The Films of Arnold Schwarzenegger*, p. 171.

101   Bly, *Iron John*, p. x.

102   Flynn, *The Films of Arnold Schwarzenegger*, p. 174.

103   Pearson, *The Hero Within*, pp. 82, 84.

104   Bly, *Iron John*, p. 6.

105   As Susan Jeffords notes, Crisp is 'the quintessential domestic Reagan enemy.' Jeffords, *Hard Bodies*, p. 142.

106   Quoted in Frank, *What's the Matter with America?*, p. 115.

107   See J. Hoberman, 'Nietzsche's Boy,' in Arroyo (ed.), *Action/Spectacle Cinema*, p. 30. 'The fear of homosexuality as an assault on gender identities,' notes Thomas Byers, 'is exacerbated both by the homophobic's perception of homosexuals as having "succumbed" to such an assault, and by the fact that a male homosexual proposition puts the straight man in the traditionally "feminine" position of the object rather than the subject of desire. Thus for the homophobic a homosexual is a "girly-man."' See Byers, 'Terminating the Postmodern,' in *Modern Fiction Studies* 41:1, pp. 14–15.

108   See Leamer, *Fantastic*, p. 211.

109   Adrian Wright makes this connection in *Arnold Schwarzenegger*, p. 131.

110   Quoted in Evans, *The Third Reich in Power*, pp. 272–3.

111   Bryson, *Made in America*, p. 422. Bush made it plain he wanted to be known as 'the education president,' but as Michael Schaller points out, 'in practice, federal policy changed little . . . and education took a back seat to most other issues.' See Schaller, *Right Turn*, p. 157.

112   Evans, *The Third Reich in Power*, p. 127.

113   Abbott and Wallace, *The Family and the New Right*, p. 10.

114   Hitler's colleague Hermann Raushning explains the purposes of marching: 'Marching diverts men's thoughts. Marching kills thought. Marching makes an end of individuality. Marching is the indispensable magic stroke performed in order to accustom the people to a mechanic, quasi-ritualistic activity until it becomes second nature.' See Gross, *Friendly Fascism*, p. 25.

115   Jeffords, *Hard Bodies*, pp. 142–3.

116   Booker, *The Seven Basic Plots*, p. 575.

117   Rushing and Frentz, *Projecting the Shadow*, p. 176.

118   *Thus Spake Zarathustra*, section 2, quoted in Ansell-Pearson, 'Who is the Übermensch?,' in *Journal of the History of Ideas* 53:2, p. 314.

119 Quoted in Nicholas Guyatt, 2007: *Have a Nice Doomsday: Why Millions of Americans are Looking Forward to the End of the World*, London, Ebury Press, p. 57.

120 King, *Spectacular Narratives*, p. 157.

121 Indiana, *Schwarzenegger Syndrome*, p. 63.

122 Quoted in Marjorie Garber, 'Sign, Co-Sign, Tangent,' in Ken Gelder and Sarah Thronton (eds), 1997: *The Subcultures Reader*, London, Routledge, p. 456.

123 Hans Blüher's *Volk und Führer in der Jugendbewegung*, quoted in Theweleit, *Male Fantasies*, p. 94.

124 Rushing and Frentz, *Projecting the Shadow*, p. 185.

125 Theweleit, *Male Fantasies*, p. 160.

126 *Ibid.*

127 See Michelle Chilcoat, 'Brain Sex, Cyberpunk Cinema, Feminism, and the Dis/Location of Heterosexuality,' in *NWSA Journal* 16:2, summer 2004, pp. 157–8.

128 Rushing and Frentz, *Projecting the Shadow*, p. 188.

129 Jeffrey A. Brown, 'Gender and the Action Heroine: Hardbodies and the "Point of No Return,"' in *Cinema Journal* 35:3, spring 1996, p. 59. Brown's essay offers an enlightening discourse on the disparate critical responses to characters such as Sarah Connor and James Cameron's almost equally 'hard-bodied' Ripley in *Aliens* (1986).

130 Quoted in Larson, 'Machine as Messiah,' in *Cinema Journal* 36:4, p. 57.

131 Byers, 'Terminating the Postmodern,' in *Modern Fiction Studies* 41:1, p. 25.

132 Quoted in Zinn, *A People's History of the United States*, p. 261.

133 Walt Whitman, 'Drum-Taps,' in Whitman, 1855/1998: *Leaves of Grass* (Oxford World's Classics Paperback Edition), Oxford, Oxford University Press, p. 221.

134 Quoted in Degler, *Out of Our Past*, p. 134.

135 Jeffords, *Hard Bodies*, pp. 162–3.

136 Starr, *Coast of Dreams*, p. 126.

137 *Ibid.*, p. 129.

138 Byers, 'Terminating the Postmodern,' in *Modern Fiction Studies* 41:1, p. 23.

139 *Ibid.*

140 *Ibid.*, p. 24.

141 Rushing and Frentz, *Projecting the Shadow*, pp. 200–1.

142 *Ibid.*, p. 200.

143 Quoted in Patterson, *Restless Giant*, p. 238.

144 Said, *Culture and Imperialism*, p. 366.

145 Booker, *The Seven Basic Plots*, p. 493.

146 Shone, *Blockbuster*, p. 205.

147 *Ibid.*

148 See Leigh, *Arnold*, p. 68.

149 Quoted in Zinn, *A People's History of the United States*, p. 107.

150 Brown, 'Gender and the Action Heroine,' in *Cinema Journal* 35:3, p. 59.

151 Campbell with Moyers, *The Power of Myth*, p. 252.
152 Bly, *Iron John*, p. 151.
153 Linda Hamilton quoted in Flynn, *The Films of Arnold Schwarzenegger*, p. 200.
154 Quoted in Gaddis, *The Cold War*, p. 261.
155 Jeffords, *Hard Bodies*, p. 177.
156 Quoted in Flynn, *The Films of Arnold Schwarzenegger*, p. 197.
157 Hoberman, 'Nietzsche's Boy,' in Arroyo (ed.), *Action/Spectacle Cinema*, p. 34.
158 Bill Clinton, 2005: *My Life*, London, Arrow, pp. 477, 502.
159 Patterson, *Restless Giant*, p. 260.
160 Quoted in Leamer, *Fantastic*, p. 228.
161 See *Halliwell's Film and Video Guide 1999*, p. 455.
162 Hoberman, 'Nietzsche's Boy,' in Arroyo (ed.), *Action/Spectacle Cinema*, p. 34.
163 Jonathan Romney, 'Arnold Through the Looking Glass,' in Arroyo (ed.), *Action/Spectacle Cinema*, pp. 34, 38.
164 *Ibid.*, p. 39.
165 From a placard carried by a Muslim demonstrator outside the film's Washington opening, quoted in Andrews, *True Myths*, p. 212.
166 Professor Richard Hofstadter, quoted in Davie, *In the Future Now*, p. 144.
167 Parker Tyler, 'From Magic and Myth of the Movies: Preface,' in Braudy and Cohen (eds), *Film Theory and Criticism*, p. 798.
168 See Maier et al., *Inventing America*, p. 1071.
169 Quoted in Andrews, *True Myths*, p. 211.
170 Arnold Schwarzenegger with Bill Dobbins, 1981: *Arnold's Bodybuilding for Men*, London, Sphere, p. 20.
171 Indiana, *Schwarzenegger Syndrome*, p. 62.
172 Quoted in Joe Matthews, 2006: *The People's Machine: Governor Schwarzenegger and the Rise of Blockbuster Democracy*, New York, PublicAffairs, p. 24.
173 Quoted in Andrews, *True Myths*, p. 214.
174 José Arroyo, 'Cameron and the Comic,' in Arroyo (ed.), *Action/Spectacle Cinema*, p. 42.
175 *Ibid.*
176 Indiana, *Schwarzenegger Syndrome*, p. 122. Emphasis added.
177 See Maier et al., *Inventing America*, p. 1053.
178 Wood, *Hollywood from Vietnam to Reagan*, p. 166.
179 Quoted in Louise Richardson, 2006: *What Terrorists Want: Understanding the Terrorist Threat*, London, John Murray, p. 118.
180 Said, *Orientalism*, p. 108.
181 Quoted in Sardar and Davies, *Why do People Hate America?*, p. 43.
182 Lewis Lapham quoted in *ibid.*, p. 189.
183 See Andrews, *True Myths*, p. 212.
184 Arroyo, 'Cameron and the Comic,' in Arroyo (ed.), *Action/Spectacle Cinema*, p. 44.
185 Quoted in Huntington, *Who Are We?*, pp. 263–4.

186 Phil Melling, 'The Adversarial Imagination,' in John Davies and Paul Wells (eds), 2002: *American Film and Politics from Reagan to Bush Jr.*, Manchester, Manchester University Press, p. 183.

187 Quoted in Wright, *Arnold Schwarzenegger*, p. 148.

188 Patterson, *Restless Giant*, p. 319.

189 Brian Neve, 'Independent Cinema and Modern Hollywood: Pluralism in American Cultural Politics?,' in Davies and Wells (eds), *American Film and Politics from Reagan to Bush Jr.*, p. 127.

190 Campbell with Moyers, *The Power of Myth*, p. 72.

191 Quoted in Simon Braund, 'Arnie,' in *Empire* 170, August 2003, p. 76.

Chapter IV

1 Armstrong, *A Short History of Myth*, p. 98.

2 Campbell, *The Hero with a Thousand Faces*, pp. 347, 353.

3 *Ibid.*, p. 350.

4 Quoted in Andrews, *True Myths*, p. 218.

5 Quoted in Blitz and Krasniewicz, *Why Arnold Matters*, pp. 163–4.

6 http://www.schwarzenegger.com/en/actor/filmography/junio.asp, accessed on 6 August 2007.

7 Howard Feinstein, 'Junior,' in Arroyo (ed.), *Action/Spectacle Cinema*, p. 51.

8 *Ibid.*

9 Leamer, *Fantastic*, p. 245.

10 *Halliwell's Film and Video Guide 1999*, p. 252.

11 Barbara Shulgasser, 'In *Eraser*, Arnold Can Even Fly,' in *San Francisco Examiner*, 21 June 1996, p. D1.

12 Trevor Johnson, '*Jingle All the Way*,' in Arroyo (ed.), *Action/Spectacle Cinema*, p. 55.

13 Barbara Shulgasser, 'Arnold: Don't Toy with Us,' in *San Francisco Examiner*, 22 November 1996, p. C1.

14 Quoted in *Halliwell's Film Guide 1999*, p. 423.

15 See Andrews, *True Myths*, p. 223.

16 Andy Medhurst, 'Batman and Robin,' in *ibid.*, p. 57.

17 Leamer, *Fantastic*, p. 267.

18 Quoted in Patterson, *Restless Giant*, p. 12.

19 See Sardar and Davies, *Why do People Hate America?* p. 5.

20 *Ibid.*, pp. 22–3.

21 Quoted in Bob Woodward, 2003: *Bush at War*, London, Simon & Schuster, pp. 96–7.

22 See *ibid.*, p. 94.

23 Soros, *The Age of Fallibility*, p. 108.

24 Armstrong, *A Short History of Myth*, p. 38.

25 Maier et al., *Inventing America*, p. 1085.

26 *Ibid.*, p. 1086.

27 Quoted in Fergusson, *Colossus*, p. 293.

28 Weber, *Apocalypses*, pp. 234–5.

29 Quoted in Simon Braund, 'Judgement Day,' in *Empire* 170, August 2003, p. 71.

30 Quoted in Braund, 'Arnie,' in *ibid.*, p. 79.

31 Quoted in Braund, 'Judgement Day,' in *ibid.*, p. 73.

32 Quoted in Sharon Waxman, 'From Pumping Iron to Pushing Political Ideas,' in *Washington Post*, 28 September 2003, p. A7.

33 All quotes are from Woodward, *Bush at War*, p. 67.

34 Ferguson, *Colossus*, p. 299.

35 *Ibid.*

36 Quoted in Jacob A. McDonald, 'Schwarzenegger "Pumps up" Deploying Guard,' online at: http://www.military.com/NewsContent/0,13319,usa1_03 1504.00.html?ESRC=army-a.nl, accessed on 29 August 2007.

37 Quoted in Blitz and Krasniewicz, *Why Arnold Matters*, p. 136.

Epilogue

1 Ronald Reagan, speaking in 1974, quoted in Guyatt, *Have a Nice Doomsday*, p. 127.

2 Bill Moyers in Campbell and Moyers, *The Power of Myth*, p. 155.

3 Quoted in Joe Matthews, *The People's Machine*, p. 257.

4 Jon Hotten, 2004: *Muscle: A Writer's Trip through a Sport with no Boundaries*, London, Yellow Jersey Press, p. 142.

5 Davies and Wells (eds), *American Film and Politics*, p. 5.

6 See Davie, *In the Future Now*, p. 7.

7 Quoted in Terkel, *American Dreams*, p. 168.

8 David Silverman's *The Simpsons Movie* (2007) visualises Arnold as president. Inevitably – and unfairly, given his acutely individualist nature – he is portrayed as an obtuse, aggressive brute entirely reliant on warmongering advisers.

9 Quoted in Terkel, *American Dreams*, p. 166.

10 T.E. Lawrence, 1935/1937: *The Seven Pillars of Wisdom*, Ware, Wordsworth Editions, p. 7.

Index